Sir William Muir

The Mameluke of slave dynasty of Egypt

1260-1517 A.D

Sir William Muir

The Mameluke of slave dynasty of Egypt
1260-1517 A.D

ISBN/EAN: 9783744741460

Printed in Europe, USA, Canada, Australia, Japan

Cover: Foto ©ninafisch / pixelio.de

More available books at **www.hansebooks.com**

1260–1517 A.D.

BY

SIR WILLIAM MUIR, K.C.S.I., LL.D., D.C.L.
PH.D. (BOLOGNA)
AUTHOR OF "THE LIFE OF MAHOMET" "MAHOMET AND ISLAM"
"THE CALIPHATE," ETC.

LONDON:
SMITH, ELDER, & CO., 15 WATERLOO PLACE.
1896.

[*All rights reserved.*]

MORRISON AND GIBB, PRINTERS, EDINBURGH

CONTENTS

YEAR A.D.		PAGE
	PREFACE . . .	ix
1097-1291.	INTRODUCTION—THE CRUSADES	xiii

CHAPTER I
640-1170. EGYPT AND THE MAMELUKES   1

CHAPTER II
1171-1260. THE EYYUBITE DYNASTY, AND SULTANATES OF EYBEK AND KOTUZ . . 6

MAMELUKE DYNASTY

PART FIRST
BAHRITE DYNASTY

CHAPTER III
1260-1277. BEIBARS   13

CHAPTER IV
1277-1290. SAÎD—KILAWUN   33

CHAPTER V
1290-1293. KHALÎL, SON OF KILAWUN .   43

CHAPTER VI
1293-1299. NÂSIR, SON OF KILAWUN—KETBOGHA—LACHÎN .   47

CONTENTS

YEAR A.D.   PAGE.

CHAPTER VII
1299–1310. Nâsir's Second Reign—Beibars II   53

CHAPTER VIII
1310–1341. Nâsir's Third Reign   66

CHAPTER IX
1341–1382. Nâsir's Sons and Grandsons   86

PART SECOND
CIRCASSIAN DYNASTY

CHAPTER X
1382–1399. Berkuck al Zâhir.   105

CHAPTER XI
The Osmanly Dynasty   117

CHAPTER XII
1399–1412. Faraj   121

CHAPTER XIII
1412–1421. Abbas Caliph—Sheikh al Mueyyad   129

CHAPTER XIV
1421–1438. Ahmed — Tatâr — Mohammed — Bursbai al Ashraf .   137

CHAPTER XV
1438–1453. Yusuf—Jakmac al Zâhir.   149

CHAPTER XVI
1453–1461. Othman—Inâl   156

CONTENTS

YEAR A.D.		PAGE
	CHAPTER XVII	
1461–1467.	Ahmed—Khushcadam	163
	CHAPTER XVIII	
1467–1496.	Jelbai—Timurboga—Kaitbai	172
	CHAPTER XIX	
1496–1501.	Al Nâsir Mohammed II.—Kansowah al Ashrafy —Jân Belat—Tumanbai	182
	CHAPTER XX	
1501–1516.	Kansowa al Ghury	187
	CHAPTER XXI	
1516–1517.	Tumanbeg	202
	CHAPTER XXII	
1517.	Sultan Selîm and the Caliph Mutawakkil	210
	CHAPTER XXIII	
	The Mameluke Race	215

APPENDIXES

I.—The Mamelukes under Osmanly Rule . . 223
II.—Memorandum by H.E. Yacoub Artin Pasha on the Mamelukes 225
Index . . . 233

LIST OF ILLUSTRATIONS

MAP OF SYRIA AND ASIA MINOR . . *Faces p.* xiii

THE IWÂN, PAVILION OR HALL OF NÂSIR MOHAMMED IBN KILAWUN, AS IN 1798 A.D. . . . *Frontispiece*

CITADEL (AS IN 1798 A.D.) FROM S.E. . . *Faces p.* 1

CITADEL (AS IN 1798 A.D.); THE RUMEILAH GATE . . „ 13

MINARET OVER MOSQUE OF NÂSIR IBN KILAWUN . . „ 84

MOSQUE AND TOMB OF SULTAN HASAN, SON OF NÂSIR . „ 96

TOMB OF BERKUCK „ 116

TOMB OF BURSBAI AL ASHRAF „ 148

MINARET OF SULTAN INAL'S TOMB „ 162

THE CITADEL; FROM THE MOKATTAM HILL „ 214

STOOL OR STAND OF BRONZE, INLAID AND EMBROIDERED WITH SILVER, FOUND IN NÂSIR IBN KILAWUN'S MOSQUE, AND SUPPOSED TO BE OF HIS AGE. PRESERVED IN CAIRO MUSEUM . . . . . „ 222

TOP OF THE STOOL IN PREVIOUS PICTURE „ 222

TOP OF A STOOL, INLAID WITH SILVER, FOUND IN THE MOSQUE OF SHABAN, SON OF NÂSIR, AND PRESERVED IN CAIRO MUSEUM „ 222

PREFACE

THE present volume contains a survey of the Mameluke dynasty, which, begun under Beibars, A.D. 1260, was brought to a close by the Ottoman Sultan Selîm in 1517 A.D. The work also completes the history of the Abbaside Caliphate down to the assumption of the title by the Osmanly Sultanate.

At the outset, I gladly acknowledge my obligations to the late Dr. Weil. For the materials of this history I am mainly indebted to the last two volumes of his great work *Geschichte der Chalifen*. These materials are rich and full; for with vast skill and labour that learned writer not only quotes his authorities as he goes along, but as a rule gives all that is most important in his Authors' very words.

The greater part of these authorities were accessible to Dr. Weil only in rare Arabic MSS., which were, with marvellous industry, sought out by him in the libraries of Gotha, Munich, Berlin, Leyden and Paris. Excepting the last fifty years of the Dynasty (for which we are mainly dependent on Ibn Ayâs and Turkish writers) the history is supported by a singular concurrence of contemporary writers, the chief of these being—

Abulfeda	born	1273;	died	1331 A.D.
Noweiry	„	1280;	„	1332 „
Ibn Batuta	„	1302;	„	1377 „

Macrizy	born	1358 or 1364;	died	1441 A.D.
Abul Mahâsin	„	1409;	„	1470 „
Ibn Ayâs	„	1448;	„	1524 „

and a dozen others. But the chief authorities are the last three given above.

Part of Macrizy, the great historian both of his own and preceding times, has been translated into French by M. Quatremere[1]; and the work is all the more valuable, because many of the more important passages are reproduced as notes in the original Arabic. Macrizy (so called from the quarter in Baalbec from which his family originally came) was himself a native of Egypt. He held office in the Cairo police, and was also Superintendent of an endowment in Damascus. His copious writings are universally held in high esteem, the annals of past times being marked by industrious research and historical judgment; while for his own day he is an unexceptionable and impartial witness.

Abul Mahâsin who survived Macrizy some thirty years was the son of the Emir Tagri Berdy, a Greek Mameluke of Sultan Berkuck. His father played a prominent part in the fortunes of Sultan Faraj; and on one occasion was pardoned at the intercession of that Prince's mother, herself originally a Greek slave-girl. Abul Mahâsin as a copious Author of high intelligence is widely relied on; and his continuation of Macrizy is especially valuable. He was a favourite at Court; and although on that account his judgment may be occasionally biassed, his testimony otherwise as a contemporaneous witness is beyond question.

Ibn Ayâs is the writer we have mainly to rely upon

[1] A portion published by the Oriental Translation Fund. Two parts. Paris, 1837 and 1840.

for the concluding period of the Dynasty. As he survived its fall, his work supplies contemporary and invaluable information at a time when other authorities fail.[1]

The following is Dr. Weil's opinion of his History, as given in the Preface to the Fifth Volume—

This volume, like the last, is devoted chiefly to the history of Egypt and Syria. But the reader will find much also relating to the border Asiatic States, as the dynasties of Timur, Osman, the White and Black Weir, the Beni Dulgadir and Karaman, and the Shereef of Mecca; as well as fresh insight into the relations of the Mameluke Sultans with Rhodes and Cyprus, Portugal, Venice, the Papacy, and other European States.

I am well aware that there are many things which yet require fuller detail and explanation than the sources at my command enable me to give. Gaps might have been filled up by conjecture, and the whole grandly rounded off as History. My object, however, has not been to frame an elaborate work like that, but in simple form to bring to light events and narratives hitherto for the greater part unknown, which had moreover to be gathered from many scattered manuscripts, and then subjected to critical analysis. The kind Reader will make allowances for the difficulty of such a task; nor will he expect from the Orientalist who has had to draw such new materials from their fountain-head, the same finished work as he would from the Historian who has found them all complete and ready to his hand.

If such be the humble view of his own work taken by the Author whose materials I have mainly depended on, how much greater cause there is for me to beg for kindly consideration at my Readers' hands. The only value I can place upon the present endeavour, is that it seeks to supply a want in our own language,—a gap,

[1] Ibn Ayâs has been published at Cairo in three volumes. I obtained a copy of it by Artin Pasha's kindness; but not until this work had been completed; so that I have hardly been able to take any advantage of it.

namely, in the history of a period of special interest, touching as it does the close of the Crusades, and embracing a Dynasty of slave Sultans unique in the annals of the world.

As the Mameluke dynasty follows close upon the steps of Saladin and his Successors,—grew in fact out of the Eyyubite Sultanate,—it is thus immediately associated with the last days of the Crusades. To illustrate this connection, I have ventured to place as an introduction to the history, part of a Lecture containing a chronological outline of the protracted struggle of the "Soldiers of the Cross," and of its final issue. The Reader may perhaps find it useful at the outset as explaining the origin and rise of the Leaders who were finally to crush the expiring efforts of that great armament of misguided Christianity.

The *Encyclopædia Britannica* has an able article on Egypt which is especially valuable with reference to the latter days and fate of the Mameluke race. The French Archæological Mission has also published several excellent numbers on the period under consideration, with beautiful illustrations, of which I have ventured to borrow some. There is also an interesting *brochure* by M. Max Herz on the Cairo Museum, with an illustrated description of its archæological contents.

Lastly I have to express my thanks to H.E. Yacoub Artin Pasha for publications regarding Cairo and the Mameluke dynasty, and for photographs of ancient buildings of which specimens are introduced into this Volume; and above all for the interesting Memorandum on the habits of the Mamelukes, which will be found as Appendix II. at the end of the book.

W. M.

EDINBURGH UNIVERSITY, 1895.

INTRODUCTION

A BRIEF HISTORICAL SKETCH OF THE CRUSADES

(Taken from a Lecture delivered to the Students of the Edinburgh University in 1894.)

IN the Preface to the *Rise, Decline, and Fall of the Caliphate* is the following paragraph :—

I may be permitted here to lament the want of any full and standard work in our own language on the Crusades, and on the Mameluke dynasty and its overthrow by the Osmanlies,—chapters not only deeply interesting in themselves, but bound up with the interests of the Eastern Churches and development of the political relations of Europe, Asia, and Egypt. . .

. . . .

. . . I purpose inviting your attention to this subject, pointing out the present defect in our literature, indicating the sources from which it may be supplied, and offering some inducement toward the study.

In our own language, Gibbon's history of the period— bright and instructive as it is, and invested with his own peculiar charm—must still be held fragmentary and incomplete; and, like other English, and indeed most European authorities, it has been drawn mainly from the Western standpoint. The most elaborate, and by far the most exhaustive treatise on the subject is by Wilken, in eight volumes. No student can pretend to any sufficient acquaintance with the history, either in its Asiatic or its Western aspect, without a thorough mastery of this great work.[1] Still more important in its Oriental bearing is Weil's *History of the Caliphs*,[2] which at this period (the Abbaside Caliphate having declined and almost vanished out of sight) is virtually a history of the Eastern Empire, —the Seljukes, Mongols, and Mamelukes. The latter half of Weil's third volume, and beginning of the fourth, are quite essential to the grasp of the successive Crusades as affected by the breaking up of the Seljuk house, the growth of the Ortok family, the fall of the Fatimide Caliphate, and the rise of the Mameluke dynasty. No writer has gone so deeply as Weil into the Oriental authorities who here are often at variance with the Western, or so thoroughly analysed the bearing of the Crusades from an Asiatic and Egyptian point of view. I therefore recommend any student who would enter on this chapter of history, to make himself perfect master of all that both Wilken and Weil have to say on the subject.

In an address like the present, which has for its object simply to direct attention to the history and results of the Crusades, any detailed narrative of the events would be altogether out of place. I will therefore confine myself to a brief chronological review. . . . The importance of the study will come home to us when we remember, *First*, that Jerusalem was held by a Christian king for nearly a century; and Syria by Christian rulers more or less for two centuries, that is, from 1097 A.D. to 1291 when Acre fell and the Crusaders were swept out of the land; and *Second*, when we take note of the vast multitudes which for two hundred years poured steadily into Palestine, numbering from first to last not less than several millions. The reflex

[1] *Geschichte der Kreuzzüge nach Morgenländischen und abendländischen Berichten*, 1807–1832. I strongly recommend the study of these eight volumes, long and laborious though the task may be, to anyone who desires complete knowledge of the subject.

[2] *Geschichte der Chalifen*, von Dr. Gustav Weil. First series. 3 vols., 1846–1851, from the rise of Islam to end of the Abbaside Caliphate. The second series covers the Mameluke dynasty till conquered by the Osmanlies, vols. iv. and v., 1860–1862.

influence upon Europe must also be held a matter of the highest historical moment.

The first idea of a Crusade arose out of the desire to protect pilgrims resorting to the Holy places there. During the tenth and eleventh centuries, there was a marked increase in these, partly from the expectation of Christ's advent at the close of 1000 years of our Era; partly, also, from the conversion of Bulgaria, which enabled pilgrims, avoiding the dangers of a sea voyage, to journey by land to Constantinople, and thence by the coast to Palestine. We read of one such expedition in the middle of the fourth century numbering 7000, of whom but a fourth returned. The enormities perpetrated in the Sanctuary by Hakem, the insensate demigod of the Fatimides, and afterwards by the Seljukes, who took Jerusalem in 1070 A.D., touched the heart of Christendom; while Peter the Hermit, by harrowing details, roused the passion for vengeance throughout every class, down to the lowest dregs of the people. In 1095. the vast assemblies at the Councils of Placenza and Clermont, thousands, both of clergy and laity, were stirred to the wildest enthusiasm by the fiery appeal of Pope Urban, who promised absolution and heavenly succour to all that joined the enterprise, and paradise for such as might fall fighting for the Cross. Marvellous was the effect. The wild cry, *Deus vult, Deus vult*, resounded all around. Men, women, and even children, flocked from every quarter to be sealed as pilgrims with the sign of the Cross, and preparations were forthwith set on foot for contingents from every land to meet the following year at Constantinople.

Meanwhile, prodigious numbers of the lower classes, " a 1096. plebeian multitude," followed in the Hermit and other leaders' train, animated by a fierce fanaticism, and, as their conduct shortly showed, slaves to rapine as well as to lower passions. They marched in several bands through Hungary, where their outrageous conduct brought the greater part to an untimely end. The first under Walter, and the second

A.D. 1096. under Peter, gave themselves up to plunder and riot, and a portion only reached Constantinople. Thence, passing into Bithynia, they took Nicæa; but jealousies broke out between the various nationalities, and they fell before the Turkish arms: "a pyramid of bones" the only relic of their misguided zeal. A few thousands were rescued by the Kaiser, but the youths and maidens—a sad foretaste— were led off to the Turkish Court. Again, a body of 15,000, and another of 20,000, taking the way through Germany where they drew the sword and committed unheard-of atrocities against the Jews, were pursued and slaughtered in Hungary; but a remnant escaped to Constantinople, and the remainder returned, a laughing-stock, to their homes. Thus, "of the first Crusaders, 300,000 had already perished, before a single city was rescued from the infidels, before their graver and more noble brethren had completed the preparations of their enterprise."[1]

First Crusade, 1097.
This miserable tale quickened the departure of the now well-marshalled forces, some 600,000, besides women, clerics, and camp followers. The leaders were princes of distinction, surrounded by brilliant companies of Knights and their attendants, the growth of chivalry; for "the Crusades were at once an effect and a cause of this memorable institution."[2] They marched, as the miserable crowds before them had done, in three bodies, and by similar routes; and, though not without severe hardships and loss, reached at last the Bosphorus. Their reception by Alexius, the Kaiser, was far from friendly, and many passages of arms with the Greeks took place before the great host was able to pass from Constantinople into Asia Minor.

Such was the route through Greece and Asia Minor, that for many years was taken by the successive expeditions which, with more or less of military discipline, sought the shores of Syria; but later on, the easier way was resorted to of a direct sea voyage. Meanwhile, we need not wonder that Alexius was dismayed at the vast armed multitudes which kept passing through his land. He had,

[1] Gibbon, chap. lviii.   [2] *Ibid.*

indeed, been long appealing to the European Powers for A.D. 1097. help against the Turks. But the unwelcome attitude of these countless hosts brought a new disquiet into his mind, and the jealousies which made the Byzantine Court often thwart their progress, fermented bad blood, and eventually led to the loss of the eastern Citadel of the faith.

It was toward the end of 1097 A.D. that the invading force, reduced in its passage through Asia Minor by fighting and desertion to 300,000 combatants, invested Antioch, and, after a siege of nine months, took it by storm, and 1098. also Edessa, with the surrounding country. Shortly after, they were in considerable danger from the Seljukes, but were able eventually to drive them off. After some delay, 20,000 soldiers, followed by as many pilgrims, marched, without serious opposition, along the sea coast of Syria towards the Holy land. It was the middle of summer when they reached Jerusalem, then in the hands of the Fatimides; and after a siege of seven weeks, took it by 1099. storm. The Sacred city flowed with blood; the Jews 15th July. sought refuge in their synagogue, but it was set on fire, and they perished in the flames. Within the next three days, 70,000 Moslems, without respect of age or sex, were put to the sword. Having sated thus their savage passions, the soldiers of the Cross fulfilled their vows, and kissed the stone that had covered Him who said, *My kingdom is not of this world, else would My servants fight.* Barbarism, cruelty, hand in hand with fanatical piety, was the strange badge of this "Holy war"; and, as we shall see, jealousy, strife, and even treachery, avarice, dissipation, and moral laxity, transpire too often, amongst the clergy as well as amongst the laity, throughout the whole course of these Crusades, and were indeed among the chief reasons that brought the cause eventually to an untimely end.

Godfrey was now elected King, and thus a Christian prince, though weak and often hard pressed, and but one amongst the independent Barons who held cities and strongholds throughout the land, occupied the throne of

b

A.D. 1099. the Holy city for fourscore and eight years, when at last Jerusalem fell before the arms of Saladin.

At first the Crusaders overran the greater part of Syria, though they never succeeded in taking Damascus. The Caliphs of Bagdad, now in abject dependence on the eastern Sultans, did not trouble themselves about the Crusade; and the Seljukes were too closely occupied with their own jealousies and dissensions to direct an army against the Holy land. But Scions of their house, and Arab Emirs of the lands around, from time to time fought vigorously, and with varying fortune, against the invaders. Tancred and Baldwin seemed at one time to be carrying all before them, when, as was the wont, they fell out among themselves, and (strange alliance for soldiers of the Cross) joined on either side by Moslem arms, fought an internecine war. Tancred became supreme in Syria; so 1112. much so, indeed, that Ridhwan and other Seljuk Emirs were fain to make him heavy payments as an inducement to grant them a truce. But this success soon roused alarm amidst the peoples of the East; and though the Caliph of Bagdad was deaf to their cries for help, a powerful army at last assembled, and repeatedly drove back the Crusading forces, led bravely on by Baldwin, with heavy loss. Dissensions, however, eventually broke up this Moslem host; and thus the Crusaders, though weakened and losing many strongholds, were still enabled to hold their own. About this time, too, Baldwin I. made a successful inroad 1118. into Egypt, and was on the very point of taking Cairo, when he died.

Throughout these first twenty years of the Crusade, the stream of Knights and Soldiers of the Cross towards the Holy land was steadily maintained, and that often in prodigious numbers. In particular, Raimond, with a host 1103. 300,000 strong, sought by a northern circuit through Asia Minor to attack Bagdad, but was routed in Armenia so fearfully that but few escaped to the shores of the Black Sea. Two other great bodies, one of them 100,000 strong, were similarly cut up in the attempt to cross from

the Bosphorus through Asia Minor to Syria, and the sur- A.D. 1103.
vivors, of whatever sex or age, sold into slavery. Such
was the wild and blinded zeal with which the heaven-born
assurances of the Papal Court had inflamed the Christian
world.

We come now to a period when the Border Emirs,
gathering strength from the dissensions of the Seljuk
House, began to inflict the first of those decisive blows
eventually fatal to the Crusade. They roused the Moslem
populations all around, and defeat upon defeat of the
Franks was the unhappy result. The Ortok clan, with
Ilghazy at their head, beat back Rogers of Antioch, and,
aided even by the Christian inhabitants, took that city for
a time. Afterwards, in the pitched battle of Danit, they 1119.
inflicted upon the Crusaders a terrible defeat, with great
loss of Knights, and of Rogers himself, of whose last
confession and communion before the fight a touching
account is given. In another sad disaster, Joscelin was 1123.
taken prisoner; and King Baldwin, sent in chains to
Harran, only gained his freedom by a compact which he
failed to fulfil. Amid all these calamities, the Crusaders
obtained a single advantage in the capture of Tyre, but
otherwise they could do little in reprisal beyond cruelly 1124.
ravaging the land.

It was now that Zenky, the terrible foe of the
Crusaders, came to the front. He was Atabek, or Major-
Domo, at one of the Seljuk Courts, and was also much
occupied with the affairs of the Abbaside Caliphate at
Bagdad. Succeeding to the Chiefship of Mosul, he entered
on a campaign against Syria. Beating the Franks at every 1126–
point, he seized many of their strongholds. While thus 1128.
pursuing a victorious course, he was called back to Bagdad,
and there detained for several years immersed in the broils
of the declining Caliphate. Eventually the city being
captured by the Seljukes, he escaped with the Caliph to 1134,1135.
Mosul. Central Asia was at this time convulsed by the
incessant irruption of Ghaznevides, Chorians, Ghoos,
Kharizmies, and other Turcoman hordes, before whom

A.D. 1136. the Seljuk dynasty came to an end. Freed thus from superior control, Zenky became the fortunate ruler of the country west of the Euphrates. And it was now that, descending like a whirlwind on Syria, he ravaged the Christian territories, and with great slaughter beat the Crusading armies back. Multitudes were slain, and many knights made prisoners. King Fulco himself was pursued and taken captive, but graciously by the conqueror let go free.

1137. About this time the Kaiser, jealous of the Crusader's claim to the province of Antioch, and with the view of securing the sovereign title recognised as his at its first conquest, marched across Asia Minor, and laid siege to the city. Having come, however, to terms with Raimond, they joined forces and, 200,000 strong, attacked Aleppo. Zenky, in alarm, appealed to the Powers around for aid. He was reinforced from various quarters, and, among the rest, with 20,000 horse from Bagdad,—all the help the Abbaside Caliphate ever gave against the Crusade. Thus strength-

1138. ened, Zenky attacked the combined army, and drove them ignominiously back to Antioch. He then went against Damascus, but the Governor with the help (strange to say) of the Franks, resisted the attack. After various victories all around, he stormed Edessa, which had been carelessly

1143, 1144. left by Joscelin undefended. The city was ransacked, but special consideration was shown by Zenky towards the native Christians and their Bishop. Shortly after Zenky was murdered by his own memlukes. The Crusaders rejoiced, but their joy was shortlived. Joscelin, hastening back with his knightly force, and aided by the Greeks, who thus quickly forgot the clemency of Zenky, retook the city. But a greater than Zenky was at hand. His son, Nureddin, coming up, attacked them in front; while the garrison from the citadel fell on them from behind. All night the battle raged. The Crusading force was cut to pieces, and only the few knights who, with Joscelin, could force their way through the enemy, escaped to Samosata. A terrible fate awaited the native Christians; for Nureddin,

incensed at their ingratitude, gave no quarter. Thirty <small>A.D. 1144.</small>
thousand are said to have been slain, and fifteen thousand
sold into slavery.

Europe was aroused by these terrible disasters. The <small>Second Crusade, 1147.</small>
Pope again sounded his heavenly summons to the battle of
the Cross; and Bernard, like Peter the Hermit, made
Europe ring afresh with the cry,—a repetition, in fact, of
what happened fifty years before. Louis and Conrad
headed the vast force thus assembled, and it marched in
great pomp, with noble ladies in its train. Against the
Jews in Germany, savage enormities were perpetrated as
before; and in Asia Minor, through the Kaiser's treachery,
even greater losses were suffered from the Turks. Hardly
one-tenth survived to reach the Holy land. Still, the
Franks were so greatly strengthened by the reinforcements
that they attempted to storm Damascus.[1] But the eastern
Barons, bribed (sad to say) by the Governor, dealt faithlessly by their fellows; the force retired disastrously, and
the newcomers sickened by the intrigues and laxity around
them, sighed again for home. Excepting the capture of
Ascalon, the campaign was one of unbroken loss and mis- <small>1149-1152.</small>
fortune. Jerusalem was twice attacked, and the land
overrun by Nureddin. Few strongholds now were left
either in the north or south to the Crusading forces, whose
rivalries, and too often worthless lives, but courted defeat,
and were fast discrediting the Christian name. In a
pitched engagement, Raimond of Antioch was slain with
all his train, and Joscelin II. carried off a prisoner in
chains, and so remained for years until his death.
Nureddin, having at last got possession of Damascus, daily <small>1156.</small>
grew in power. A truce made by him about this time
was faithlessly broken by King Baldwin, who fell upon an
unsuspecting Moslem camp that trusted to it. Shortly
after, the Franks paid dearly for this act of treachery.

---

[1] Saladin was present at this battle with his father. It is curious
to read that the enthusiasm of the citizens was kindled by the holding
up of Othman's Coran, the same copy so recently lost in the conflagration of the great Mosque.

A.D. 1156. The King escaped with difficulty from Nureddin's hands; but a body of his knights was captured, marched with ignominious pomp through the Damascus streets, and then in retaliation put to death. Even when success was near at hand, as in the siege of (northern) Cæsarea, the opportunity was, by the jealousies of the Barons, lost. But the cause, sunk thus low, was anew strengthened by a fresh contingent under Dietrich of Flanders. Nureddin, too, fell sick, and in one engagement was nearly taken prisoner. But fortune turned again, and in a raid against Armenia, Rainald fell into the enemy's hands, and was led off in chains to Aleppo. A year or two of inaction followed; but the time was made good use of by Nureddin to consolidate his rapidly increasing realm.

Third Crusade, 1158.

1169. At this point, Egypt comes upon the stage as bearing on the fate of the Crusade. In the decrepitude of the Fatimide dynasty, Nureddin and King Amalrich both set their heart upon it. The Caliph's Vizier sought aid from each against the other, and each in turn invaded the land. At last a friendly treaty was concluded with both, which Amalrich was the first to break, ravaging the country and exacting largesses from the Court. The wretched Caliph appealed to Nureddin, sending locks of his ladies' hair in token of extremity. Nureddin gladly despatched his general Shirkoh to the rescue, before whom Amalrich, crestfallen, slipped away. Shirkoh thus became supreme

1170. in Egypt, and shortly after his nephew, Saladin, succeeded to his place. Next year the Caliph died. So ended the Fatimide dynasty.[1] And Saladin became Lord of Egypt. He was of Kurdish blood, and though at first little of a soldier, was not long in distinguishing himself by the able defence of Damietta against the Franks, and he soon displayed all the qualities of a great ruler at once in council and in war. Jealous of the independent attitude of his viceregent, Nureddin repeatedly summoned him to submission; and the position of Saladin was rapidly becoming hazardous, when he was happily relieved of the danger.

[1] Having lasted 272 years.

For just then Nureddin died,—a grand, true, and faithful A.D. 1171.
prince. And so Saladin was left at peace in Egypt, where
he signalised his reign by schools and hospitals and other
improvements.

Fortunately for Saladin, dissensions in the family of 1176.
Nureddin enabled him to extend his sway over Syria, and
eventually as far as Mesopotamia and Mosul. He was
recalled to Syria by a fresh invasion of the Franks, who
arrived in bodies both by land and sea. At first these,
with the miraculous fragment of the Holy cross, drove all
before them; but, as usual, they wasted their energies in
wrangling and useless raids. Attacked at Paneas, they
suffered a sad defeat, losing Honfroi and a multitude of 1180.
knights. A fortress built on the Jordan to threaten
Damascus was stormed, and the King himself on one
occasion escaped with difficulty. The Franks were fast
sinking into a weak and helpless state. The guardians of
the throne about this time were (as Gibbon puts it) successively a leper, a child, a woman, a coward, and a traitor;
while the Barons and Knights, of whatever order, instead
of rallying to its defence, did little else than quarrel for
the supremacy, and, indeed, were too often taken up by
cupidity, jealousy, strife, and licentious lives,—unholy
defenders of a Holy land! The Pullanes too (half-caste
progeny of native mothers), grown up now a disreputable
and disloyal race, added to the insecurity of the Franks.
The wonder is that the kingdom hung so long together;
which, indeed, it never would have done had there not
been an unceasing flow, year by year, of Knights and
Pilgrims for its defence. Things, however, were now
coming to a bitter end.

Satisfied with his victories, Saladin entered into a 1182.
truce, and returned to Egypt. He was, however, shortly
after recalled to revenge an attack on the Sacred environs
of the Hejâz by Rainald, who, having fitted out a fleet at 1183.
Ayla, devastated the coasts of Mecca and Medina. He was
driven off with great loss, and a multitude of his followers
were taken captive, some of whom were sacrificed at the

A.D. 1186. shrine of Mina. Saladin, resenting the despite thus done to his Faith, inflicted reprisals on the Crusaders' territory, and, being now secure throughout the East, gathered his forces from all sides, resolved to make a final end of the Crusading rule. Against Rainald he was specially incensed, not only for the attack on Arabia, but for repeated seizure of caravans with Moslems on their pilgrimage to Mecca. Against the advice of Raimond, who had lately made peace with Saladin, King Veit marched upon Tiberias, where Saladin, having taken the city, was raiding 1187. all around. The armies met at Hittin, where the Crusaders, blinded by the smoke and heat of the kindled grass, suffered a crushing defeat. The King and the Grandmaster of the Templars, with all survivors, were taken captive. Rainald was slain by Saladin, as he had sworn, with his own hand. The captives were sold as slaves; but the Knights of both Orders, to avenge the inroad on the Sacred territory and attacks upon the Moslem pilgrims, were hewn in pieces before Saladin's eyes. The King alone was taken honourably to Damascus, and freed on promising to give Ascalon up.

Saladin now scoured the land, and recovered most of the strongholds still in the Crusaders' hands. Unwilling to besiege the Holy city, he offered to make concessions if it were but ceded peacefully. His advances were declined, and so at last Jerusalem was invested; and, after an eight 2nd Oct. days' siege, becoming untenable, the keys were delivered 1187. up to Saladin. A cry of anguish rose from the miserable inhabitants, and of wailing from the women clothed in sackcloth. The Sacred places were desecrated, the churches turned into Mosques, the crosses torn down, and the bells destroyed. But the people, on payment of a light ransom, were allowed free departure. The conduct, indeed, of Saladin and his brother Adil on this occasion is praised for their care of the poor Christians, and for the convoy provided for their departure.

1188. Saladin made good use of his victory, and left little of importance throughout Syria in the Crusaders' hands besides Antioch, Tyre, and Tripoli. Boemund was A.D. 1188. besieged in Antioch; but, on surrendering all his Moslem captives, and promising to retire if not soon relieved, Saladin admitted him to a seven months' truce. Another Crusade, however, was at hand. The loss of Jerusalem and its desecration after having been a Christian capital for nearly a century, the slaughter of Knights, and the loss of Syria, fell like a thunderbolt on Europe. The Pope fulminated his Bulls afresh, and (forgetful of the past) reiterated the promise of Divine aid and victory. He also imposed fresh burdens on the people, of which "Saladin's tenth" survived a welcome remnant for the treasury of Rome. The cry resounded through Europe, and though at first there was much dissatisfaction, especially at the faithlessness of the Pullanes, multitudes at last assembled, and carrying, like their predecessors, cruelty and rapine in their front, set out upon the fourth Crusade. Many went by Fourth sea; the rest, by land, fought with the Greeks, as their fore- Crusade, 1189. runners had done a hundred years before, and after similar perils and privations, reached, but a remnant, the Holy land. Thus reinforced, the Franks invested Akka. There Saladin inflicted severe loss upon them; but they were too many for him, and so, sick and disheartened, he retired from the scene. The siege was prosecuted with vigour. Hunger and hardship were bravely borne by the forces as they held their ground around the city; but there is also the usual story of dissension; Cœur-de-Lion, for example, and King Veit arrayed with their followers in arms, against Conrad and Philip of France. There is also the same sad tale throughout the army of mingled fanaticism and sin, of masses and prayers, hand in hand with vice and riot. After two years the Moslem garrison, in the last extremity of want, surrendered upon favourable 1191. terms. These were faithfully carried out by Saladin, who forthwith set all the Christian captives free, while the cruel Richard put the garrison, two or three thousand in number, to death, excepting such as could give a heavy ransom. After some fresh hostilities, in which Saladin

A.D. 1191. retaliated by taking the lives of such Crusaders as fell into his hands, and the loss of Ascalon (which Saladin, with a heavy heart, to safeguard Egypt, took and razed to the ground), a three years' truce was concluded between the contending parties. Soon after, Saladin died. A noble prince: in virtuous living, not, indeed, to be compared with Nureddin; but gentle and forbearing, though ever stirred by a lofty ambition and by the aggressive spirit of Islam.

1193.

1193–1196. The truce was fortunate for the Moslems, who were at that moment seriously weakened by the death of Saladin and by the discord which, as usual, rent his large family, till at last his brother Adil gained the ascendency. But the Crusaders were in no case to profit by such opportunity; and we may say, indeed, that the fate of the Crusade was henceforth but a foregone conclusion. Their land was waste, and their hold alone maintained by the few strongholds yet left in their possession, and by the ceaseless flow of fresh Crusading bands. The fifth Crusade, composed of German levies, under Henry VI., was ill-received by the Italians, French, and English. Bad blood and disunion again paralysed their efforts. Beyond the capture of Beyrut,[1] little else was gained, and the new-comers, disheartened, soon began to return again to Europe. Meanwhile, Adil was achieving a grand and undisputed rule from Georgia to Aden, before which the weak, divided, and desultory efforts of the Franks were powerless.

Fifth Crusade, 1197.

Sixth Crusade, 1200. The sixth Crusade, an overpowering force, was diverted, on reaching Venice, from the Holy land by the ecclesiastical rancour that ruled against the Greek Church. Constantinople was besieged and taken with terrible slaughter and calamities, and remained under the Roman hierarchy for half a century, when it again reverted to the Greeks. From first to last this Crusade, supported by the Papal

---

[1] Two ships had long lain in wait outside the harbour to decoy Crusading vessels and carry their passengers into Beyrut, where as many as 14,000 were, on its capture, found in captivity. Some say many more.

Court, was an iniquitous work, which but tended to the A.D. 1200. eventual downfall of the Eastern bulwark of the Christian faith. About this time, also, we read of the Children's 1212. Pilgrimage, which ruined disastrously the lives and virtue of thousands of girls and boys. Some 30,000 were seized on their voyage to Egypt, and there sold as slaves; sad illustration of the fanatical darkness in which the Crusading spirit had shrouded Europe, and its melancholy results.

Little time elapsed before there was a new inroad into Syria. A great army, headed by four kings, assembled at Akka. After ravaging the Holy land, they advanced on Egypt, and laid siege to Damietta. In a few months they forced the defences that barred entrance, and invested the city. Hearing of their success, the Pope sent Cardinal Pelagius as his representative, who immediately assumed the management of affairs. After two years of heavy fighting and bloodshed, the city, and eventually the citadel also, fell into their hands, whereupon Pelagius was glorified by the Pope throughout Europe as a second Joshua. Another year passed, and the opportunity of further advance was lost in the usual quarrels and jealousies; —Pelagius spending such time as he could spare from fasts and masses in bitter dissensions with the other leaders. The Sultan, in distress, made repeated offers to cede Jerusalem if they would but retire; but, against King John's advice, the offer was rejected by the Cardinal. After the King with many thousands had retired in disgust, Pelagius at last advanced from Damietta upon Cairo. But the Egyptians, attacking the force before and behind, cut off both advance and retreat. Reduced to terrible straits, it was only by the clemency of the Sultan that they were not utterly destroyed, but were allowed to return unmolested to Syria. So ended the grand scheme of the Papal Court, all chance of success being lost by the ambition and perversity of Pelagius; while the forbearance of the Sultan, who granted an eight years' truce, has been justly lauded on every hand.

The sons of Adil, who died of grief at the taking of 1222.

(Seventh Crusade, 1217. 1218. 1220. 1221.)

A.D. 1222. Damietta, fell into discord among themselves; but little advantage was taken of it till Kamil at last gained
1227. supreme command. Between him and Frederick II., who made his Crusade about this time, friendly relations sprang up; so much so, indeed, that Jerusalem, with the
1229. surrounding lands, was restored to his possession on condition of equal rights and freedom to the Moslems, and also that the city should remain unfortified. Frederick was now crowned King of the Holy city, and this concession was enjoyed for fifteen years, till at last the Mongols swept before them all away. But Frederick, being under the Pope's displeasure, the Holy places were for a time under the Papal ban; and Frederick, in consequence, was ill-received by the Knights, who are said even to have planned his assassination. The Chiefs of Antioch, Tripolis, and Beyrut, independent one of another, thought little of combined action. Miserable contentions and abandoned living still weakened the Crusading arm; little more than raids and plunder were attempted, and that often with serious loss.[1] Meanwhile, the Crusade was again vigorously preached in Europe; but the new levies were, during the next ten or fifteen years, diverted by the Pope to Crusades against the Albigenses, the Pagans of the north, and suchlike objects of Papal displeasure.

1239. About this time the Franks embraced the cause of Ismail, who rose in rebellion against his nephew, the Sultan Eyyub,—an alliance so hateful even to Ismail's own followers, that their desertion on the field of Ascalon led to
1240. the Christians' shameful overthrow. The Sultan, nevertheless, came to peaceful terms with them; but the restless Knights continued hostile raids against Kerak, and even among themselves. We blush to read that 2000 prisoners
1243. were slaughtered by them at Akka, and still worse, that a body of captives brought in on promise of being baptized,

---

[1] In repelling an attack of the Mongols on Jerusalem, 2000 of the Moslems were mercilessly cut to pieces by the Pullanes; who, we are told, were more dreaded by the inhabitants of Syria even than the Mongol hordes.

were also put to death. A yet darker season was at hand A.D. 1240. in the eruption of the Charizmian hordes, who now at last reached Syria and fell upon it like an avalanche. They destroyed Jerusalem with horrible barbarity, slaying 7000 Christians, and carrying off the maidens into captivity. These barbarians formed an alliance with the Egyptian Sultan; and, commanded by Beibars, his Mameluke general, routed a combined army of Franks and Moslems near to Joppa, where the Christians, being again deserted by their Moslem companions, met with a terrible and bloody overthrow.

We come now to what may be called the last Crusade 1247. upon the Holy land, namely, Louis' first campaign. Passing on to Egypt, he attacked Damietta with the same early success, and the like eventual disaster, as in the case of Pelagius thirty years before. The army was defeated in an advance on Cairo, the fleet destroyed, and Louis taken prisoner. He was well treated by Turan Shah, who, for this act of kindness, was slain by Beibars; and Beibars thus succeeded to the Sultanate, the first of the Mameluke dynasty. In wretched case Louis and his Barons got back to Syria, and after further misfortunes, home to France. Long afterwards, Louis engaged in a second 1270. Crusade, but that being against Tunis, requires no further notice here, except that it was marked by the same disunion as of old, and had an equally unfortunate end.

The remainder of our story is one melancholy tale 1263. of decadence, hastened by the fatal discord and internal *et seq.* warring of the Hospitallers with the Templar Knights. "Foes to themselves," said Beibars, "their own strife and folly are their downfall." In his four memorable 1262-campaigns, Beibars destroyed their chief remaining strong- 1269. holds excepting Tripolis and Akka. The women and children from all quarters were sent as slaves to Tyre. At Antioch there is a sad tale, the whole body of the Crusaders —soldiers, priests and monks, and Christian citizens—on its capture, were put to death or reduced to slavery.

In 1289, Tripolis at last was stormed with terrible 1289.

A.D. 1289. massacre, thousands of women and children being driven into slavery. Still Knights and Barons courted attack on their yet remaining places on the coast by frequent raids and breach of truce, till at last Akka alone remained, the centre to which all fled for safety; and that was now besieged. It was a vast, magnificent, and voluptuous city, as grandly described by Wilken; crowded by Franks from every quarter as their last resort; Crusaders all, but yet, as the historian tells us, even in the throes of last existence still a prey to dissensions, jealousies, greed, and dissipation.[1] The Grandmaster of the Templars, anxious to save this great city, sought the Sultan, and brought from him pacific terms; but he was disowned as a traitor by the infatuated leaders, who drove him back upon the Sultan's Court. The first attack was repelled, but at the cost of 2000 lives. Despairing now, this last Crusading band resolved to die, and there is an affecting scene of their last confession and

1291. communion. The city fell (strange to say) on the same day, and same hour of the day, as a hundred years before it had been captured from the Moslems. A few escaped by ship. A thousand fled for the moment into a fortified place, but in the end all met their fate, and not a soul survived. A melancholy tale.

So ended the great Crusade. "By the command of the Sultan, the churches and fortifications of the Latin cities were demolished; a motive of avarice or fear still opened the Holy sepulchre to some devout and defenceless pilgrims; and (as Gibbon finishes the sad story) a mournful and solitary silence prevailed along the coast which had so long resounded with the WORLD'S DEBATE."

Such is a brief outline of the Crusades. I have had occasion repeatedly to notice the jealousies and discord which led to misfortune and defeat. But above and beyond these, the grand cause that rendered success impossible was the absence of any supreme and recognised ruler. There was no common authority from first to

[1] Wilken, viii. p. 793.

last, which could prevent disorder, enforce obedience, or command united action. The Crusaders came from the various lands of Europe; as such they had each their separate interests, and not less so the various knightly Orders. Too often, as we have seen, they fought one against the other. The "King" of Jerusalem had little authority beyond his own environs. Antioch, Tripolis, Edessa, and other strongholds were independent of one another, sometimes even hostile, and the Kaiser was jealous of them all. Under a common Prince, with recognised authority, success was possible. Torn by factions and contending interests, defeat was in the end inevitable.

The Crusades from first to last are a chapter unique in the history of the world; a chapter also, of which, especially in its Oriental aspect, there is, as I have said, much need of a well-digested work in our own language. Such an undertaking would afford occasion also for reviewing the effect of that great and protracted warfare upon the social state of Europe, as well as upon the Churches and Communities of the East. With the latter, persecution, loss, and decadence; with the former, some advantages as well as many evils.

The Crusades it was that roused the Western world from a long sleep of listlessness. It was they that first brought the Principalities throughout Europe into common action with a grand though mistaken object, and endowed them thus with a fresh political life. A new interest was by them created and quickened in the East, extending historical and geographical knowledge both as to place and people, and enlarging ideas in respect of the language as well as the manners and habits of the Asiatic world. Again, while the Crusades gave an insight into the defects of the Moslem faith, they furnished some bright examples of generosity and virtue even in the hostile ranks. They promoted trade and mercantile activity, and thus increased the wealth and capital of Europe. They contributed to the revival of the fine arts, and the prosecution of such scientific branches as astronomy, mathematics, medicine, pharmacy, and natural history. Above all, the Crusades gave a last blow to the Feudal system. The multitude of serfs that flocked to the banner of the Cross threw aside their servile bonds and assumed an attitude of independence; while the system was still further loosened by the frequent sale of feudal properties as the Knights and Barons left their homes for the East.

On the other hand, the Crusades aggravated the intolerance of the day, and promoted deeds of bloodshed and cruelty in the Christian ranks as appalling at times as those of their enemy; while we also have the strange combination of fanatical piety hand in hand with the lowest vices of humanity. Indeed, it is often difficult to recognise the Faith of Jesus, either in the religion which, throughout these two centuries, the Popes and their Councils kept sending back to the land of its birth, or in the agencies by which it was sought to establish it there. And while it might have been expected that the constant falsification of the Heavenly promises made by the Roman conclave would have weakened, if not altogether destroyed, faith in the guidance of the Western Church, we find, strange to say, that the Crusading sentiment had the directly contrary effect, introduced the reign of inquisitorial terror, filled the coffers of the Roman See, and riveted the shackles of Papal dominancy.

CITADEL (AS IN 1798 A.D.) FROM S.E.

ERRATA ET CORRIGENDA.

Page	Line				
7	18	*For* Adlil	*read* Adil		
40	28	,, Mokallam	,, Mokattam.		
40	28	,, Frontispiece	,, p. 214.		
41	9	,, outside	,, in.		
49	Margin	,, 1297 Novr.	,, 1296 Decr.		
80	11	,, Citadel	,, City.		
81	21	,, 14th	,, 4th		
81	28	*delete* the word Hill.			
81	30	*For* pp. 466, 467	*read* pp. 60, 100 et seq.		
81	31	,, Max Henry Le Caise	,, Max Herse; Cairo, 1896.		
117	11	,, twelfth	,, thirteenth.		
150	7	,, thirty-five	,, seventy-five.		

THE MAMELUKE DYNASTY

1260–1517 A.D.

CHAPTER I

EGYPT AND THE MAMELUKES[1]

SHORTLY after the Prophet's death, during the Caliph- <small>A.D. 640.</small> ate of Omar, Egypt was conquered from Mucoucus the Roman Governor by Amru, and for two centuries remained a province ruled by the Caliphs of Damascus and Bagdad. Towards the end of the ninth century, the Egyptian governor Ibn Tulûn, son of a <small>868–905.</small> Turkish slave, threw aside the yoke of the now decrepid Caliphate, and himself mounted the throne. His splendid administration is still marked by the magnificent Mosque which he built in Fostat, and

---

[1] Mameluke (*memlook*, the past participle of the verb *malak* to possess) signifies a slave. It is from the same root as *Málik* an owner or king. We shall call the slaves memlukes, as shorter and more akin to the original, and the Emirs or leaders Mamelukes.

which to this day bears its great founder's name.[1] The Tulunides after a time suffered Egypt to fall back into the Caliph's hands; but again it became independent under another Turkish Governor, Ibn Toghej, first of the Ikshidite line so called from his Ferghana lineage. Eventually the Fatimide (or Shiea) Caliphs, having defeated the Aghlabites of Tripolis and Kairowan, turned their arms eastward, conquered Egypt with southern Syria, and fixed their seat at Cairo,—*Câhira*, "the Victorious,"—which has ever since remained the capital of Egypt, and in the famous Mosque and College of Al Azhar contains a memorial of their rule. The Fatimides held the throne for two hundred years, but towards the end of that time becoming, like the Caliphs of Bagdad, weak and imbecile, they fell into the hands of Turkish Viziers who, keeping their masters in subserviency, themselves assumed the rule.[2] Such was the state of things at the time our history begins. But before passing to it, a few words may be of use to introduce

A.D. 868-905.

933-970.

[1] It is in Fostat, the ancient capital, a little above the modern Cairo; "the largest Mosque in Cairo, and as presenting the earliest specimens of the pointed arch, noteworthy in the history of architecture."—*Enc. Brit.*

[2] The Fatimide Caliphate was an offshoot of the Ismailians, a transcendental sect of the Shiea, or Alyite, faith. It arose from the Berbers of North Africa adopting a "*Mehdy*," who fled from Arabia in the beginning of the tenth century, and recognising him as their Caliph at Tripolis. Some sixty years afterwards, the Fatimide Caliphs (so called as descended from Fâtima, the Prophet's daughter) conquered Egypt and southern Syria. See the *Caliphate*, Relig. T. Society, London 1892, ch. lxxi.

to the reader the strange Mameluke race of which we write.

For several generations the Caliphs of Bagdad had fallen into the dangerous habit of attracting to their capital thousands of slaves with barbarous names from Turcoman and Mongol hordes. These they used both as bodyguards and also as contingents to countervail the overweening influence of the Arab soldiery, whom in the end they superseded altogether. From the bondmen, they became the masters of the Court, fomented riots and rebellion, and hastened the fall of the effete Caliphate.[1] The same habit, with the same eventual result, was followed by the Fatimide Caliphs; and after them likewise by the Eyyubite dynasty who, being strangers in the land, were glad of the support of foreign myrmidons. Conquered tribes in Central Asia were nothing loth to sell their children to the Slave-dealer, who promised them prosperity in the West; and the tidings which spread from time to time of fortune to be gained in Egypt, made his task an easy one. It was thus that not only prisoners of war, but children of the Eastern hordes, kept streaming to the West, where they were eagerly bought, sometimes at enormous prices, both by Sultans and Emirs.

The thousands who thus, with uncomely names and barbarous titles,[2] began to crowd the streets of

---

[1] *Caliphate*, pp. 589, *et seq.*
[2] I have throughout softened and abbreviated the names and titles.

Cairo, occupied a position to which we have no parallel elsewhere. Finding a weak and subservient population, they lorded it over them. Like the Children of Israel, they ever kept themselves distinct from the people of the land; but the oppressors, not, like them, the oppressed. Brought up to arms, the best favoured and most able of the Mamelukes when freed became at the instance of the Sultan, Emirs of ten, of fifty, of a hundred, and often, by rapid leaps, of a thousand.[1] They continued to multiply by the purchase of fresh slaves who, like their masters, could rise to liberty and fortune. The Sultans were naturally the largest purchasers, as they employed the revenues of the State in surrounding themselves with a host of slaves; we read, for example, of one who bought some six thousand. While the great mass pursued a low and servile life, the favourites of the Emirs, and specially of the Crown, were educated in the arts of peace and war, and, as pages and attendants, gradually rose to the position of their masters—the slave of to-day, the Commander, and not infrequently the Sultan of to-morrow.

From the first, insolent and overbearing, the memlukes began, as time passed on, to feel their power, and grew more and more riotous and turbulent, oppressing the land by oft-repeated pillage and outrage. Broken up into parties, each with the name of some Sultan or

[1] A title of command.

leader, their normal state was one of internal combat and antagonism; while, pampered and indulged, they often turned upon their masters. Some of the more powerful Sultans were able to hold them in order, and there were not wanting occasional intervals of quiet; but trouble and uproar were ever liable to recur.

The Eyyubite princes settled their memlukes, chiefly Turks and Mongols,—so as to keep them out of the city,—on an island in the Nile, whence they were called *Bahrites*, and the first Mameluke dynasty (1260-1382) was of this race, and called accordingly. The others, a later importation, were called *Burjites*, from living in the Citadel, or quarters in the town; they belonged more to the Circassian race. The second dynasty (1382-1517) was of these and, like the *Bahrite* dynasty, bore their name.[1] The memlukes were for the most part attached faithfully to their masters; and the Emirs, with their support, enriched themselves by exactions from the people, with the unscrupulous gains of office, and with rich fiefs from the State. The memlukes, as a body, thus occupied a prominent and powerful position, and often, especially in later times, forced the Sultan to bend to their will.

Such is the people which for two centuries and a half ruled Egypt with a rod of iron, and whose history we shall now attempt to give.

[1] *Bahr*, a sea or river, whence Bahrites, as living on the island. *Burj* (Boorj), a tower or case-mate, whence Burjites (Boorjites).

CHAPTER II

THE EYYUBITE DYNASTY, AND SULTANATES OF EIBEK
AND KOTUZ

1171–1260 A.D.

A.D. 1169. It was about the middle of the twelfth century that Nureddin and King Amalrich both turned a longing eye towards Egypt where, in the decrepitude of the Fatimides, dissension and misrule prevailed. The Caliph in alarm sought aid first from one and then from the other; and each in turn entered Egypt ostensibly for its defence, but in reality for its possession. A friendly treaty was at last concluded with both; but it was broken by Amalrich, who invaded the country and demanded a heavy ransom. In this extremity, the Caliph again appealed to Nureddin, sending locks of his ladies' hair in token of alarm. Glad of the opportunity, Nureddin despatched his general Shirkoh to the rescue, before whom Amalrich crestfallen retired. Shirkoh having thus delivered the Caliph, gained his favour, and, as Vizier, assumed the administration. Soon after he died, and his nephew Saladin A.D. 1169. succeeded to the Vizierate. The following year the Caliph also died; and now Saladin, who had by vigorous measures put down all opposition, himself as Sultan took possession of the throne. 1170. Thus the Fatimide dynasty which had for two centuries ruled over Egypt, came to an end.[1]

Saladin was son of a Kurdish chief called Eyyub, and hence the dynasty is termed *Eyyubite*. His capital was Cairo. He fortified the city, using the little Pyramid for material; and abandoning the luxurious palace of the Fatimides, laid the foundations of the Citadel on the nearest crest of the Mokattam range, and to it transferred his residence. After a prosperous rule over Egypt and Syria of above twenty years he died, and his numerous 1193. family fell into dissension. At last his brother Adlil, gaining the ascendency, achieved a splendid reign not only at home, but also in the East from Georgia to Aden. He died of grief at the taking 1218. of Damietta by the Crusaders, and his grandson Eyyub succeeded to the throne. It was now that the Charizmian hordes fell upon Syria, and, with horrible atrocities, sacked the Holy City. 1240. Forming an alliance with these barbarians, the Sultan sent the Mameluke general Beibars to join

---

[1] I have ventured to give a good deal here in the words of the Lecture on the Crusades.

A.D. 1240. them against his uncle the Syrian prince Ismail, between whom and the Crusaders an unholy union had prevailed. Near Joppa the combined army of Franks and Moslems met at the hands of Beibars and the Eastern hordes, with a bloody overthrow;
1246. and thus all Syria again fell under Egypt. To establish his power both at home and abroad, the Sultan bought vast numbers of Turkish memlukes; and it was he who first established them as *Bahrites* on the Nile. His son Turan was the last Eyyubite Sultan. In his reign Louis invaded Egypt, and advancing upon Cairo, was defeated and taken prisoner. Turan allowed him to go free; and for this act of kindness, as well as for attempts to curb their outlawry, he was pursued and slain by
1250. the Bahrite memlukes, who thereupon seized the government.

The leading Mamelukes chose one of themselves, the Emir Eibek, to be head of the Administration. He contented himself at first to govern in the name of Eyyub's widow, who indeed had been in complicity with the assassins of her stepson Turan. The Caliph of Bagdad, however, objected to a female reigning even in name, and so Eibek married the widow; and still further to conciliate the Eyyubites of Syria and Kerak, elevated to the title of Sultan a child of the Eyyubite stock. This concession notwithstanding, Nâsir the Eyyubite ruler of Damascus, advanced on Egypt but, A.D. 1251. deserted by his Turkish slaves, was beaten back by Eibek who returned in triumph to the capital. He soon found it, however, impossible to hold the turbulent memlukes in hand for, with the victorious general Aktai at their head, they scorned discipline and defied authority. Eibek therefore compassed the death of Aktai, on which the Bahrite Emirs all rose in rebellion. They were defeated. Many 1254. were slain and cast into prison; the rest fled to Nâsir, and eventually to Kerak. Among the latter were Beibars and Kilawun, of whom we shall hear more hereafter. Eibek was now undisputed Sultan, recognised as such by all the Powers around. And so he bethought him of taking a princess of Mosul for another wife; on which the Sultana, already estranged, caused him to be put to death; and she 1257. too, in the storm that followed was assassinated by the slave girls of still another wife.

Eibek's minor son was now raised by the Emirs to the titular Sultanate; and Kotuz a distinguished memluke of Charizmian birth, persuaded to assume the uninviting post of Vicegerent.[1] The Eyyubite prince of Kerak, in whose service many of the Bahrite memlukes still remained, attempting with their help to seize Egypt was twice repulsed by

[1] He belonged to the royal Charizmian house; which being defeated, he was carried a prisoner to Egypt, and there sold as a slave.

A.D. 1259. Kotuz, and thus obliged to disband the Bahrites, who returned to their Egyptian allegiance. Their return was fortunate, a time of trial being at hand. For it was now that Holagu with his Mongol hordes, having overthrown Bagdad, and slain the last of the Abbasides, launched his savage troops on the West. He fulminated a despatch to Nâsir the Eyyubite head of Syria, in which he claimed to be "the scourge of the Almighty sent to execute judgment on the ungodly nations of the earth." Nâsir answered it in like defiant terms; but, not being supported by Kotuz, had to fly from Damascus
1260. which was taken possession of by the Mongol tyrant. After ravaging Syria with unheard of barbarity, Holagu was recalled to Central Asia by the death of Mangu. Leaving his army behind under Ketbogha, he sent an embassy to Egypt with a letter as threatening as that to Nâsir. Kotuz, who had by this time cast the titular Sultan aside and himself assumed the throne, summoned a council and by their advice put the embassy to death. Then awakening to the possibilities of the future, he roused the Emirs to action by a stirring address on the danger that threatened Egypt, their families and their faith. Gathering a powerful army, the Egyptians advanced to Akka where they found the Crusaders bound by a promise to the Mongols of neutrality. The two armies met at Ain-Jalût, and

there, after a fiercely-contested battle, and mainly A.D. 1260. by the bravery of Beibars as well as of Kotuz himself, the Mongols were beaten and Ketbogha slain. On the news reaching Damascus, the city rose upon their barbarian tyrants, and slew not only all the Mongols, but great numbers also of the Jews and Christians who, during the interregnum, had raised their heads against Islam.

Following up their victory, the Egyptians drove the Mongols out of Syria, and pursued them beyond Emessa. Kotuz, thus master of the country, re-appointed the former Governors throughout Syria, on receiving oath of fealty, to their several posts. For his signal service, Kotuz had led Beibars to expect Aleppo; but, suspicion aroused of dangerous ambition on Beibars' part, he gave that leading capital to another. Beibars upon this, fearing the fate that might befall him at Cairo, resolved to anticipate the danger. On the return journey, while Kotuz was on the hunting-field alone, he begged for the gift of a Mongol slave-girl, and taking his hand to kiss for the promised favour, seized hold of it while his accomplices stabbed him from behind to death. Beibars was forthwith saluted Sultan, and entered Oct. 1260. Cairo with the acclamations of the people, and with the same festive surroundings as had been prepared for the reception of his murdered predecessor.

CITADEL (AS IN 1799 A.D.): THE BEMBER AH GATE.

PART FIRST

THE BAHRITE OR TURKISH DYNASTY

1260-1382 A.D.

CHAPTER III

BEIBARS

1260-1277 A.D.

BEIBARS BANDUKDARY,[1] first of the long line of Bahrite Mameluke Sultans, who for a century sat upon the throne of Egypt, had been purchased as a slave by Sultan Eyyub; while yet young he distinguished himself in the war with Ismail and the Crusaders, and then rose to high dignity. He was among those who conspired to take the life of Turan, the last Eyyubite prince. Under Eibek's Sultanate, he joined the disloyal party of Aktai, and on Aktai's assassination fled the country with

A.D. 1260.

---

[1] A Persian term signifying "holder of the gun."

A.D. 1260. the Bahrite fugitives. Under Kotuz, as we have seen, he regained his position as commander of the army; and on Kotuz' assassination was unanimously elected Sultan.

After his triumphal reception at the capital, Beibars made ample amends for whatever excesses he may have before committed in company with his Bahrite brethren. By wise administration, he succeeded in establishing his popularity and power both at home and abroad. He lightened the taxes which had made his predecessor's reign unpopular; gained confidence by judicious measures and the fair advancement of his memlukes; and conciliated Syria by the prompt recognition and friendly treatment of the local Governors. Damascus alone stood out; but there too the Emirs were gained over and the recalcitrant governor carried a prisoner to Cairo. He fostered public works, beautified the mosques, established religious endowments, improved canals, harbours and fortifications, and added to the security of the kingdom by a swift post between Damascus and the capital.[1]

1261. In the year following his enthronement, Beibars conceived the design of re-establishing the Abbaside Caliphate which, two or three years before, had been swept away and the whole Abbaside house destroyed by Holagu at Bagdad. He required his throne to be

[1] Despatches were received in sixty hours.

thus strengthened against the jealousies of former comrades, as well as against efforts of the Shie-ites to restore the Fatimide dynasty. A.D. 1261. A Caliph of the Orthodox faith would put an end to such intrigue, and confer legitimacy upon the Crown. Hearing, therefore, that an Abbaside still survived the Mongol massacre, Beibars had him brought in triumph from Syria to Cairo. At his approach, the Sultan with his Court went forth in State to meet him, while even the Jews and Christians carrying aloft the Law and Gospel followed in his train. He was then installed as Caliph, Beibars and the officers of State swearing fealty to him; while he in turn conferred on Beibars the sovereign title. At public worship, after the established ritual of reading the Coran and invocation of blessing on the Prophet and on the lineage of Abbas, the Caliph offered prayer for the welfare of the Sultan. Some weeks passed, and the royal party, having witnessed a festive combat on the Nile, assembled in a garden outside Cairo where the Caliph invested Beibars with a robe of honour and the glittering badge of Imperial State. He then presented him with a pompous patent, in which was enforced at great length the duty of warring for the faith and other obligations which now devolved upon him.[1] Then with sound of trumpet and shouts

---

[1] A very lengthy affair, copied verbatim both by Macrizy and Noweiry.

A.D. 1261. of joy from the crowds around, the procession wended its way through the carpeted streets, back to the Citadel,—the Sultan in front, next the Caliph and Vizier on horseback, while the rest followed on foot; a scene, we are told, impossible to describe. The Sultan then set out with a powerful army, intending to establish the Caliph in possession of Bagdad, as of old. At Damascus, however, he was warned that a powerful Caliphate set up there might endanger Egypt's independence. Jealous, therefore, of his protégé he left him there to march across the desert with a Bedouin and Turkish force; but on his march the new Caliph was attacked by the Mongol Governor and, deserted by his followers, perished upon the road.

On the tidings of this disaster reaching Cairo, another scion of Abbaside descent was elevated to the Caliphate (1263 A.D.). But, although he performed all the functions devolving on the office, Beibars took care that he should occupy a very different position from that of his predecessor. A mere creature of the Court, he was kept under restraint,—a *détenue* in the Citadel. Throughout the Mameluke dynasty, though the position varied under different Sultans, the office remained but a shadow and a name. The Caliph was brought out on important State occasions to complete the surroundings of the Court, and at every fresh succession to the Sultanate, as head of the Moslem faith, to grant its recognition of the title; and that was all. A.D. 1261.

However just his general administration, Beibars was not long in betraying, whenever his jealousy was roused, the treachery and disregard of life so characteristic of the race. He listened readily to suspicious tales, and not only kept changing his Viziers and Governors lest they should become too powerful but would cast them into prison whence sometimes they never again came forth. The most painful feature was the perfidy by which he did not scruple to attain his object. The biographers give many instances. The most notorious is that by which he drew into his net Moghîth, the Eyyubite Prince of Kerak. After various attempts, he sent him a despatch in which, under the most solemn protestations, he swore to be true and faithful to him.[1] Still doubting, but with no alternative, Moghîth repaired to the Sultan's camp in Syria, where Beibars, receiving him with all honour, accompanied him on horseback to his tent. There he was suddenly seized, and sent in fetters to Cairo,

---

[1] Noweiry, who himself saw and copied the original, gives it verbatim, and Weil's translation fills two pages. Beibars swears that, should he break the oath, he would dismiss his slaves and slave-girls, and walk thirty times barefoot as a sinner to Mecca.

Moghîth was accused of sending his son to Holagu beseeching him to spare Kerak; but even assuming such communication, that would not have justified the perjury.

A.D. 1261. where he was either murdered or starved to death. The Governor left by him at Kerak refused to give up the citadel to the faithless Sultan, and so it had to be taken by storm. The family of Moghîth, however, was kindly treated, though his son, on coming of age, was on mere suspicion cast into prison. After this it is needless to give other acts of perfidy; but the cruel finesse of the following may justify the exception. Wishing to be rid of the christian Patriarch of Bagdad, whose friendship with the Mongols alarmed him, Beibars fabricated a letter thanking him for secret intelligence. He then arranged that the carrier should be waylaid, and the letter laid before the Mongol Governor of Bagdad, who, before the facts transpired, had the Patriarch beheaded as a traitor.

1262, 1263. Beibars was at this time in great dread of the Mongols, whose empire under Abagha extended from the Oxus to the Indian Ocean. This led to friendly relations with Abagha's enemy, Berekh, Prince of Kiptchak. The same fear induced friendly relations with the Keisar, who was now recovering from the Sixth Crusade and the terrible calamities inflicted on Constantinople by the Papal Court. So friendly were the communications, that the Keisar built a mosque for the Moslems at his capital; and obtained from Beibars a Melchite Patriarch for

those of that persuasion in his realm. Beibars A.D. 1262.
busied himself also with envoys to Spain, Naples,
and the Seljukes of Asia Minor; wherever, in fact,
he might gain support against the dreaded Mongols.
But, after all, there was no present cause of alarm,
the Mongols having enough to do at home; and
so things remained till towards the close of his
reign.

We turn to the great Crusade, and to the four 1263.
memorable campaigns by which the Christian power 1. Campaign.
was brought by Beibars near to its end. With Kerak
conquered, and the Mongols held in hand by Berekh,
he was now able to bring down the whole power of
the Sultanate upon the Crusaders, who, besides other
causes of offence, were specially obnoxious for their
friendly relations with the Mongols. He had already
proposed an exchange of prisoners; but as the Franks
demurred, he now upbraided them for their want
of pity towards their own brothers in the faith; and
so he kept all his Christian slaves in hard labour
on the fortifications of Damascus. The immediate
cause, however, of his first campaign against
them, was their alleged breach of treaty in
failing to give up certain strongholds. To mark
his displeasure, Beibars now ravaged the country
in all directions, and demolished the Church of
Nazareth.

The second campaign was opened early in the

A.D. 1265.
II. Campaign.
Feb.

following year by the siege of Cæsarea, which, notwithstanding the heavy fortifications of Louis, was, after five days, stormed and dismantled; Beibars himself encouraging the troops, not only by his brave example in the field, but by himself labouring with them at the demolition of the walls. Then he attacked Arsuf, a maritime citadel a little

April.

to the south. It was manfully defended by the Hospital Knights for forty days; while, on the opposite side, there was a marvellous outburst of fanatical zeal, roused by the fakeers and dervishes, and even by the women, who joined in working at the approaches under ground. Beibars, at the last, had to open negotiations with the garrison. Spared their lives, they were forced to labour at the destruction of their citadel and then, as trophies with broken crosses and inverted banners, made to grace the Conqueror's return to Cairo. Before leaving the field, Beibars rewarded the leading Emirs, some fifty or sixty in number, by endowing them in fieff with the fertile lands in Palestine of which he had now stripped the Crusaders. Copies of the roll in which he recorded the gift were distributed amongst his followers. This document describes in boastful terms the grandeur of the Sultan's reign, establishing, as it did, the true Faith by the overthrow of its Tartar and Crusading foes, and also the loyal services of the Emirs, "who glittered like

stars in the heavens, and had now received their A.D. 1265.
due reward."[1]

In the spring of 1266 A.D., Boemund Sixth of Antioch having, with both Orders of Knights, attacked Hims, Beibars sent a force to relieve it; and then, with all the troops at his command, set out upon his third campaign. He visited Jerusalem, and at Hebron gave gifts to the guardians of the grave of Abraham, forbidding them, at the same time, to allow Christian pilgrims to visit it. Then he crossed the Jordan by a bridge lately built by him, a little above the Dead Sea,[2] and

1266. III. Campaign.

---

[1] Written in Beibars' extravagant style, it is quoted by Macrizy, with the names of the grantees and titles of the several domains assigned to each. It occupies several pages of Quatremere, part ii. pp. 11-15.

[2] The bridge stands to the present day, and the centre arch has an inscription, stating the architect's name who built it, by order of Beibars, dated 671 A.H. (1273 A.D.); see picture and article by Clermont Ganneau, *Journal Asiatique*, 1888, p. 305, "Pont de Lydda." The inscription is in clear Arabic letters, four lines, with figure of a lion on either side.

See also Quatremere's *Macrizy*, ii. p. 26, and *Palestine Exploration Fund*, July 1895, p. 253, where, in an article entitled "Stoppage of the Jordan in 1267 A.D.," Colonel Watson, C.M.G., quotes the account of Noweiry (d. 1332) as to how the Jordan was temporarily cut off, as in the days of Joshua, which is briefly as follows:—

"In February 1266 A.D., the Sultan Beibars ordered a bridge of five arches to be built over the Jordan near Duma; and a marvellous thing happened, the like whereof was never heard before. After being erected, one of the piers got displaced, and the Sultan being angry, sent the builders back to have it righted; but the current was so strong as to interfere with their work. When, lo! after a time, on the night of December 8, 1267, the water ceased to flow; and the bed being dry, they lighted fires and torches, and hastily using the opportunity, completed repairs that would otherwise have been impossible. Riders sent

A.D. 1266. advanced from thence to Ain-Jalût and the Lake of Tiberias. The Egyptian forces, after the relief of Hims, having devastated the Crusaders' lands from north to south, were now assembled before Safed, a hill fortress beyond Tiberias. Here Beibars pressed forward the siege with his usual zeal and devotion, labouring himself at the bombardment, and assiduously attending the sick and wounded. Naphtha was discharged into the fortress, and the fighting was fierce and sanguinary. After three weeks thus passed, an amnesty was granted, allowing the garrison to pass out empty-handed. They were nevertheless all beheaded—some two thousand Templars and others—on a neighbouring hill. The reason assigned for this savage act is that the prisoners carried arms and valuables away with them, or that some Moslems were found imprisoned in the citadel; but such excuses will hardly suffice to clear the Conqueror from the dark blot that rests not only on his humanity but on his faith.[1]

to find out the cause discovered that a mound some way up had fallen into the channel and dammed the water up. By degrees the mass melted into mud and broke away. And so, at the fourth hour of the following day, the flood came down upon the bridge, with a volume as high as a lance. But the repairs had been completed, and only the scaffolding was carried away. Truly," concludes Noweiry, "a marvellous thing; and the bridge is there to the present day."

[1] Weil iv. 54 sums up the reasons assigned for this act of incredible cruelty with impartiality. Two of the garrison were spared at the entreaty of an Emir; but Macrizy says one embraced Islam, and the other was sent to carry the tidings to the Crusading army.

Safed was now rebuilt, and on its walls engraven a vainglorious tale of the "Alexander of his age and Pillar of the Faith," who had turned chapels into mosques, the clangour of bells into the cry of the Muedzzin, and the reading of the gospel into the recitation of the Coran, and so forth; ending with "Victory rests with the faithful, even to the Day of Judgment."[1] A.D. 1266.

It is about this time that we have the first mention of Armenia in relation to the Mamelukes. In 1262 A.D., King Haiton, in company with the Seljukes of Asia Minor (both under Mongol influence), invaded the coasts of Syria and threatened Aintab. Beibars forthwith sent an army against them, on which the Armenians sought aid both from the Tartars of Asia Minor and from the Crusaders of Antioch. With this help they made a fresh inroad on the frontier, and laid siege to Harim, but owing to the snow and severity of the season, were obliged to retire. Beibars had now his turn of vengeance, ravaging not only the confines of Armenia, but the Crusading districts of Antioch, Akka, and Cæsarea. Two years later, in the autumn after the capture of Safed, Beibars sent a force through the Cilician passes into Armenia, where Haiton, failing timely help from the Mongols, was defeated, one of his sons slain, and the other taken captive to Egypt. The whole land from Adana to Tarsus was 1263,1264. 1266.

---
[1] The inscription occupies nearly a page in Weil.

A.D. 1266. devastated with bloodshed and rapine, and the capital, Sîs, subjected to all the penalties of war. An Armenian stronghold held by the Templars was stormed, the men all slain, and the women and children taken captive. Beibars himself inflicted a terrible fate on Kara, a Christian village on an eminence north of Damascus, against which there was a charge of catching Moslem travellers and selling them as slaves. Their cloister was set on fire, the inhabitants sold as captives, the monks cut in pieces, and the church turned into a mosque. The youths were all sent as memluke slaves to Egypt, where some of them rose to distinguished rank. Beibars, having fallen from his horse, was carried in a litter back to Egypt; and in the following year, Haiton having submitted himself to the demands of the Sultan, his son was released and peace restored. But he had to forswear his alliance with the Mongols, and give up many of the frontier strongholds which he had received from them. It had been well both for the Armenians and for the Crusaders, had they kept aloof from Mongol influence which could not fail to embitter the Egyptians, and in the end to cause the fall of both.

1267.   In 1267 A.D. fresh ravages were made by the Syrian troops up to the very gates of Akka, but with no very marked result. It was in the following year that we come to the memorable fourth campaign. Early in the spring, after storming Shekîf, A.D. 1268. and falling without warning upon Jaffa which had given him serious umbrage, Beibars advanced on Tripolis and Antioch, resolved to wreak his vengeance on Boemund their Chief, for his support of the Mongols in their attack on Syria. The land was accordingly laid waste around Tripolis, towns and villages ransacked, and all Franks falling into their hands slain. The army then advanced on Antioch. The Governor in a sortie was taken prisoner, and Beibars, willing to come to terms, sought through him to make the authorities surrender. Failing in this, he invaded and stormed the city. Egress was 19th May. barred, and the inhabitants, — over one hundred thousand, including monks and priests,—slain or taken captive. Next day the garrison surrendered to save their lives, and were distributed, some eight thousand, besides women and children, with the other surviving inhabitants, as slaves amongst the army. The citadel was set on fire, and the flames spreading, the city was reduced to ashes.[1] The Conqueror then sent a letter to Boemund derisively commiserating with him on the sad fate of his Capital, in terms that overflow with vainglorious taunt and irony.

During the next two or three years military operations against the Crusaders were steadily pursued. One stronghold after another, succour

[1] The sad account should be read in Wilken, vol. viii. pp. 520 *et seq.*

A.D. 1269-1271.

from the West notwithstanding, fell into the Sultan's hands; and in his elation, especially after the capture of Akkar (between Tripolis and Hims), he dictated another insulting letter to Boemund: "Our yellow flag hath overthrown thy red, and Allah Akbar hath put to silence thy church bells."[1] While thus engaged, Beibars fitted out a fleet against Cyprus, which had given substantial aid to Akka, but it was wrecked by a storm as it approached the island.

These were the last proceedings during the present reign against the Franks. Continuous reinforcements from the West, and fresh apprehensions from the East, led Beibars to conclude a ten

1275.

years' treaty with Tyre and Akka; and some little time after, Boemund dying, Tripolis was also admitted as a tributary to peaceful terms. Besides these three cities, little now remained to the Crusading arms.

The Ismaelites settled in Syria, as tributary to the Crusaders in return for their protection, had long been the object of Beibars' enmity and of repeated attack upon their strongholds. On terms, however, being made with the Hospi-

---

[1] It is interesting to note that a town called Cosseir, belonging to Wilhelm, was spared on the production of a document in which the Caliph Omar had secured it to the Christians; but shortly after even this was seized on some pretext, and Wilhelm carried off to Damascus.

tallers, they now became subject to the Sultan. A.D. 1275. Eventually they resigned all their fortresses and in return received lands in Egypt. Their power was crushed, and they gradually disappeared, though we still find mention of them in the fourteenth century, and indeed some few survive to the present day.[1] It is characteristic of Beibars that he himself was not above making use, through them, of the assassin's dirk.

Relieved now of apprehension from the Franks, Beibars was able to turn his arms against the Mongol hordes which began to press upon the West. At the head himself of a strong battalion, he dashed fearlessly through the Euphrates, 1273 A.D., and drove the invaders completely back. The next two years he spent in various successful expeditions on the borders of Asia Minor; and in a fearful raid upon the Armenians for alleged neglect of treaty, Sis and Massîssah were given over to rapine and flames, and the whole land from Tarsus to Adana devastated. The booty was so great as to cover all the open ground in Antioch.

1273–1275.

Towards the close of his life, warlike measures were set on foot against Nubia, to avenge raids frequently made on Upper Egypt. The result was all the more successful from the dissensions that prevailed in the reigning family, which henceforth became entirely

[1] Burkhardt mentions several hundred families at Massiat.

A.D. 1272-1276. subservient to Egyptian rule. The Nubians were defeated in a pitched battle beyond Dongola; and as they refused Islam, they were forced to submit to the poll-tax payable by Unbelievers, and to a tribute of elephants, giraffes, and Nubian rarities, together with half the produce of the soil. The army returned laden with booty and slaves. We may remark this as the first occasion since the rise of Islam in which Nubia, notwithstanding frequent attacks, became really subordinate to Moslem control.

1276, 1277. The last campaign of Beibars was in some respects the most remarkable. The year before he died, a strong force had been despatched into Asia Minor to support the minor Seljuk prince of Cæsarea against a Mongol deputy who had usurped the government. The following spring, Beibars himself, after a grand review, set out with a heavy force, and advancing through Cilicia, completely defeated the Mongol army near to Ablestin. As he approached Cæsarea, the inhabitants, headed by the judges and nobles, came forth with music and

April. joyful shoutings to meet him, and thus festively conducted him into their city. After a few days spent there in royal state, he found his position so insecure that he retired by the Blue River, and spent some time at Harim. Meanwhile Abagha with a great army had hastened from the East to avenge the defeat of his troops and restore the Mongol rule. Arriving at Cæsarea, thus deserted by Beibars, he inflicted on its Moslem people a terrible revenge for the welcome accorded to the Egyptian Sultan, slaughtering multitudes of the residents there and around.¹ Such were the barbarities of the Mongol hordes upon Armenia; and such the faithlessness of Beibars, who thus hastily left the city which had welcomed him, to its fate; rejoicing only that the enemy he feared for Syria had turned its steps instead towards Asia Minor.

_{A.D. 1277.}
_{May.}

Returning leisurely to Antioch, he spent a month in the groves surrounding the city, and then set out for Damascus. There he rested, and gave a feast of his favourite Cumiz milk (the Tartar food) to his Emirs. An over-draught brought on fever, and about a fortnight after he died. Another account, however, is that the bowl of which he drank was one poisoned for an Eyyubite Emir, of which the Sultan also by inadvertence drank.²

_{June.}
_{19th.}
_{1st July 1277.}

So died Beibars in the zenith of his glory. Brought by a slave merchant with another boy from

---

¹ The numbers are given at 200,000, some say even 500,000; admitting all exaggeration, the carnage must have been terrible.

² The accounts vary. The writers of the day may naturally have refrained from a record so damaging to the Sultan. On the other hand, subsequent historians, as Macrizy, relate that the gallant deeds of an Eyyubite prince had roused the jealousy of Beibars, who thus got rid of him. Another curious statement is, that being an astrologer,

A.D. 1277. Kiptchak, he was originally sold at Damascus for 800 silver pieces, but returned for a filmy defect in one of his blue eyes. Dusky in complexion, he was tall and of a commanding voice, brave and energetic, and ever on the move. Mounted on horse or dromedary, he used to see for himself all that was going on, whether at Cairo, Alexandria, or elsewhere. Fond of travel, it was said of him, "A day in Egypt, a day in the Hejâz; here in Syria, now in Aleppo." He was addicted to a Tartar game like tennis, to which he would devote two days in every week. At his first rise to power, two of the Egyptian Sultans fell under his hand or that of his fellow-conspirators; and in the end, from the slave-boy of yesterday, he rose to be a great and noble Sovereign, ruling uncontrolled from the Euphrates to the Nile, from the confines of Asia to Sawakin on the Red Sea. Barring the few strongholds still in the Crusaders' hands, his authority was everywhere unquestioned. A strong opponent of Shieism, he was the liberal supporter of the four Orthodox schools; and, as we have seen, established an Abbaside Caliphate, though but a shadow and a name. An exemplary Moslem, he made the pil-

the Sultan had learned that in the present year a prince was to die of poison at Damascus, a prediction which caused him much disquiet and led to his casting the predicted fate upon the Eyyubite, of whom he was besides jealous. It is not easy to account for the rise of such stories unless there were some foundation for it in fact.

grimage to Mecca, and established many religious institutions. A.D. 1277. He had (apart from slave-girls) four wives of noble Tartar descent, and a family of sons and daughters, which is all in his favour, although in Moslem society (and specially so with the Mameluke surroundings) the female sex is so entirely hidden that little or nothing is heard of the domestic life of either Sultan or Emir. Beibars was a model Mameluke, both in virtue and in vice; he was not free from conduct not even named in the West, and his cruel exactions, treachery, and murderous acts have left a foul stain on his otherwise fair name as a brave, wise, and commanding Monarch.[1] His grand achievements, his unceasing activity, his public works and religious endowments, as well as his constant appearance in public and association with all around him, caused his immanity to be forgotten; and his name is heard to this day in the coffee-shops of Cairo as one of the best and greatest Sultans that Egypt has ever seen.

[1] In summing up his character, Macrizy mentions his forcing money from the rich by such horrid cruelties that many lost their lives. Also unheard-of enormities against the Jews and Copts of Cairo; wood was gathered in a furnace, and the wretched creatures were about to be cast therein, when, at the entreaty of the Atabek, he "pardoned" them, and contented himself with the lash, under which many lost their lives; Quatremere, ii. 154; see also p. 16, where the same thing is attributed to imputations of incendiarism. One hopes the tale is overdrawn; but that it should have gained currency at all, is evidence of the character for cruelty attributed to the Sultan.

A.D. 1277. There is little doubt that Beibars looked for the Sultanate to continue in his line, and accordingly, some years previously, had proclaimed his eldest son, Saîd, while yet a boy, Successor to the throne. The year before his death, he had him married with great festivities to a daughter of Kilawun, in hope, no doubt, of securing that leading Emir's support to his son's administration. The body of Beibars was embalmed and buried at Damascus; but his death was not known to the public till nearly a month had passed, for a litter had been despatched to Cairo, carrying, as was supposed, the sick Sultan, and it was not till the 30th July that Saîd mounted the throne.[1]

---

[1] In connection a story is told of Beibars having some nine years before left his camp at Arsuf, and travelled unknown to Cairo, where, watching how things went on, he remained concealed in the Citadel, the army believing all the time that he lay sick in camp.

CHAPTER IV

SAÎD—KILAWUN

1277–1290 A.D.

SAÎD, a vain and foolish youth, nineteen years of age, A.D. 1277. was cruel and treacherous like his Father, but utterly devoid of the Father's ability. Under the influence of his Mother, a few weeks after assuming the sceptre, he poisoned his Father's Vizier and cast others of his Father's officers into prison. Then yielding himself to the counsel of his young memlukes, he alienated the great body of the Emirs, who began to fear his designs against them. To divert their attention, a campaign was started for Armenia; but Saîd, with his Mother, remained behind at Damascus. Meanwhile the leaders with the army and Kilawun at their head, made aware of Saîd's unfriendly intentions, hurried back, and marching straight for Cairo, barred the city against him. He gained entrance, however, by stealth into the Citadel, but, after a week's siege, was allowed to abdicate and retire to Kerak. His uneventful reign had lasted little more than two years.

A.D. 1279.
Nov.

KILAWUN, the leading Emir, and father-in-law of Saîd, was now called on to take the reins, which he did at first as *Atabek*, or guardian, of another son of Beibars,—a mere child. But shortly after, dropping the pretence, he assumed the Sultanate in his own name.

1280.

The following year, Sonkor, governor of Damascus, rebelled, and set himself up as Sultan. This threw Kilawun into distress, for he feared the adherents of Beibars' family, as well as the approach of the Mongols, and the Bedouins also, who would gladly have seen the kingdom of Syria independent as in former times of Egypt. After repeated engagements, Sonkor was obliged to fly, Damascus was reoccupied, and peace restored. The rebellious Emirs both of Egypt and Damascus, and eventually Sonkor himself, were treated with magnanimity and restored to favour,— a well-advised, as well as generous, course, by which the Sultan gained their affection and support.[1]

1280.

Peace had hardly been restored, when the Mongols began again to fall upon the Syrian border with the same outrages as twenty years before. The district of Aleppo was visited with such savage cruelty that the people fled south; while Damascus fell into so great a terror that multitudes escaped

---

[1] Among the inhabitants of Damascus thus pardoned was Ibn Khallican the great historian, who, as chief Cazie of the city, had given a *fatwa* in favour of Sonkor's claims.

for refuge into Egypt. Kilawun repeatedly led his A.D. 1280. troops against these hordes; but they retired for the moment without coming to any decisive battle. The Hospital Knights of Markab had taken advantage of this invasion to plunder the Moslems in their vicinity. For this imprudence they were now attacked by the Sultan. But having sued for peace, were admitted to a ten years' truce; and so was also Boemund of Tripolis, for the Sultan was still in dread of the Mongols.

About the same time a conspiracy was formed against the Sultan's life. It is remarkable as having been discovered by friends of Kilawun in Akka, where the conspirators confided to the Franks that it was useless to treat with the Sultan, as his life would soon be cut off,—showing a freedom of communication between the Emirs and the Franks one would hardly have looked for. The conspirators confessed, and sought for mercy, but were all put to death. The suspicion extended to a number of memlukes, who were cast into prison, while several hundred adherents of the Beibars family escaped to the Mongols. The party thus attached to the late Sultan's house, and called after one of his titles *Zâhirites*, maintained a permanent position in the politics of the State, as we shall hereafter see.

The Sultan then revisited Damascus to solemnise 1281. the obsequies of Saîd, who had died at Kerak, and

A.D. 1281. whose remains were now carried by his Mother to be laid beside those of his father Beibars. While there, the Mongol hordes, under Abagha and his brother Mengu-timur, again poured into northern Syria. Straining every nerve, Kilawun gathered an army of Egyptians and Syrians, Bedouins and Turcomans, 50,000 strong, and with it advanced to Hims. There Mengu met him with an equal force, one-third of which were Georgians, Armenians, and Greeks.

Oct. A fierce fight ensued, which at the first declared itself against the Sultan; so much so, that in despair he took refuge with a thousand horse on a neighbouring height. But the Mongols hastening for plunder to Hims, reversed the fortune of the day. Mengu was unhorsed and wounded; his army fled, and was cut to pieces; and shortly after, he died, either from grief or of his wounds. The following year Abagha also died.

The Egyptian triumph marks an important epoch in the destinies of the East. If, as seemed at one time likely, fortune had told otherwise, not only might Egypt have fallen into Mongol hands, but the Christian tendencies of Abagha might have changed the fate of Syria. For while some of the Eastern potentates were gradually affecting Islam, Abagha stood firm in his preference of the Christian faith. Indeed, throughout his reign, he kept sending embassies—as in 1267 and 1276 A.D.—to the Pope and other European Courts, in which he urged a fresh A.D. 1281 Crusade and war with Egypt. His brother, on succeeding to the throne, adopted the Moslem creed, with the corresponding name of Ahmed; and communications, though not always of a friendly character, passed between him and Kilawun. But taken captive, he was put to death by his nephew Argun, who was as favourable to Christianity as had been his father Abagha. Like him, he not only sent deputations to the christian Courts, but (1291 A.D.) offered to place the resources of his kingdom at the service of the Pope with the view of driving the Egyptians out of Syria; and he even intimated the intention, so soon as Jerusalem should again fall into Christian hands, of being himself baptized.[1] But the negotiations came to nothing. Hostilities were dropped between Kilawun and the Mongols. No attempt was made to avenge the defeat of Hims, and the conversion of the Mongol house to Islam soon established matters on the same footing as they had been upon before.

Kilawun kept up the friendship which Beibars had formed with the Prince of Kiptchak, who,

[1] Argun favoured both Jews and Christians. A Jewish chancellor had a distinguished rôle at Bagdad; and we read of Christian missionaries being well received in Persia. The communications of the Mongol princes with the Pope and European Courts are of singular interest; two original letters of Argun and Oeljeitu in the Mongol tongue, to Philip the Fair, are still extant (Weil, iv. p. 152). Abagha had a Christian wife, an illegitimate daughter of the Keisar.

A.D. 1281. announcing that he had become a Moslem, begged that a suitable title and escutcheon might be conferred upon him. Embassies were also received from Yemen, with gifts of eunuchs, elephants, spices, and parrots. There was correspondence even with the King of Ceylon, through whom Kilawun sought to encourage commerce with the East. Friendly relations were at the same time maintained with Constantinople and various European Courts. Towards the close of his life, the Sultan concluded commercial arrangements with Genoa, and even entered into a kind of defensive treaty with Castile and Sicily.

But not the less, relieved as he now was from fear of the Mongols, did he turn his army, wherever 1285. opportunity offered, against Christianity in the East. His treatment of Armenia was in the last degree threatening and oppressive; and it was only by a crushing tribute, and the surrender of all Moslem captives (while the Armenian captives were kept in slavery), that Leo obtained a truce. With what still remained to the Crusaders in Syria, Kilawun lost no opportunity of mortal conflict. He was ready, indeed, as occasion offered, to enter into treaty with them; but it was not difficult at the convenient time to find pretext, or it might sometimes be good cause, for evasion. Latakia was seized though included in the treaty of Tripolis; and Tripolis itself was attacked on an apparently insufficient cause.¹ It was a grand A.D. 1289. city, populous and well defended; but, though helped from Cyprus, it was, after a month's siege, taken by storm, the male inhabitants massacred, and the women and children reduced to slavery. Not long after, some Moslem merchants having complained of being outraged on their approach to Akka,² the long-looked-for opportunity was taken of proclaiming a campaign against this, the last seat of the Crusades. The project, however, was not popular with the Emirs, who feared the strength of the citadel. The Sultan accordingly obtained from the Law officers a deliverance that the insults offered to the merchants formed a ground sufficient for Jehâd; and having accordingly proclaimed a Holy war, he set out, with great preparations, for the siege; but he died on the 1290. way, and left the task for his successor.

During this reign there were two rather fruitless campaigns against Nubia, and warfare also against the Bedouins, who kept Palestine and Upper Egypt

---

[1] On the death of Boemund, his sister claimed the succession. Bertram of Ghibelet was promised the Sultan's aid to oppose that claim, on stipulation of becoming tributary. But Boemund's sister having waived her claim, Bertram thought himself released from the compact, and this Kilawun seized as the *casus belli* for which he had been waiting.

[2] The most received account is that there really were excesses committed on some Moslem traders by certain rapacious servants of the Pope, sent, in the train of a bishop, to Tripolis. For other accounts, see Wilken, vii. pp. 721 *et seq.*

A.D. 1290. in continual alarm. There was also fighting at Mecca, where Yemen contested with Egypt the supremacy of the Holy city. But with Kilawun these things were secondary to the war in Syria. He possessed no fewer than twelve thousand memlukes, Circassians as well as Mongols. Between three and four thousand of these were quartered in the Citadel, and hence (as we have seen) called *Burjites*; so named as distinguished from the *Bahrites*.[1] These memlukes, their great numbers notwithstanding, were kept in perfect order, and we hear as yet of none of the excess and outrage which by and by made the very name a terror.

Kilawun is praised by the historians of the day as a mild and upright ruler. He certainly deserves the commendation when compared with others of his race; but, as we have seen, he could be cruel and treacherous and, as occasion required, could also cast aside the most sacred oaths. He was not so bloodthirsty as Beibars, but towards Christians he was less tolerant, for he excluded them from all share in public offices, and his treatment of the Crusaders was vindictive and to the last degree remorseless. Jealous, and at times tyrannical, some of his punishments were barbarous

---

[1] See above, p. 5. Kilawun gave his slaves a lighter dress, with turbans more suitable for the climate. The previous style affected more the European military costume. For the Citadel barracks at foot of the Mokallam Hill, see *Frontispiece*.

in the extreme. For example, a bandit stretched upon a camel's back (a punishment we begin to hear too much of) was paraded about the city streets till he died; and a Christian was buried alive for having married a Moslem, while the poor woman had her nose cut off.[1] But, with all his defects, he was a wise and beneficent monarch. The memorial which chiefly claimed the gratitude of the people was an immense edifice built outside the city for a hospital, college, and mausoleum. Spacious rooms were fitted up with beds for the sick, whether rich or poor, and specially for women; while there were lectureships, laboratories, and every sort of medical appliances. In the mausoleum, fifty Coran readers were ever at their sacred duty. The library was plentifully furnished with works of every sort, and supplied with librarians at public call. There were lecturers for the several Orthodox schools of theology; while a Children's seminary, Infant school, and Orphan asylum complete a description reminding us of like institutions nearer home. Architecture began now to receive attention from abroad, with fruits that rapidly developed in the coming reigns. For these and other public services, Kilawun's name has survived in Cairo to the present day.

A.D. 1290.

Kilawun was aged seventy when he died. One 1290. 10th Nov.

[1] Moslems may marry Christian women, but Christians are forbidden to marry Moslem women.

A.D. 1290. of his titles was Alalfî, or the Thousander, from the heavy price paid for him when a beautiful youth.¹ He left three sons and two daughters. On the death of his eldest son, he had the next, Khalîl, proclaimed as his Successor. In later life he took to wife the daughter of a Mongol prince, who, like many others, had wandered into Egypt, and by her had a son called Nâsir, of whom we shall hear more hereafter.

¹ A thousand golden pieces were on two occasions given for him. This being one of his *royal* titles is suggestive, showing as it does that, instead of being ashamed of their servile origin, the Mamelukes gloried in it.

CHAPTER V

KHALÎL, SON OF KILAWUN

1290-1293 A.D.

KHALÎL succeeded peacefully. He wanted his father's A.D. 1290. grace and wisdom, and was of an arrogant and ruthless nature. Finding the patent of appointment unsigned by Kilawun, who would have preferred Nâsir had he been of age, the young Sultan put the Vizier to death, and conceived a cruel hatred towards all the adherents of his Father, whom he removed from office, and in their stead appointed minions of his own. He had no respect for life, and indulged in such caprice, that after incarcerating an opponent, he would anon restore him to favour, and sometimes again seize and torture, and even put the wretched man to death. The page is full of such enormities.

In one thing, however, he followed close upon his 1291. Father's steps, and that was in the resolve to drive the Crusaders out of Syria. He inaugurated the design by a solemn service in his father's mausoleum, and distributed largess to the Cazies and Doctors of the law.

A.D. 1291. Then he summoned to Damascus all the governors of Syria, requiring them to furnish the heavy draught for dragging to the walls of Akka the material and machines of war. The city was then invested and ninety-two catapults set against its ramparts. There was a brave defence, as well as help from Cyprus; but fatal jealousies (the bane of the Crusaders from first to last) prevailed even in this their dire extremity, and great numbers of the garrison sailed away. 18th May. After a siege of three-and-forty days the place was stormed—a tale of terror, for the men were all slain or taken prisoners, and the women and children sent in slavery to Egypt. Even the Knights, to whom a safe-conduct had been promised, were mercilessly butchered.[1] The city was burned, and the walls dismantled. It had been in the Crusaders' hands just one hundred years. All places still held by them were now abandoned,[2] and the fate of Beyrut in cold-blooded slaughter vies with that of Akka. On Khalîl's return, Cairo was decked out, and grand festivities prepared for his reception. A crowd of captive Franks in fetters graced the triumphal entry, followed by their conquerors carrying the banners of the Cross reversed,

---

[1] The reason given is, that when the enemy rushing in abused the women and children, the Christians closed the gates upon them and slew the guilty Moslems. See Wilken, viii. p. 765. See also Weil, note iv. p. 181—a tale of horrors.

[2] Tyre, Sidon, Haifa, and Athlith are named.

and their victims' heads aloft upon their lances. A.D. 1291.
Thus, after two centuries of a chequered life, maintained by means abhorrent from the teaching of the Prince of peace, the great Crusade came to a sad end; and (as Gibbon closes the melancholy story) "a mournful and solitary silence prevailed along the coast, which had so long resounded with the *World's debate.*"

With nothing left to occupy him in Syria, Khalîl 1292. now turned his arms against the Mongols; and religious services were again repeated in the mausoleum to rouse enthusiasm for a fresh Jehâd. From Aleppo, the Egyptian forces proceeded to storm Kalaat Rûm, where the whole garrison, Armenians and Mongols, were slain and the women carried off as slaves. In the height of his vanity, Khalîl wrote a circular to his Governors announcing that he had changed the name of Kalaat Rûm to Kalaat Muslimin (citadel of the Moslems), and glorifying himself as "destined to conquer the East from the rising of the sun to the going down of the same." But immediately the Mongols appeared, though too late to save the city, he forthwith left and retired to Syria.

After some unimportant expeditions the young 1293. Sultan returned to Cairo, and crossed the Nile on a hunting expedition. While thus engaged he was assassinated by a party of Emirs, who could no

A.D. 1293. longer endure his overbearing and cruel treatment. These, again, were pursued by the favourites of Khalîl,—the Emir Ketbogha being at their head. The chief conspirator was put by them to death, though he pleaded in their presence that the iniquities of the late Sultan had left them no alternative;—his shameless licence with the youths around (he cried) and indulgence even during the Fast in wine, besides the inhuman treatment of his Father's friends, casting some into dungeons and then putting them to death, justified the act. It was all too true, but it did not serve to save him.

The Sultan's body, left for two days upon the ground, was buried by a villager on the spot; but eventually transferred by his followers to his vault outside Cairo. He left two daughters, but no son. His reign lasted about three years.

The name of Khalil is naturally exalted by Moslem writers as that of a successful combatant in the interests of Islam. But it may no less be remembered that the final blow to the soldiers of the Cross was dealt by one of a character so low as that which the same historians ascribe to the Sultan Khalîl.

CHAPTER VI

NÂSIR, SON OF KILAWUN—KETBOGHA—LACHÎN

1293–1299 A.D.

THE next five years give us little more than a A.D. 1293. tale of conspiracies and assassinations following one hard upon another. NÂSIR, Kilawun's younger son, now nine years of age, was, on his brother's death, unanimously elected Sultan; and (though destined to reign two-and-forty years) was deposed after a year by Ketbogha, and he again by Lachîn, when, on the murder of the latter, Nâsir, as we shall see, was called again to the throne.

This first Sultanate of Nâsir was but nominal. Dec. Ketbogha as Regent, and Shujai governor of the city as Vizier, held the reins in their own hands. They put to death, with horrid cruelties, all they could lay hands upon connected with the conspiracy against Khalil. Eight of these had their hands and feet cut off, and then, stretched on camels, were paraded about the town till they expired. Even the favourite Vizier of the late Sultan, having in-

A.D. 1293. curred their jealousy, was laid hold of, and tortured to death for his vast treasures.

Soon, however, jealousies sprang up between the two. Shujai had all the *Burjites* in the Citadel at his command; while Ketbogha, himself a Mongol, was supported by the rapidly increasing Mongol party. An attempt by Shujai to entrap Ketbogha as he entered the Citadel led to an open conflict: the Citadel was besieged and Shujai assassinated. Left thus alone, Ketbogha aspired to the Sultanate, and to attain his end made friends with Lachîn and other conspirators against the late Sultan. This so offended the adherents of Kilawun's house that, joined by the discontented factions, they rose in rebellion against Ketbogha, attacked the markets and public offices, and made the city for a day and night the scene of tumult and disaster. The rulers, at last put to flight, were caught, and their leaders slain or mutilated.[1] The outbreak afforded Ketbogha fair excuse for holding that the administration was no longer safe in the hands of a child; and so Nâsir was deposed and sent away to Kerak.

1294. Dec.

KETBOGHA, thus elevated to the Sultanate, was weak enough to fill the offices of State with his own creatures, as well as raise a great number of his own

---

[1] Macrizy tells us that some had both hands and feet cut off, and tongues cut out, and others hung up at the city gates. Some three hundred were treated thus.

slaves to be Emirs, and thus alienate the older nobility. A.D. 1294. He was unfortunate, too, in the welcome given by him to the Yurats—a wild Tartar tribe of some eighteen thousand families which, expelled from Persia, he now settled in Syria. Though gradually adopting the Moslem faith, this horde was hateful to the people for their heathen habits, especially that of feeding on horse-flesh; and Ketbogha's adoption of the race caused him much obloquy. A prolonged 1295. famine, succeeded by the pest, also occasioned much distress and loss for which, as usual, the Sultan was held responsible.[1] To meet the deficit of revenue, he made a circuit with his army through Syria and extorted what he could from the various provinces. But his overbearing treatment continued to alienate the Emirs; and on a hunting expedition at Hims he was set upon in his tent, and barely escaped by flying to Damascus; where, finding that Lachîn was the popular candidate, he gave himself up and swore allegiance to him as his Successor.

LACHÎN, or LAJÎN, thus by general consent elected 1297. Nov. to the Sultanate, had been at first a slave of Eibek and then of Kilawun by whom he was freed, and then gradually rising to the Emirate, eventually became

[1] The price of a water-melon rose to 100 dirhems. In Cairo 17,500 died of the pest in a single month; and Ibn Ayâs says that altogether 70,200 died. The dead bodies, lying all about, were cast into the river or devoured by dogs, which again were killed and eaten by the starving poor.

A.D. 1297. Governor of Syria. He was well received on his return to Cairo; and was there inducted by the Caliph who followed, as he rode through the city, in his train. The people were pleased because, on the return of plenty, he was able to remit all outstanding taxes occasioned by the dearth.[1] But Lachîn soon fell helplessly under the influence of one of his slaves called Menkutimur. Raised to high office, this minion became the real ruler; and, by treating all around him with capricious severity and exaction, roused dangerous dissatisfaction.

1298. To divert the attention of his embittered Court, Lachîn organised an expedition against Armenia. The time was favourable, for the kingdom was just then the subject of a contested succession; and Ghazan ruler of Persia, its ally, was engaged with enemies in the East. The King of Armenia sought by submissive terms to stay the attack; but that would have defeated Lachîn's object to keep the Emirs out of his way; and so the army went on, ravaged the land from Sîs to Adana, and returned to Syria laden with spoil. The Sultan sent them back again to capture certain strongholds; one of which, Nejimeh, was besieged for forty days before surrendering.

1299. Jan. In the beginning of the following year, Lachîn sent off Kiptchak, a leading Emir, with a force to

[1] The ardeb of wheat fell from 160 to 20 dirhems.

Aleppo on the rumour of a Mongol attack, but in A.D. 1299. reality with secret orders that he and his friends should be poisoned or otherwise made away with. Anticipating the danger, Kiptchak, with his Emirs and their memlukes 500 in number, escaped to Persia; there, being well received by Ghazan, they stirred him up to an attack on Syria; the result of which, however, belongs to the following reign.

The rule of Lachîn, or rather, one might say, of Menkutimur, continued to embitter the Emirs whose revenues were affected by a new distribution of the various claims upon the public domains.[1] At last two of the leaders, unable longer to stand their affronts, took advantage of the absence of the army to assassinate the Sultan as by night he played at chess in the Palace; and, immediately after, Menkutimur also. They then assumed the government; but after three days' rule, the troops, re-entering Cairo, put them both to death. It was then resolved to recall Nâsir from Kerak, and meanwhile a Council of eight conducted the administration.

Lachîn is praised as an exemplary Moslem, indulging neither in wine nor forbidden games, and

---

[1] There were twenty-four endowments (*carât*), ten for the Emirs, ten for the army, and four for the Sultan and his Court. The latter were reduced or redistributed in a way that alienated both the Emirs and the army.

A.D. 1299. fasting three months in the year. He had for his wife a daughter of Beibars. His chief fault lay in the facile elevation of his own memlukes, and the way in which he became the passive agent of Menkutimur. Otherwise he bears a character much above that of the ordinary Sultan.[1]

[1] Curiously enough, Western authorities will have it that Lachin was a German converted to Islam. But this must be fable, as we have native authority for his history from the time he was bought as a slave-boy, then probably not more than eight years of age. Some say he was a Greek.

CHAPTER VII

NÂSIR'S SECOND REIGN—BEIBARS II

1299–1310 A.D.

RECALLED with cries of joy to the throne NÂSIR, yet A.D. 1299. but fourteen years of age, was of necessity in the Feb. hands of his ministers. Sallar was Regent, and Beibars president of the Palace. As such, the latter had the *Burjite* memlukes at his command; the former, the independent Emirs. Each sought, as usual, to outvie the other in the elevation of his followers; and jealousies were becoming rife when attention was called off to fresh and dangerous ravages of the Mongols.

The chronic hostility of Central Asia had been Autumn. quickened of late by the attacks of the Sultan on Armenia, by the reception at Cairo of rebel Mongols, and now by the cry of Kiptchak and his brother refugees. News of the inroad thus precipitated, reached Egypt in the autumn of 1299 A.D. Setting out with a powerful army, the Sultan made but

A.D. 1299. little haste, and was besides detained on the way by a dangerous conspiracy of the Yurat leaders who, joined by discontented Emirs, plotted to assassinate the Sultan and his ministers, and to restore their friend Ketbogha to the throne. The conspirators met with condign punishment, and the army passed on. News that Ghazan, with 100,000 Mongols, had passed the Euphrates now hastened the Egyptian march, and the two armies met at Salamia, to the north of Hims. There the Egyptians, being but a
23rd Dec. third of their enemy, suffered a crushing defeat and fled panicstruck. The Mongols, though with the loss of 14,000, carried all before them; and Damascus, deserted by its troops and by all who could escape, was in terrible consternation. But Ghazan, when he reached the city, graciously received
30th Dec. a deputation of the leading men, and stopped all further outrage. For this end a royal Firman proclaimed in the Omeyyad Mosque protection for all, even for Jews and Christians, and good government throughout Egypt so soon as it came under Mongol rule.[1] Though Damascus was thus saved, its environs, and indeed the whole of Syria, had a sad experience of rapine and plunder. A Mongol

---

[1] The long Firman is given by Noweiry in full, abounding in texts of the Coran and abuse of the Egyptian Government. In promising protection for Jews and Christians, an interesting saying is quoted from Aly : "The People of the Book pay tribute that their blood may be as our blood, and their goods as our goods!"

Viceroy was placed over it, and Kiptchak rewarded with the government of Damascus, though the citadel still held out.[1] For the moment it seemed to all intents as if the land had passed into Mongol hands. Ghazan, however, was content for the present to threaten an early return, and after a month retired.

A.D. 1300.

Feb.

Meanwhile the Egyptian troops, casting aside their arms and uniform, had fled from the battle-field in utter confusion past Damascus to Cairo, which the young Sultan reached with hardly a follower about him. Measures were immediately taken to repair the disaster. Prodigious exactions supplied the means,[2] and in a couple of months the army left to reconquer Syria; but the Mongols had already left, and so Damascus was reoccupied and Syria restored without further fighting. Kiptchak and his fellow-exiles were pardoned, but Damascus now suffered again from its Egyptian masters; for such of the inhabitants as had stayed on and been friendly to the Mongols, were now visited with terrible retribution. And as Ghazan had promised to return again in the autumn, the city was kept in a state of chronic terror. Heavy

March.

---

[1] It was now the custom to place the citadels in Syria not under the city Governors, but under separate Commanders.

[2] Such an enormous amount of gold was raised and put into the market to equip the troops that, compared with silver, the dinâr fell from 25 to 17 dirhems, and the rate was eventually fixed at 20.

A.D. 1300. burdens, too, were laid both on Egypt and on Syria.

It was not till late in the year that Ghazan again marched westward, but the winter proved so severe that, after an attack on Antioch, he retraced his steps. Up to this time Ghazan, though a Moslem, had hoped, like his predecessors, for the aid of christian Powers in wresting Syria from Mameluke domination. As late as 1302 A.D. we read of embassies to the Courts of England and France; and there is a correspondence extant in which he complains bitterly that the West held back from his support.[1] Despairing at last of Western aid, he thought of making peace with Egypt, and accord-
1301. May.
ingly sent an embassy with a despatch, in which, after reproaching the Sultan for unprovoked attacks upon his territory, he threatened reprisals if his terms were not agreed to. In Nâsir's name a
Oct.
haughty answer was returned;—Ghazan was reproached with the sins of his father and of his heathen ancestors, and upbraided for making common cause with European Powers which fought against the Caliph and his faith; but while scorning threats of an attack, the message ends with the assurance that

---

[1] See M. Rémusat in *Mem. de l'Acad.* vol. vii. p. 388, where King Edward's reply, 12th March 1302 A.D., is mentioned. There was still a Crusading spirit abroad, and Genevese ladies even were prepared to join the enterprise.

should Ghazan change his tone, the Sultan would A.D. 1301.
be as ready for peace as he.¹ On receipt of this
intemperate despatch, Ghazan resolved on war; but
he meanwhile allowed a year to pass in peace.

The interval was improved by Egypt in a well- 1302. Feb.
planned attack on the Bedouins who, pretending a
government of their own, infested the whole of Upper
Egypt. Sallars and Beibars themselves took the field;
and the army in three divisions closed in upon the
enemy from all sides, slew mercilessly every Bedouin
in the land, and carried off their women captive.
Another expedition chastised Armenia for its support May.
of the Mongols; and advancing towards Sîs, cruelly
devastated that unhappy land again. Somewhat
later, a fleet was despatched against the Templars, Oct.
who still occupied Aradus,² and from thence made
raids upon the coast. The island was now taken,
and the Christian inhabitants slain; while only 280
who occupied the tower survived as captives. So
ended this unhappy remnant of the great Crusade.

At last came the long-threatened attack of the 1303.
Mongol host. Ghazan, however, retired from it
before reaching Syria, and left the command to his
father-in-law Kotlushah. It was spring when the

---

¹ The despatch, a model of Oriental pomposity, occupies *nine* pages of Weil, and is weary reading. It abounds with quotations from the Coran.

² *Ruád*, opposite Tertosa (Tartus).

Egyptian army, with Nâsir, now a youth of eighteen, at its head, marched from Damascus,—from which in terror every soul that could had fled;[1] and that same evening, at the plain of Merj Soffar, they met the Mongol army which, with its Armenian and Georgian contingents, was 100,000 strong. Next day the battle was fought. At first it seemed as if the Egyptians would again be beaten, for the right wing turned and fled. But the rest stood firm, and beat back with fearful slaughter the crowded hordes, which on the following day escaped in part with difficulty and loss into the desert.[2] Nâsir returning to Damascus, there spent a month in triumph, and sent a despatch to Ghazan which vies with that of Beibars to Boemund in the bombast of its exultation, and the threat of overthrowing Asia to its farthest end. The rejoicings on the way to Cairo were truly Oriental. The road was so laid with carpets that the hoofs of the Sultan's charger did not touch the ground; and he entered the capital in such triumph "as had not been ever seen before."[3]

---

[1] The consternation at the Mongols' near approach was so great that 500 to 1000 pieces were offered for any kind of beast to ride away upon, and men deserting their families took refuge in the citadel.

[2] Noweiry and Abulfeda, two of our authorities, were present in this battle.

[3] The rejoicings were followed by an earthquake; and Macrizy adds that the music and rejoicings throughout the land were so extravagant and undevout, that men might have been thankful even for an earthquake to put an end to them.

In Persia there was a different tale. At Tabriz A.D. 1303. the wailings lasted for weeks. Ghazan, sick with grief, retired from public view. A new army was gathered in the hope that Europe would aid in a fresh attack on Syria; but Ghazan died before the design could be carried into execution. He was a good and just ruler, and the best of the Ilkhans. The Mongol power in Persia had now reached its height; but what with troubles at home and at Herat, the West was spared from further attack in that direction.

During the next two years, the unfortunate 1304,1305. Armenians were again attacked for having joined the Mongols. The country was as usual plundered, and the fortress of Tell Hamdun taken and destroyed; the Armenian chiefs who defended it were put to death, excepting one who saved his life by embracing Islam. Peace was restored on the Prince of Sîs paying up the arrear of tribute that was due. A campaign was also led against the Druses in their mountain retreat of Kesrawan.[1]

About this time, severe restrictions were issued against Jews and Christians, which owed their origin to a somewhat unexpected cause. The Court of Arragon having sent an embassy for the reopening of certain Churches and the release of a Christian prisoner, the prayer was granted; but

[1] Between Tripoli and Damascus.

A.D. 1305. as the party on its return was embarking at Alexandria, the Sultan bethought him that a ransom should have been demanded for the captive, and sent to bring him back. The Spaniards not only refused, but carried off the messengers from Cairo with them. This roused Egyptian hostility against the Christians; and, reclamation from European powers notwithstanding, the intolerant rules of Omar II. were reimposed.[1] Not only were these mercilessly enforced, but popular attacks upon the Christians were allowed, if not encouraged, by Beibars. They were rigidly debarred from public office and employment. The restrictions as to dress and riding were sternly enforced; and such churches and synagogues as had been built since the rise of Islam, were to be demolished. An edict to this effect was promulgated throughout the kingdom, from the Euphrates to Nubia, and the position became so intolerable that great numbers emigrated or were driven over to Islam. The edict, it is true, like similar edicts before it, gradually fell into abeyance, but the chances of its reinforcement hung continually, like the sword of Damocles, over the heads of the unhappy people.[2]

[1] See *Caliphate*, p. 377.

[2] It may be of interest to give an outline of the edict. To distinguish Jews and Christians at a glance, the latter must wear

During the next few years, party spirit ran A.D. 1305. so high between Beibars and Sallar and their respective factions, that it came often near to an open fight. A campaign having been set on foot against Yemen for withholding its tribute, Sallar sought by taking the command to regain the chief power; but Beibars, seeing the design, interposed; and so the project fell through. Nâsir was not only deprived of all hand in the affairs of State, but to lessen his influence was kept so short of means as to be often half-starved. A Vizier who, touched by his want, ventured to advance him money for presents to his ladies, was seized by Sallar and tortured to death; and all the while Sallar was amassing vast treasures for himself, and on a pilgrimage to Mecca spent them in

a blue turban, the former a yellow one; their women must be recognisable by a peculiar covering over the breast. Forbidden to carry weapons or mount a horse, they might ride on mules, but only sideways, and with no decoration on the saddle. They must give way to Moslems, and leave them the middle of the road. In assemblies, they must rise up before Believers and subordinate the voice to theirs. Palm Sunday must not be observed with any public festivity. Christians are prohibited the use of bells for worship; nor may they in any way attempt the conversion of a Moslem. They are forbidden to possess Moslem slaves or captives, or anything that may have fallen to Moslem arms as booty. Should they resort to a public bath, they must have a bell tied about the neck. They are forbidden Arabic inscriptions on their rings, nor may their children learn the Coran. They may exact no heavy work from Mussulman labourers; and any familiarity with a Moslem female is to be met by death.

Kerak and Shaubek were the only places where the edict was not published, as being very largely peopled by non-Mussulmans.

A.D. 1308. princely style and benefactions to the needy there.

As Nâsir advanced into manhood, he felt the indignity the more thus cast upon him. Seeking to get rid of his two masters, he plotted with the Governor of the Citadel, within which they lived, to arrest them both. But this coming prematurely to light, it would have fared badly with the young Sultan, had not a popular demonstration been aroused in his favour. He was forced, however, to send his immediate attendants into exile, and the state of things became for him even worse than before.

1309. For another year he submitted to this treatment, more as a slave than ruler; till at last, enduring it no longer, he set out as if on pilgrimage to Mecca,—a religious obligation which could hardly be denied him. But on reaching Kerak, he sent a despatch to Beibars and Sallar in which, declaring his intention to remain where he was in peace, he desired that all matters of moment should be reported to him, but left the administration in their hands, and bade the Emirs and memlukes be obedient to Sallar as Regent. In reply, the Emirs expressed astonishment at what they called his childish play, and intimated their resolve that he must either return or resign the Sultanate. On this, Nâsir sent back the insignia of State, and repeated his desire to end his days at Kerak. But room for A.D. 1309. compromise had closed; after a long debate between the various factions on receipt of Nâsir's first despatch, Beibars had already been elected Sultan.

BEIBARS II., bought as a slave by Kilawun, and raised by him to nobility and office, became now April. the first Sultan of Circassian birth. He accepted office hesitatingly, as he feared opposition from Syria; and indeed, excepting Damascus, the other Governors still held by Nâsir, and were only induced by his express desire to submit to the new rule. But Beibars was unfortunate. The Nile failing to rise added the usual unpopularity to his difficulties. Then hearing of communications made by Nâsir with Syria, his former friendly attitude gave way to suspicion. He demanded restoration of the treasure, the memlukes and the stud, which Nâsir had taken with him to Kerak; and at last the correspondence grew so embittered, that Nâsir imprisoned the Sultan's envoy and even threatened to seek for refuge with the Mongols.

For Nâsir now saw that the only chance of safety lay in claiming the active support of the chiefs of Syria, who, as adherents of Kilawun's house, were for the most part on his side. At the invitation of Kara Sonkor governor of Aleppo, Asendimur of Hama, and other Syrian governors, he was on his way to Aleppo when a second des-

A.D. 1309. patch, urging him to hasten his journey, was intercepted by the Governor of Damascus, who bribed the messenger to carry in its stead a forged letter in Kara Sonkor's name, bidding him return to Kerak. There he received from Beibars an angry despatch, threatening armed attack if he failed to give up certain refugees. Nâsir sent a humble and deprecatory reply, which for the moment disarmed the Sultan's suspicions. Meanwhile he still busied himself with preparations for returning to Syria, Beibars being kept in ignorance of the design.

When at last, all being now ready for a rising, Nâsir set out for Syria, Beibars realising his danger, sent an army after him; but the greater part of it went over to Nâsir. Beibars himself remained inactive at Cairo, seeking for safety in a grandiloquent proclamation of his rights by the shadowy Caliph. His pompous edict was derided by the people ;—" The Caliph !" they cried, " who is he ? He is but lord and master of the winds !" Sallar, too, whom Beibars had long suspected, remained in his house prepared to welcome Nâsir back to Cairo.

Meanwhile Nâsir, as he marched from Kerak to Syria, was daily met by crowds of returning followers, so that he entered Damascus in such festive and regal pomp, that unheard-of sums were given for roofs to behold the procession from. Akush,

the Governor, fled at his approach ; but, on re- A.D. 1310.
ceiving a rescript of pardon backed by a solemn
oath, he came and offered Nâsi royal gifts of
horses, camels and treasure. And now from every
quarter proofs of similar loyalty poured in.

Beibars, deserted thus by his followers, fled to
Suez from whence he sent to implore the returning
Sultan's pardon. This, Nâsir stil fearing opposition at his Capital, not only granted but promised
him a Syrian command. On hearing this, he
hurried back to Gaza, but (as we shall see) was
made prisoner there. So ended Beibars' unfortunate
reign of little above a year.

CHAPTER VIII

NÂSIR'S THIRD REIGN

1310–1341 A.D.

A.D. 1310. March. Now his own master, Nâsir was not long in betraying some of the worst features of his race, as a jealous, cruel, suspicious and avaricious tyrant. Relieved of anxiety now by the friendly attitude of his capital, he began to regret the clemency promised to Beibars, and had him brought up in fetters. He then reproached him for the niggardly treatment of past years. "Remember," he said, "when I once asked for a roasted goose, thou madest answer:—'What will he do with a roasted goose? will he dine twenty times a day?'" Though Beibars confessing it all, yet pleaded for mercy, he was lashed and carried off to the Chamber of death. When half suffocated the cord was loosened and the Sultan, having again upbraided him, had him strangled before his eyes and the body cast into a stye. His property was confiscated, and his slaves distributed among the Emirs.

Sallar, notwithstanding his support and friendship, fared no better. He had welcomed Nâsir with every token of festivity and princely gifts. But his death was predetermined, though postponed for a safer time. Meanwhile, at his own request, he was appointed Governor of Shaubek. The summer was spent by Nâsir in ridding himself, too often by cruel death, of Beibars' party whom he feared. In the autumn, now safe, he sent a messenger to summon Sallar. His followers, apprehending danger, urged his flight to Yemen; but after some hesitance he obeyed the call. On reaching Cairo, he was cast into prison, and, deprived of food, died within a fortnight of starvation there. He is praised as a noble, brave, generous, and upright ruler. His wealth was fabulous, treasure, jewels, slaves, and stud, gathered as Regent, while barely allowing Nâsir wherewithal to live;—a poor excuse, however, for such a tragic end.[1]

A.D. 1310.

Sept.

While painfully suspicious of the influential

---

[1] Sallar was a Yurat slave bought by Kilawun. I have not thought fit to dwell on the details of his death, which may possibly have been exaggerated. Nâsir is said to have sent him a tray which the famished chief eagerly opened, but found the dishes filled, one with gold, another with silver, and a third with pearls and jewels. He had gnawed his palms, his fingers half-bitten still in his mouth, and so forth. He left, they say, 800 millions of gold. Allowing for all exaggeration, there was here enough to tempt Nâsir's avarice, and cause his death, besides the niggardly treatment during his second reign. Sallar was also an accomplice in the assassination of Nâsir's brother.

Emirs around him, and ever ready to coerce them, Nâsir treated with singular wisdom and forbearance the conspiracy of a powerful faction to supplant him by a Brother's son. Having summoned the culprits to his presence, he pardoned some and exiled others, but took no life. It was otherwise with Kara Sonkor, to whom he owed so much, and whom he now treated with unworthy jealousy. He sought to put him off his guard by promotion to a government in Syria; but discovering the trap, the Chief made his escape with a body of discontented Emirs to the Court of Oeljeitu (brother of Ghazan), whom they induced to make a raid upon Syria. The Sultan marched for its relief, but found the enemy had retired, and so instead he went to Kerak, and thence on pilgrimage to Mecca. During the next year or two, renewed expeditions were sent against unfortunate Armenia. Malatia was invested; and, timely capitulation notwithstanding, was plundered by the outrageous troops, who carried off the Christians as slaves into captivity.[1]

Though Oeljeitu never came to actual hostilities with Egypt, yet having zealously adopted the Shiea

---

[1] Abulfeda was present and sought in vain to prevent the troops from violence, and to enforce the truce. Abulfeda was now Governor of Hamah, the seat of his forefathers. Asendimur, his predecessor, notwithstanding his recent support of Nâsir, had met the same fate as Kara Sonkor. Abulfeda tells us he was imprisoned at Kerak, and never again appearing must there have met his end.

creed, he sought to spread it westward, and like A.D. 1310.
his predecessor had designs on Syria and Egypt.
He sent embassies, as Ghazan had done before, to the
Pope and European Courts, offering 100,000 horse
to aid in the recovery of Syria and punishment of
ungodly Egypt; but his negotiations met with little
favour, and he died without effecting anything.[1]
His son, Bû Saîd, returned to the Orthodox faith;
and being engaged with the Uzbecs, and anxious also
to keep secure the Syrian frontier, now felt it his
best policy to seek the friendship of Egypt. It
being equally the object of Nâsir that his disaffected
subjects should no longer have a safe retreat at
the Mongol Court, peace was readily concluded.
To such an extent, indeed, was the friendship
carried that by consent the insignia of both
kingdoms were recognised at the Meccan pilgrimage.
Another, and but too characteristic, proof of their
mutual understanding may also be found in the
assassination of Timurtash, a rebel Mongol who had

---

[1] Interesting details of these negotiations are given by Rémusat, *Mem. de l'Acad. des inscript.* vii. pp. 389 *et seq.* In the Paris archives is a letter to Philip the Fair, dated May 1305. The embassy to England was answered by Edward II., November 1307, which shows the Khan's anxiety to join the Christians in overthrowing the Mamelukes; and a letter to Pope Clement V. evinces the same desire. His diatribes against Egypt led to the notion that he was himself inclined to Christianity, which was not the case. After the death of his Christian mother he became, like his brother, a zealous Moslem, but of the Shiea sect.

A.D. 1310. been given asylum at Cairo. In return for his head, Bû Saîd promised that of Kara Sonkor, whose death Nâsir had long attempted at the assassin's hand. On hearing some time after of Kara Sonkor's death, the Sultan, his hatred still unquenched, cried out:—"Oh, that it had been by mine own sword, and not another's!"[1] Egypt now remained safe from Mongol attack till the time of Tamerlane.

1336. The dissensions which followed the death of Bû Saîd caused Nâsir to turn an ambitious eye towards Persia. He took the part of Hasan the Greater, against Hasan the Less,—son of the Timurtash whom he had assassinated, and at the report of whose mysterious reappearance he was dreadfully alarmed. Eventually he sent a force to support Hasan the Greater, on promise of being recognised as supreme at Bagdad. His name had accordingly been already adopted in the Persian mint and public Prayers, when the contending factions came to terms; and

1341. so, shortly before his death, the Sultan's grand expectations came to nought. His altered relations with the Mongols never interfered with his standing friendship for their enemy the Uzbec prince, whose daughter (after much haggling as to the

[1] Kara Sonkor was now Governor of Meragha. He died six years after, but whether a natural death, or by Bû Saîd to fulfil his promise, is uncertain. Nâsir is said to have bribed over a hundred assassins to destroy him; for, as we are told, "assassins were the arrows of Nâsir" (*Mem. Arch. Fr.* Tome vi. p. 429).

price demanded) he had some years before (1320 A.D.) A.D. 1310. obtained as his bride.

Armenia was, during this reign, repeatedly attacked by Egyptian troops; and it suffered also from the Mongols who, since their conversion to Islam, instead of being its defenders, made it now the object of hostile inroad. In 1320 A.D., weakened by internal division on the succession of the minor Leo V., it was attacked by a Syrian army, the city plundered, the palace fired, and the country raided. A year or two after, the Sultan sent an expedition 1322. ostensibly to enforce tribute, but chiefly to take advantage of any opportunity which the hostilities between the Uzbecs and Bû Saîd might offer for his own advancement in the East. Deserted now by their former allies, and the subject of chronic devastation, the Court of Sîs was glad to make peace on any terms. Some years later Leo, in hopes of assistance from a Crusade projected by Philip VI.,[1] assumed a too independent attitude; and to punish certain aggressions on the border, Nâsir sent an army which, advancing into the country, destroyed Ayas; but on the submission of Leo it retired, and hostilities ceased for a time.

In the affairs of Mecca and Medina, Nâsir took the deepest interest; and disunion among the contending Shercefs enabled him the easier to maintain

[1] Upon the death of Pope John XXII., this project came to nothing.

A.D. 1310. his ascendency. At one time, however, Oeljeitu gained over the Shereefs to his Shie-ite heresy, and had his name substituted for that of the Sultan in the public Prayers, but the Bedouins attacked his troops. Nâsir soon regained his position as head of the Holy places; and in a time of famine royally supplied the people of Mecca with corn.

To the south, repeated expeditions reached as far as Suakin, partly against the Bedouins who were ravaging, as usual, Upper Egypt; partly against Nubia, which Nâsir attempted to put under a Mussulman king. Nubia was thus kept unsettled for a time; but eventually things reverted to their previous state.

1316. In Syria there occurred a wild rising of the Druses who, in a great body, plundered Jebelah; and, having slain many of the people, retired with the shout, "*There is no God but Aly!*" They were put to flight by the Governor of Tripolis; and Nâsir sought by most stringent measures to suppress their strange tenets, even threatening death for the attempt to spread them.[1]

1308. As in other directions, so also in North Africa, Nâsir extended his rule westward. For many years,

---

[1] They held Aly to be "the Creator of the heavens and of the earth," and his Successors to be Divine; they also believed in transmigration of the soul. They explained the Coran allegorically, and allowed the use of wine.

his nominee was Governor of Tripoli, and aided by A.D. 1308–1320.
Egypt, held possession even of Tunis for a time; but in the end, he was expelled. In Arabia Felix, the Sultan interfered in disputes among the local Rulers, 1325. hoping thus to secure a voice in the local administration, as well as in the commerce of the East; but his army was ill received, and had to retire through the desert not without difficulty and loss.

Such is a brief outline of the foreign policy of Nâsir. Though upon the whole successful, he was himself no warrior. Excelling not in the field but in diplomacy, he was ever ambitious, but not always honest and straightforward. Embassies were frequently exchanged with the Powers around. The Emperor, Ibn Taghluk, sent a deputation twice 1381. from India seeking for co-operation against the Mongols. With the Byzantine Court there was a common interest in fear of the steady movement westward of the Turcoman hordes. By the Pope, Nâsir was asked to treat his Christian subjects 1327. kindly, with the promise that the same should be done for Moslems in the West. Similar deputations 1330. came from France and elsewhere, which sought even the restoration of Jerusalem and the cession of a landing-place for pilgrims, a request which was indignantly refused.

However unenviable was still the position of Christians in Cairo, it must be admitted that Nâsir himself

A.D. 1310. used his best endeavours to do them justice. He early tried, but in vain, to allow them the liberty of wearing white turbans. Later on, an unfortunate incident occurred to stir up the too ready anger of
1314. the people. The carpets and lamps of a Moslem fane having been lent for use at a Christian festival, a fanatic and his followers attacked the worshippers and destroyed their Church. The Sultan in anger threatened to cut out the fanatic's tongue, but in the end cooled down and sent him away with a
1321. solemn warning. Worse times, however, for the poor Christians were at hand. A few years passed, and the cry was raised against the forbearance shown them ; and notwithstanding every effort to quell the tumult, some threescore Churches were destroyed. Then there happened a conflagration in the city ; and other fires breaking out here and there roused the cry that the Christians were the incendiaries, which some under torture confessed to being. Nâsir, with his Ministers' support, stood bravely up for justice ; but unable to stem the angry tide, had at the last to allow the obnoxious laws stringently to be put in force. So sad was now the Christian state that none dare venture forth but in the yellow Jewish garb. The Vizier, a pervert still suspected of Christian tendencies, was attacked by a great body of memlukes ; but here again Nâsir showed his firmness, and brought the rioters to justice.

Another proof of his impartiality is that shortly A.D. 1323. after, a fanatical Soofie at Damascus seeing a Moslem kiss the hand of a christian Secretary as he passed, in indignation cut the Secretary to pieces.[1] The Sultan, unmoved by the heated cries in favour of the fanatic, had him hung up at the city gate. With similar firmness the leaders of a dangerous 1327. outbreak at Alexandria were treated.[2] And again at Damascus, when another christian Secretary, having, 1340. under the rack confessed to a conflagration, was with his friends put to death and a heavy tax laid on the community, the Governor was by the Sultan severely called to order.

Three Viziers of Christian descent were nevertheless put to death under this reign, partly in punishment for cruel administration, partly (we are told) for the vast treasures amassed by them. One is such a tale of horrors that, if but half of what is told be true, it casts a lurid light on the barbarity of the day. Nashju, himself a pervert raised to the highest 1340. offices of State, resorted to such inhumanities of the rack and lash as to arouse the anger of the people.[3]

[1] An incidental proof that the regulations against employment of Christians fell constantly into disuse.
[2] The cause is singular. An envoy from Constantinople listened with a crowd around to a story-teller but, when the rest joined in at the benediction of the Prophet's name, he was silent;—at which the people rose in tumult upon all the Christians in the place.
[3] He would wrap his victim's hand in cloth steeped in boiling rosin. The mother of his predecessor was stripped, seated in boiling

A.D. 1340. Nâsir long refused to credit his guilt; and, as usual, there was treachery and swearing on both sides to produce evidence true or false. At last he was arrested; and a golden cross, wine, and swine's flesh (secret signs of Christianity) found in his house roused the indignation of the crowds to such a pitch that all night long, with flags and torches, they shouted around the Citadel. The Sultan was in the end forced to condemn Nashju; and not only he, but his mother and brothers with him, were put to death. Buried in the Jewish cemetery, his grave had to be long watched lest the body should be taken up and burned.

Nâsir's treatment of the Christians around him was no doubt partly due to their official competency and to his belief that they were loyal, but more perhaps to their being beyond his jealousy. In regard to his Emirs, and indeed to all around, so long as there was nothing to arouse his suspicion or his avarice, Nâsir may be praised. But otherwise he could show himself a treacherous and bloodthirsty tyrant. We are told of no less than a hundred and fifty instances of death by poison, starving or assassination. The case of Tengiz must here suffice. Bought as a slave by his predecessors, he served Nâsir faithfully eight-and-twenty years as Governor of Damascus, when in the last year of his Sovereign's

oil and so tortured that she miscarried, and so forth. The details of this miserable case occupy six pages of Weil.

life, he fell. The tale is strange and dark almost beyond belief. Besides his bravery in battle with the Mongols, he had endangered his life in the negotiations which (it will be remembered) enabled Nâsir, when in peril at Kerak, to gain over the Syrian Emirs; and in return was rewarded with the Viceroyalty of Syria. There, practically independent, he was often summoned as a counsellor to Cairo. Nâsir took Tengiz' daughter as his Queen and, at an expected birth, invited Tengiz to come with his family to the Capital. As he approached, the Sultan went out in State to meet him, and with high festivity led him up into the Palace, where his reception with royal gifts and entertainments exceeds description. The Sultan's daughters were bade to call him "Uncle" and to kiss his hand, while two of them were affianced to his Sons. After enjoying for a time such untold favour and distinction, Tengiz departed, and added as to the Sultan he said goodbye,—" I have but one wish left, and it is to die before thee!" "Forbid it!" exclaimed Nâsir, "for who then would support my widows, and who sustain my Son with honour on the throne?" A year had hardly passed before this fond affection turned into jealousy and hate. The reasons alleged would seem altogether beside the mark;—displeasure, namely, at the severe treatment of the Christians accused of incendiarism, and devotion of the fine imposed on them to the re-

A.D. 1340.

1339.

A.D. 1340. storation of the great Mosque, instead of being sent to him. Nâsir is also said to have been annoyed at Tengiz desiring to put off the bridal festivities till a season of less distress. At last the Sultan desired him to bring his Sons to Cairo and have the marriage there. But by this time treachery had poisoned Nâsir's ear, and Tengiz perceived that his time too had come. Suspicious now of his Viceroy, and fearing that he might rebel, the Sultan sent a force to seize him at Damascus, and was so overjoyed when he heard that his victim was being brought along in fetters that he had the good news proclaimed. Carried thus to Cairo, and interrogated by the Counsellors of State, the wretched captive was able to give so good an account of himself, and so well rebut the accusations made against him, that they begged he might be allowed to end his days in peace. But, deaf to their entreaty, Nâsir despatched the miserable object of his jealousy to Alexandria, where he was beaten and tortured to disclose his supposed confederates and

1340. his hidden treasure. He was then put to death, and with him fell several Emirs who shared his confidence and his friendship. The property of Tengiz and those condemned with him was so vast, that Nâsir could afford to bear with equanimity the reproaches which some even dared to offer at Tengiz' cruel fate.[1]

[1] Weil tells the story at inordinate length,—eleven pages; but it is very illustrative both of Nâsir and his times.

And so it was with rich and powerful Emirs A.D. 1340 throughout the reign. He suffered them to gather wealth, and in due time, on some charge or suspicion, took their lives and seized their riches. He would veil his designs sometimes for years, till the occasion came and then woe to the wretched victim. But while with the rich or with such as excited jealousy, he was a wayward, capricious and cruel tyrant, towards the rest of the world he is praised as a wise, just and able ruler. Obnoxious taxes swept away; Emirs' appanages, eating into the revenue, cut down; field measurements and assessment revised; departmental expenditure reviewed;— such were among the wise measures of the day. During a severe famine, grain was imported from Syria; the rich also were forbidden to sell their hoards above a certain price; a measure which, however opposed to economic principles, had yet the result of making food more available to the people at large.

The public works of Nâsir, constructed at immense expense, and some with such forced labour as risked life itself among the multitudes driven to the task, contributed to the prosperity of the country, the fruitfulness of the land, the beauty of the Capital, and convenience of the people. The important canal from Fuah to Alexandria, on which a hundred thousand toiled, not only opened up to the country maritime

A.D. 1340. traffic direct from the sea, but rendered a barren waste both arable and populous; while villas and gardens beautified its banks. Roads also at safe level throughout the land, and especially a dam along the right bank of the Nile, afforded at once means of communication and protection from the swelling flood. Then, both within and without the Citadel, mansions were built for the Sultan's wives and concubines, slave-girls and children; especially the far-famed *Casr Ablac*, or White Castle, after a model at Damascus, for which architects and masons were summoned from Syria, and its completion celebrated by royal festivities. No fewer than thirty Mosques, besides fountains, baths, and schools, were founded by him; while portions of the great Mosque and other buildings in the Citadel still bear the Sultan's name.[1] Beautiful remains also, in stone, in marble and in brass, with delicate tracery and inscriptions, exquisitely ornamented stands and lustres,[2] with other rarities, still remain to attest the progress at this time of artistic taste and execution borrowed however mainly from surrounding lands, and have left the name of *Nâsir Mohammed ibn Kelawun* as perhaps the best known of bygone rulers in the Capital. Nor was his care confined to Cairo, for in the chief cities of Syria, and at Mecca, measures

---

[1] Materials from the ruined Cathedral of Akka adorn this Mosque.
[2] See examples at end of volume.

were taken to promote embellishment and public works. A.D. 1340. It may be added, as showing the extent to which private as well as public money was now lavished on architecture, that the Sultan's two chief Ministers (of whom we hear more hereafter) vied with each other in the grandeur of their edifices, the remains of which have carried down their names also to the present day.[1]

All this must have weighted the burdens by which the people were ground down to poverty. But not only so; there was added to it the extravagance of a sumptuous Court, which might have been held quite fabulous unless attested by contemporary writers. On pilgrimage, the Sultan's table was supplied throughout the Arabian desert with a garden, as it were, of flowers and fruits. The journey of one of his Queens to Mecca cost

[1] The French *Mission Archæologique* gives us much that is interesting on these ancient remains, and on the architecture in the Citadel bearing Nâsir's name. Very beautiful illustrations of the edifices, carving, and inscriptions may be seen in Tome vi. 14th Fascicule, such as the Mosque, Dewan, gate of the Citadel, etc., all bearing the Sultan's name. At p. 86, Tome xix. are three inscriptions from the Citadel wall, as entered by Saladin's gate, in glorification of Nâsir. In Tome iii. pp. 60 and 101, there are other interesting notices, among which one of the "Emerald Gate," the mansion of the Sultan's daughter married to Kausun. It is remarkable that there are still remains of the *Beisan* Palace purchased by that Emir, as well as of the Hill palace, *Casr Beshtak*, bearing his rival's name. These are the two ministers noticed above. (*Troisième Fascicul.* pp. 466, 467.) See also beautiful illustrations in the *Catalogue Musée National de l'Art Arabe*, par Max Henry Le Caire.

A.D. 1340. 100,000 golden pieces; and the bridal outgoings for each of his Daughters 800,000. The marriage of a Son was celebrated with regal splendour. The palace was lighted by three thousand tapers; the nobles passed before, with their memlukes, each holding a flambeau in his hand. When this had lasted well into the night, the ladies of the Emirs assembled in the great Hall, and bowed as they passed each holding her wedding gift; and then (contrary to all Eastern propriety) forming into rows, danced with tabret and song before him. A devoted lover of horses, and of all kinds of animals, he spent large sums upon them, and on hawks for the chase; and indeed he lavished money on whatever to his taste approved itself.[1]

But in the midst of all this state, Nâsir himself was plain and unadorned. With no personal pretensions, short in stature, spot-eyed, and lame in one foot so that he must lean on a staff or attendant as he walked, he yet dispensed with every kind of adornment either in dress or equipage, while both he lavished on his trusted memlukes. The position of the memluke became thus more than ever attractive; and so, tempted by the vast sums offered by

[1] He gave 30,000 golden pieces for a horse he fancied; 10,000 was an ordinary price, and so with other animals. Macrizy tells us that 18,000 loaves of sugar were provided for his Son's marriage-feast, and 20,000 beasts slain. Such are samples of the boundless extravagance attributed to him.

the Sultan's agents and the glowing accounts that A.D. 1340. thus reached to Turkestan, multitudes sold their sons and daughters to be carried to the Egyptian Court, and themselves crowded to the land of promise.

To provide for such a Court there was needed an extravagant expenditure; and, as we have seen, in raising it little regard for what was right,[1] and sometimes even for life itself, was shown. But along with all this, when not misled by covetous or vindictive feelings, wisdom and justice guided the Sultan's reign. He had himself studied law and theology at Damascus, and obtained a diploma there; and so now whenever the Jurists interfered, he held his hand. Great offence was given to the Cazie[2] of Damascus by the appointment there of a christian Copt as private secretary; Nâsir was angry at first, but in the end gave the office to the Cazie's son. He disliked the Hanefite Cazie because of his hostility to the Christians, and being thwarted by a decision[3] of his, deposed him

---

[1] I read in Ibn Ayâs, who gives a very sad account of the morals of the ladies of the day, that a heavy tax was allowed by the Sultan to be laid upon all women of high rank and their daughters indulging in unchastity, and that a female official was appointed to administer it. This is one of the very few notices the historian gives of the state of female society.

[2] *Cazie*, a judge, so pronounced in Central Asia; but in Western lands, *Cadie* or *Kadi*.

[3] The Sultan allowed one of his favourites to take part of the lands of an endowment, giving an equivalent in other lands; an exchange the Cazie declared to be against the law, and refused when threatened to alter his decision, which greatly displeased the Sultan.

A.D. 1340. for a time. The Shafie-ite Cazie he was partial to, but because of the shameless life of his son, was obliged to send him and his family away to Damascus. The Caliph, on account of his open support of Beibars, was kept with his family in one of the Citadel towers, and latterly (1337 A.D.), suspected of disloyalty, was banished to Upper Egypt. The people are said to have been sorry for him; but the Caliph could hardly have been much missed at Cairo. The Sultan's appreciation of learning is shown by his treatment of the historian Abulfeda, and his restoration to the government of Hamah, originally conferred on the family by their ancestor Saladin's brother. Given the title of Sultan, he was invested with the trappings and emblems of royalty, and rode as a prince through the streets of his city. The highest titles were assigned to him by Nâsir, who even addressed him as "brother,"—a singular instance of the Sultan's trust and favour towards a powerful Ruler continued to the end.

For Nâsir was jealous even of his own Sons, so that till the eve of his death he nominated none as his Successor. Ahmed, the eldest, a wretched specimen of slavery to the lowest forms of vice, was banished to Kerak as his father failed to sever him from the company of a memluke youth. Anuk, another son, clung similarly to a singing girl.

In 1341 A.D. Nâsir was seized with an illness,

MINARET OVER MOSQUE OF NÂSIR IBN KILAWUN.

which gradually increased till he used to fall off into A.D. 1341. swoons. These he sought to conceal, but still alarming reports created serious disturbances in the city. The two leading ministers, Beshtak and Kausun, both married to daughters of the Sultan, but at deadly feud against each other, sought to take advantage of the emergency; and this state of things, prolonged from day to day, hurried on so dangerous a crisis that the dying monarch at last summoned a Council, and in their presence June. invested his son, Abu Bekr, with the sword of State. A day or two after, with pious and repentant sighs, he died at the age of fifty-eight, having been forty-eight years Sultan; but of these, his own master, only thirty-two.

A great Prince, whose tyranny and oft-repeated deeds of cruelty cast into the shade his virtues, Nâsir died with a name more feared than loved. Buried without pomp in his father's mausoleum, none even of his own family were present. And so a biographer says of him,—" Lord of many lands, he died as one forlorn, was washed and laid out as an outcast, and buried as a homeless one." A life of strange vicissitude, of much that is to be well spoken of, but of more that is to be condemned, and passions of anger and jealousy in the last degree to be denounced;—the biography of Nâsir ibn Kelawun is one well worthy of careful thought and study.

CHAPTER IX

NÂSIR'S SONS AND GRANDSONS

1341–1382 A.D.

A.D. 1341. FOR the next forty years the Sultanate was held by the house of Nâsir; in the first score by eight of his sons successively, and in the second by his grandsons;—from first to last a miserable tale. They rose and fell at the will of the Mameluke leaders of the day, some mere children; the younger, indeed, the better, for so soon as the puppet Prince began to show a will of his own he was summarily deposed, or he was made away with, few of such as reached maturity dying a natural death. The Emirs rose and fell; each had his short day of power; then deposed and plundered, exiled or strangled, others succeeded but to share their fate. There were short intervals of able rule; but for the most part, murders, torture, execution, crime, and rebellion were throughout the period rife. The tale is sad and unattractive, and will be disposed of as briefly as the history admits of.

Nâsir, as we have seen, on his deathbed nominated not his eldest son, but ABU BEKR, twenty years of age, to be his Successor. This youth had already at Kerak shown himself cruel and overbearing; and his first act as Sultan was that of a savage tyrant. For some slight that had been shown him, he had his father's Chancellor nailed down on a camel's back and paraded through the streets, while his children were brought out and slain before his eyes.[1] Beshtak was by his jealous rival Kausun seized and carried off to Alexandria, where by the Sultan's command he was put to death, and his vast possessions seized. At last, misguided by the youths with whom he spent his nights in dissipation, Abu Bekr fell foul of Kausun, and sought to lay hands upon him. But timely warned, Kausun gained over the great body of the Emirs, and sending the young tyrant, with his grown-up brothers, to be confined at Coss in Upper Egypt, so closed a reign of but two or three months' duration.

A.D. 1341.
June.

Kausun, now supreme, raised KUJUK, another son of Nâsir, six years of age, to the throne; and the Caliph, approving Abu Bekr's deposition for his evil life, confirmed the choice. The new reign opened with the usual overthrow of all in power. One of

August.

---

[1] Besides the slight, the Chancellor had detained and ill-treated one of Abu Bekr's servants who had fled to him. This is all that is alleged for such incredible bloodthirstiness.

A.D. 1341. the late Sultan's favourites, bound on a camel, and followed by crowds with torches, breathed his last upon it. Kausun now lived in dread of Ahmed, the eldest son of Nâsir, still at Kerak, and sought to entrap him by promise of the crown if he would come to Cairo. But Ahmed, upon the alert, stayed on at Kerak. Kotlubogha an Emir sent with troops against him, was gained over by Ahmed; and through him most of the Emirs in Syria also to the same side. The two parties tried conclusions there, and Ahmed's gained the ascendency. Kausun in difficulties would now have gladly recalled Abu Bekr from Coss to the throne; but he had already by his secret command been there put to death. Deserted by his followers, he was seized and sent to Alexandria, where he met the same fate as Beshtak.[1]

1342. Jan. The child Kujuk, after a reign of five months, was upon this deposed, and a deputation sent by the leading Emirs to AHMED, now twenty-four years of age, and living still a life of shameless self-indulgence at Kerak, inviting him to come to Cairo and ascend the throne.[2]

---

[1] Kausun was unpopular among the Emirs because he was not a proper memluke, not having been *bought* as a slave; for he had come to Nâsir of his own accord in the Mongol princess' suite, and thus had voluntarily made himself over to the Sultan. He had not the social elevation of a *purchased* slave!

[2] Among the Emirs here mentioned was the second husband of Ahmed's mother. As a slave-girl she used to sing to the Emirs, for she had a beautiful voice; Nâsir, taking a fancy to her, married her; divorced by him, she married this Emir.

But he had no wish to go; indeed but for Kausun's A.D. 1342. hostility he never would have thought of the throne; and so to the deputation he replied that he would stay where he was till the Syrian Emirs had joined him, meanwhile desiring that the oath of allegiance might be taken at Cairo. His Brothers, now returned from Coss, joined the rest in urging him to return; and so after long delay he at last started with a March. few followers, and entering the Capital at night in a Bedouin's garb, retired to a Brother's house. He did not for days show himself either in Mosque or Palace or any public place, and by this strange conduct gave much offence. At last he was installed; but abandoning himself still to his Kerak voluptuaries, he left the rule to Tushtumur, Kotlubogha and other Emirs, who committed unheard-of atrocities against their opponents.[1]

Tushtumur, gaining the ascendency, sent away April. his colleagues to commands in Syria, and so ruled supreme. But Ahmed becoming jealous, shortly after assumed the reins himself, cast Tushtumur into prison, and caused Kotlubogha, Governor of Damascus, to be arrested there. But even now, with a free hand and none to control him, the

[1] It was by them that Kausun, Altunbogha, etc., were now murdered in prison. At Abu Bekr's mother's desire, the Governor of Coss, for having at Kausun's command put her son to death, was paraded about the streets for days, and still surviving was after a week strangled.

dissipated tyrant's love for Kerak still prevailed. Leaving Aksonker a leading Emir as Regent, dressed again as a Bedouin, and mounted on a dromedary with but a couple of attendants, he rode off to Kerak, where he retired into privacy and was seen by none but his familiars. Cairo left to itself, fell into confusion and disorder. A letter signed by the chief Emirs demanded his return as needful for Egyptian rule; to which he replied that he had Syria as well as Egypt to govern, and would remain where he was so long as he pleased. Tushtumur and Kotlubogha were carried in chains to Kerak and beheaded there. Their families were sent away to Damascus, robbed even of their clothing, and in so sad a plight that the Syrian Emirs, roused to indignation, forwarded a despatch to Cairo demanding the appointment of another Sultan. On its receipt the leaders, their patience now exhausted, deposed the still absent Ahmed, who thus after a dissipated and cruel reign of half a year, was succeeded by another Brother.

This was ISMAIL, who, though but seventeen years of age, was exemplary and mild in his administration; the only member of his house indeed in whom cruelty, avarice, and treachery were not the leading features. He re-entered the deserted Palace, and commenced his administrations hopefully; but he was not allowed a peaceful reign. One of his Brothers rebelled, and lost his life in the struggle. But

Ismail's chief anxiety arose from the intrigues kept up by the deposed Ahmed, which led to the siege of Kerak. That strong fortress held out for a year, when at last it fell. Ahmed was put to death, and his head despatched to Cairo. At the sight of it, the young Sultan trembled violently, and became deadly pale. From that moment he lost his sleep, and died within a year. He was devoted to his harem, and had lost his heart to a black slave-girl whose lute charmed and soothed his later days, and that is all we are told of his domestic life. Much influenced by his attendants and Harem, Ismail's weak administration tempted misrule around; but apart from the siege of Kerak, little of moment occurred during these three years, beyond risings amongst the Bedouins, and unimportant fighting on the Syrian border. The finances became so low that the young Sultan had to give up an intended pilgrimage to Mecca, where Yemen again began to seek supremacy. Yet so great was still the Mameluke prestige abroad, that another Embassy, laden with rich gifts, arrived from India, to obtain the Sultan's recognition of Ibn Toghluk's succession, as well as his confirmation by the Caliph who, though thus revered abroad, was made at home but little mention of.

A.D. 1342.

1344. July.

Two other Brothers succeeded, SHABÁN and then HÁJY, slain each at the end of a year; a time of debauchery, murder and misrule, worse if possible even

1345. August.

than anything that had gone before. Shabân assassinated two of his Brothers, one of whom (Kujuk, former Sultan) was strangled in his bed. His vices and cruelty became at last so unbearable, that discontent spread from Egypt to Damascus. Alarmed at the report of this, he became afraid of his two remaining Brothers, and was on the point of treating them as he had done the others, when the inmates of his harem interposed and saved their lives. Disorder throughout the kingdom caused so great a fall in the revenue, that the annual Pilgrimage had to be given up; and yet the luxury of the Court and splendour of the ladies' wardrobe exceeded anything ever seen before. At last the Emirs of Syria (all of them Mamelukes of vast influence in Cairo) rose against Shabân and demanded his abdication. Attacked in his palace and deserted by his followers, he fled to his harem where he was pursued and put to death. The reign of his brother HÂJY, an abandoned youth of fifteen chosen to succeed, was even worse. Emirs all around were put to death, both at the Capital and Alexandria. The Regent, a Circassian by birth, desirous of promoting those of his own blood at the expense of the Turkish faction, excited the jealousy of the latter. These accused him to Hâjy, who put him off his guard by the offer of Gaza, and then treacherously slew him. The young Sultan spent fabulous sums upon his slave-girls, especially on one who had been the favourite mistress successively of the two Sultans before him.¹ At a time when people were starving from a prevailing dearth, he abandoned himself to the frivolities and dissipations of his mistresses, singers, musicians, jugglers and others, on whom he squandered great sums of money. Having on one occasion divided amongst his favourites the whole treasure of a condemned Emir, two of his trusted memlukes warned him of the dark clouds gathering around. In his scorn, he was on the point of destroying them; but they, effecting their escape, roused the Emirs all ready for revolt. Assembled in hostile array, these demanded Hâjy's resignation. He rode out against them, but deserted and unhorsed, was put to death, pleading in vain for mercy.

A.D. 1347.

The Circassian memlukes would now have elected Hosein, but the Emirs preferred HASAN, a younger brother of twelve, as an easier tool to work with. Then followed the usual outrages against the favourites of the late Sultan. The gay courtiers and slave-girls were plundered of their last dirhem to supply

1347. Dec.

---

¹ Fabulous gifts were lavished on this slave-girl, one consisting of pearls costing 400,000 silver pieces. She had a turban which the three Sultans, one after the other, had adorned with pearls worth 100,000 golden pieces. Two of his friends who persuaded him to put away this girl, as well as two others to whom he was devoted, were the following year with others invited to a feast, and there for their good advice, assassinated.

A.D. 1347. the empty treasury. For example, Hâjy's clown, a wretched hunchback, was beaten and tortured for his money, till in agony he expired. The Circassian memlukes, too, who had favoured Hosein, were pursued and distributed among the Turkish Emirs. The present reign was quieter than the last, but that was mainly due to the appalling visitation—the *Black Death*—which, in its deadly march from the far East to the Mediterranean laid 1348,1349. its millions in the dust.[1] The mortality was nowhere greater than in Syria, and for the time nothing else was thought of. Apart from the

[1] Macrizy tells us a great deal about this terrible pestilence. Appearing in China some seven years before, it spread through Tartary to Constantinople, and thence over Europe and Syria; while according to other accounts, it reached Syria from India through Persia and Mesopotamia. From Syria where few towns escaped, it passed on to Egypt, but lost its virulence as it went south. At Cairo, from November to January, 1000 to 1500 died daily, and once as many as 20,000; the dead were carried on rafters, 30 to 40 being cast into a single grave. In Aleppo 500 died daily, and in Gaza 22,000 in one month. In Egypt the plague attacked with boils, both cattle and fish, the watercourses being full of dead fish. Even the vegetable world was smitten and dates became uneatable from worms. At Cairo the illness began with women and children, and then passed on to men. The roads were strewed with corpses which they feared to remove, for the very touch brought on fatal boils. The Capital became empty, for the Sultan and all who could fled. The total mortality here reached 900,000. Property passed often through seven or eight hands, and you might see labourers mounted on officers' horses. The land was waste, there being none to till it. Corn was cheap enough, but meal almost unprocurable, there being few hands left to grind it. The virulence of the disease gradually diminished in the spring of 1349 A.D., and shortly after it altogether ceased.

recurring atrocities of the Bedouins, and a deadly A.D. 1349. quarrel in which the Governor of Damascus was slain by the Emir of Tripoli, there is little for the first three years to record. Then the Regent being absent on pilgrimage, Hasan himself assumed the reins. Though outrages during this period are not wanting, they were of a less marked character than usual, and a victory at Mecca over the Yemen 1350. troops, and at Sinjar over the Turcomans, gave some *éclat* to the young Sultan's sceptre. But his Ministers still interfering, he plotted their arrest; and this coming to their knowledge, he was attacked, deposed and interned in a private dwelling-house, after a reign of four years, of which only in the last was he possessed of any real power.

Another young son of Nâsir, SALIH by name, 1351. fourteen years of age, whose Mother was daughter of Aug. the fated Tengiz, was now placed peacefully on the throne. He reigned three years, which, apart from Mameluke plots and cruelties, was an uneventful time. In the continual rise and fall of Emirs at Cairo, their occasional rebellion in Syria, their flight, pursuit and, it may be, death, there is little that would interest the reader. The Vizier, a Christian pervert, who had amassed an enormous fortune, was accused by a rival of being still a Christian. Not only the wretched man, but his family and dependants also, were horribly tortured, till property worth

A.D. 1351. two million golden pieces was disgorged, after which he was banished to Coss. The Christian community suffered much at this period. Envied for their honest gains, they were stripped of all, their Churches demolished, and the former cruel regulations again stringently enforced. This, with the destruction of Bedouin hordes which as usual infested Egypt, is all that the youthful Salih's reign is remarkable for. At last, he was tempted himself to assume the power; but falling into a dissipated life, he plotted to seize the Courtiers who were in his way. These anticipating danger, sounded the trumpet of rebellion, put the Sultan under arrest, and reappointed Hasan in his stead.

1354. Oct.

HASAN had spent his season of seclusion and restraint, but with little profit, in study and devotion. His second reign lasted six years. Becoming a miserable debauchee, he allowed his Emirs to rule,—a succession of tyrants who practised inconceivable atrocities.[1] His Sultanate is bare of incident, excepting a defeat at Mecca, and a fresh

---

[1] Shicku, the Chief of the day, had a deposed rival paraded through the city. After that (so we are told) his head was shaved and bored in various places: into the punctures venomous insects were inserted; then a burning brass plate was applied, which caused the creatures to bore deeper in till the poor man died. Shicku paid the penalty of his inhumanities, being cut down in Court. And yet he is praised as an exemplary Believer, having not only endowed a theological school with reciters of the Coran, but laboured with his own hands at the pious work of building the cloister.

MOSQUE AND TOMB OF SULTAN HASAN, SON OF NÂSIR.
(MINARET TO LEFT, PART OF ORIGINAL BUILDING.)

invasion of Armenia where Tarsus, Adana and A.D. 1354. Massîssah were seized and garrisoned by Moslem troops. At last he was attacked by his leading Emir, Yelbogha, to whom he had given offence; and having been cast into prison, was never seen again.

Two grandsons of Nâsir now succeeded to the 1361. Sultanate. First MOHAMMED son of Hâjy, a youth of March. fourteen, who after a couple of years was deposed as wanting, and kept in confinement. SHABÂN followed, 1363. a child of ten years, preferred as such to his father Hosein, who himself never reached the throne. He reigned (if one might use the word) fourteen years, longer in fact than any other of the family. In the constant downfall of leading Emirs, and sad end of the Sultan himself, the tale differs little from that which has gone before. The early years were uneventful, the later stormy both at home and abroad. Yelbogha (Al Jahjawy) was at first the dominant Emir; but his atrocities so transcended even the barbarous precedents of the age [1] as to 1366. arouse the hatred of the people, who rallied to the support of the young Sultan when Yelbogha rebelled and would have raised another Brother to the throne. The tyrant was defeated, and his head exposed upon a burning torch. His memlukes, however, remained dominant and in their wild excesses had the city at

[1] His savage cruelty was such that many had their tongues cut out simply because they had offended him.

7

A.D. 1367. their mercy. At last they too attempted to dethrone the Sultan; but the troops and citizens, who could no longer bear their riot and outrage, put them to flight. The leaders were all drowned, beheaded or banished. Among the latter was Berkuck who, after some years' imprisonment, escaped to Damascus, where we shall hear more of him hereafter. Things now went on pretty much as before, the only remarkable incident being that, on the death of the Sultan's mother, the ruling Emir who had married
1373. her and claimed her estate, rose in rebellion, was worsted, fled, and falling with his horse into the Nile, was drowned.

Some events of external interest may here be
1364. briefly noticed. The Governor of Bagdad having rebelled against the Ilkhan Oweis, sought the aid of Egypt, proclaimed the Sultan as his Sovereign, and coined money in his name. His deputation was returned with rich gifts, and with the escutcheons both of the Sultan and the Caliph. The Ilkhan sent an Embassy in complaint to Cairo which was ill received. But the ambitious designs of Egypt came to nought, for the rebel Governor was beaten, and Bagdad restored to the Eastern Empire.
1365. While Yelbogha was yet in power, Cyprus with the Venetians and the Knights of Rhodes schemed a Crusade against Egypt. Landing at Alexandria,

they plundered the city for three days and, before A.D. 1365. troops could arrive from Cairo, had sailed away with 5000 prisoners. Yelbogha vented his anger against the Christians by exacting from them large sums to fit out a fleet and ransom the captives. A friendly Embassy of Franks offering reparation, and asking 1368. that the Church of the Resurrection might be reopened, was detained at Cairo by Yelbogha, while he busied himself with preparations for hostilities.[1] Getting no reply, the Cyprus fleet raided the Syrian coast, and again attacked Alexandria, but was repulsed with loss. Hostilities continued thus throughout the year; but peace was at last restored, and the Church reopened to the pilgrims.

Armenia not having been included in this treaty, 1369. the forces of Egypt and Syria were now brought to bear on that unfortunate land. In 1369 it was overrun by the Governor of Aleppo, who captured Sîs, but again retired. A few years after, Cilicia 1374. was anew attacked, when King Leo VI. retired to a hill fortress, but was taken prisoner and carried off to Egypt.[2] Sîs was now placed under a Mameluke 1375.

[1] This Embassy demanded hostages before leaving Alexandria; and it illustrates Mameluke duplicity that Yelbogha sent, ostensibly as hostages, a company of condemned criminals, gaily dressed out; and to deceive the Franks the better, had them followed by women and children as if their families.

[2] He remained in captivity till 1382 A.D., when at the instance of John I. of Castile he regained liberty; but forbidden to return to Armenia, wandered about Europe till he died at Paris 1393 A.D.

A.D. 1375. Emir; and poor Armenia, destined for ages to be the cruel sport of Mameluke and Osmanly despotism,
1378-1381. ceased to be a Christian State. Some years later (it was during the following reign) the Syrian Chiefs made repeated raids on the Turcoman house of Dilghadir in Asia Minor, but were driven back so disastrously that Aleppo was even placed in jeopardy. This marks a new epoch in the relations between Egypt and the Turcomans of the North. Hitherto, as Macrizy remarks, the Turks of Asia Minor had been a wall of defence to the Egyptian frontier. Henceforth they became hostile to Mameluke rule, and eventually the cause of Egypt's downfall.

1366. Early in Shabân's reign an important expedition by land and sea was sent south as far as Suakin, for the protection of Upper Egypt and the Nubian border from the alarming outrages of the Bedouins.[1] It was successful, but the barbarous cruelty of the Governor of Assouan so enraged the surrounding tribes that they rose upon the Egyptians and, having slaughtered them, left the city in flames.

1376. We are now drawing near the close of Nâsir's line. It was not only rebellion and misrule which

(*Vahram's Chronicles of Armenia*, by C. F. Neuman; Oriental Fund, London, 1831.)

[1] The details of the ascent of the Nile, and passing of the cataracts, remind one of the Gordon campaign in our own day.

at this time affected the land, for sore famine and A.D. 1376. pestilence again prevailed. Tushtumur, the Prime Minister, was stricken by the plague; and on recovery piously planned a pilgrimage to Mecca. The Sultan and Caliph both accompanied him, and they set out with vast pomp, and a great multitude of memlukes. On reaching Ayla these demanded money and rose upon the Sultan, who in alarm escaped by night to Cairo. Meanwhile, apparently in concert, a similar plot was taking place at Cairo; for the memlukes had also risen there, and giving out that the Sultan was dead, attacked and slew his favourite Emirs and proclaimed his son Aly in his stead. The Sultan on reaching Cairo had fled to the house of a singing-girl, where discovered in female attire, he was tortured for his treasure, and at last strangled by a memluke whom he had raised to the Emirate. The people lamented his death for, though weak and avaricious, Shabân was mild and gentle compared with those who had gone before him.

ALY, but six years of age, thus set up by the Cairo rebels, was inaugurated on the spot by a Caliph extemporised for the purpose, and entered on his reign;—a troubled period of six years. Shortly after, the other party with Tushtumur at their head, made their appearance from Ayla, and sought to place the Caliph, who returned with them, on the throne. They fought and after repeated encounters were defeated, 1377. March.

A.D. 1378. when Tushtumur was sent away as Governor to Damascus. The memluke party which thus had gained the ascendency now stormed for money, and at the point of the sword secured 500 golden pieces a head by robbery of the Orphan chest. The events that follow are but a kaleidoscope of the rise and fall of ruling Mamelukes, of riot, treachery, extortions, exile and bloodshed.[1] At last, Berkuck and Berekh (who had been banished on the fall of Yelbogha Jahjawy), gaining the countenance of the Syrian Chiefs, became supreme at Cairo. But outrage still continued, and the Citadel itself was the scene of riot. Berkuck plotted to seize Berekh; but he escaped, and followed by his Turkish adherents gave battle to Berkuck and his Circassian band. Berkuck was beaten and sent a prisoner to Alexandria, where he was put to death.[2]

1379.

1380.

[1] A characteristic story may be mentioned here, namely, an attempt to place on the throne the son of a divorced wife of Nâsir, who declared that she was *enceinte* by him when she joined her second husband. The Caliph declared the lady's conduct a scandalous breach of Moslem law. It is rare that we find the Caliph thus interfering; but he was here in entire accordance with Moslem law.

[2] Apparently by Berkuck's command; but he denied it, and laid his death at the door of the Governor of Alexandria, Bu Khalil, a learned writer, whom he made over to Berekh's memlukes. These after parading him on a camel cut him in pieces.

This parading on a camel, so often mentioned now, is explained by Macrizy to have been a horrid spectacle. The victim was first stretched upon a board, on which he was fixed by iron nails through the arms and feet. The whole was then fastened on a camel's back and the victim paraded through the city;—a sad picture of the barbarism of the age.

In the following year the young Sultan died, A.D. 1381. when his brother HÂJY, aged six, succeeded. But memluke risings again broke out; and an attempt was made on Berkuck's life. Accordingly, towards the end of 1382 A.D., Berkuck, in a Council of Emirs 1382. and Sheikhs and in presence of the Caliph, announced that both for peace at home and prosperity abroad, the Sultan must be a man and not a child. The assembly agreed, saluted him as their Ruler, and so the little Sultan was led back again into the Harem.

Thus ended the house of Kilawun; and with it the *Bahrite* or Turkish dynasty came to a close, having lasted for 122 years. The Sultanate passed henceforth into the hands of the *Burjite* or Circassian race, which held it, as we shall see, for 135 years, that is till the close of the Mameluke rule.

PART SECOND

THE BURJITE OR CIRCASSIAN DYNASTY

1382–1517 A.D.

CHAPTER X

BERKUCK AL ZÂHIR

1382–1399 A.D.

It is a relief to pass from upstart Emirs, creatures A.D. 1382. of the day, ruling in the name of boyish Sultans, to a line of Sovereigns ruling in their own name and by their own right; although the change may not have always brought much benefit to Egypt. Such was Berkuck. He was bought by Yelbogha (Al Jahjawy) twenty years before from a Chersonese slave-dealer; and was banished, as we have seen, on his Master's murder. Returning, he fell into 1367. the ranks of Shabân's memlukes, and joined the outbreak that dethroned him. In the turmoil which 1376.

A.D. 1382. followed, he rose rapidly to be a ruling Emir, and having crushed his rival Berekh, became supreme. The slave of yesterday was immediately recognised
Nov. as Sultan by the Emirs of Egypt and by the Governors throughout Syria, many of whom (a suggestive lesson) had held distinguished commands while Berkuck was but a menial memluke, and in the common ranks. After three days' retirement (a practice followed now on each succession) Berkuck issued from the Palace in great pomp, and having been duly done homage to by the Caliph, the Judges and other High officials, distributed the usual gifts and announced the preferments of office. In the follow-
1383. ing year a plot was detected to murder him and
Aug. raise the Caliph, Mutawakkil, to the throne. Summoned to the Sultan's presence, the conspirators, on threat of torture, confessed; on which Berkuck was so enraged that he rushed at the Caliph with his sword; but, held back, sentenced him to death. The Jurists approved; but, the Cazies differed, on the ground that a Caliph had the power to seat and unseat Monarchs (a strange deliverance at this time of day); and so Berkuck contented himself with setting up another Caliph in his stead, and condemning one of the conspirators to death. A reign of terror now began to alienate the leading
1386. Emirs. The Chamberlain, for example, on mere suspicion of a design to restore one of Nâsir's

descendants to the throne, was nailed down with A.D. 1386.
two of his memlukes all three upon a single camel,
paraded, and then put to death. Many were fettered, tortured or banished for no sufficient cause.
The same barbarous rule extended to Syria, where
Governors from being suspected and accused, were 1389.
turned into rebels; till at last the whole province,
with hardly an exception, rose against the Sultan,
whose treacherous designs to decoy his victims to
Cairo and there destroy them, hastened his fall.
A rebel force under Yelbogha (Al Nâsiry) of Aleppo,
and Mintash of Malatia, attacked Damascus; and
having beaten the Sultan's troops, took possession
of the city. They then advanced on Cairo, where
the utmost confusion prevailed. Berkuck's behaviour
was feeble and cowardly in the extreme; he wept
like a child; fawned upon the Caliph Mutawakkil,
whom he had so lately threatened to slay, and
never ventured beyond the Citadel. At the last
moment, he sent a submissive message to Yelbogha,
who spared his life and sent him prisoner to
Kerak. Cairo was for days abandoned to riot
and plunder; till at last, Yelbogha, resisting the
cry of the Emirs that he himself should be Sultan,
restored Hâjy, the child deposed by Berkuck, as the June.
best entitled to the throne.

Yelbogha, as Hâjy's Atabeg or Major-domo,
assumed supreme authority, and Mintash now felt

A.D. 1389. himself powerless. He sought in vain that Berkuck should be put to death, which Yelbogha, holding him to be a sort of counterpoise to Mintash, firmly refused. But he imprisoned Berkuck's followers, and dispersed the whole body of Circassian memlukes. In the end, Mintash, unable longer to bear the supercession, raised the standard of rebellion, and gathered all the disaffected, including even Berkuck's Circassian followers, to his side. Yelbogha now delayed too long. He sent the Caliph to reason with Mintash, who complained that Yelbogha had broken faith with him, and lorded it over the young Sultan. Fighting went on for several days, and Yelbogha, beaten at last, was sent a prisoner to Alexandria. Mintash, now the Atabeg, indulged his power in plundering and imprisoning all around. Even Berkuck's Circassians, to whom he owed so much, became with others the subject of horrible cruelties ;—the hands of many being cut off, and the people threatened with death for carrying any weapons about with them. The Governor of Damascus, a follower of Yelbogha's, was by a treacherous letter put off his guard, seized and put to death; by all which excesses Mintash did himself more harm

1389. than good. Troops were at last sent to Kerak to
Sept. put Berkuck to death ; but favoured by the inhabitants, he escaped to Syria, and there found himself rallied round by increasing numbers. Min-

tash alarmed, began with the Caliph's help to preach A.D. 1389. a Holy war against the apostate Sultan, and soon gathered a strong force with which he marched to Syria. The two came to a pitched battle near Gaza; Berkuck's troops were there put to flight by Mintash, who pursued them towards Damascus, and the day seemed lost. By a lucky chance, Berkuck with a small following came upon the royal tent, where was lodged the young Sultan with the Caliph. He took possession of it and, treating the inmates kindly, was rapidly joined by troops from all directions. Mintash returned too late from his victorious pursuit, and the battle raged again next day, but without result. A storm having forced Mintash back upon Damascus, Berkuck promptly took the opportunity, instead of continuing the battle, to turn his face towards Egypt, and with an ever-increasing force advanced towards Cairo. The young Hâjy, still a youth, whom he carried kindly with him, now resigned in his favour, and proclamation was made in camp that Berkuck was again Sultan. Mean- 1390. while Cairo had been in sad tumult, fear, and uproar. But so soon as it was known that Berkuck was approaching, the city turned out in grand festivity, and welcomed him back with rejoicing to his Palace. Hâjy, who rode in the procession by his side, was provided with a residence in the Citadel, and there for many years he lived in good repute.

A.D. 1390.
Jan.

Reseated thus, by marvellous good fortune, upon his throne, Berkuck sought by every possible means to ingratiate himself with his subjects. He scattered benefits all around, even amongst former enemies; but it was more from motives of expediency than natural kindness and goodwill, for he was still uncertain as to the attitude of Syria. Things, however, did not go well with Mintash there. Losing Damascus, most of his forces went over to the Sultan; but he soon gathered another army, to which Turcomans and Bedouins, besides memlukes of the Kilawun house, readily flocked. Thus equipped, he again took the field against Yelbogha who commanded the Sultan's Syrian army. A bloody but indecisive engagement was fought at Salamich; and so hostilities went on till Berkuck, doubtful of Yelbogha's faith, resolved himself to take the field. Before leaving Cairo, his memluke ferocity betrayed itself in the inhuman torture of all he had suspicions of, especially the friends of Mintash, many of whom were put to a cruel death.[1]

[1] Some curious details are given of sumptuary regulations enforced against the ladies by Kemisbogha, the Governor now left at Cairo. They were forbidden to visit cemeteries, or join parties on the Nile. Their dress had become of such extravagant dimensions as to require for sleeves and skirts, 72 ells of cloth 3½ broad. Running in the opposite direction, Kemisbogha reduced the stuff to 24 ells. The Sultan on his return cancelled the order. Macrizy tells us that in his time, he saw some ladies in short and narrow dresses which they called "Kemisbogha skirts."

At Damascus Berkuck was well received, for he A.D. 1391. July.
published there, as suitable for the moment, an
amnesty to all however implicated; and then marched
northward to Aleppo. Mintash meanwhile had gone
over to the Bedouins; and so dissatisfied was the
Sultan with Yelbogha's pursuit of him that, on
returning to Aleppo, he was seized and, with many
of his favourite Emirs, put to death. Such was the
ingratitude shown by the Sultan to the Chief who
had in time of peril befriended him. At Damascus
too, the proclamation notwithstanding, and also on his Dec.
return to Cairo, many Emirs of whom Berkuck was
jealous, especially all Yelbogha's friends, were pursued, exposed on camels and put to death. Mintash prolonged his border hostilities two years
more, when the Bedouin chieftain, his ally, bribed
by the Sultan, betrayed him to emissaries who
carried him to Aleppo. There to revenge his 1393.
treason, he was tortured with fire and the rack
till in agony he expired. His head, after being
paraded throughout Syria, was hung up at the gate
of Cairo, and then given his poor widow to bury.

In the following year, a learned Shereef, descended 1394.
from Aly, was accused of having plotted with the
Arabs to restore Syria and Egypt to the Prophet's
family. Along with a friend to whom he had
promised office under the new rule, he was put to
the rack to reveal their supporters. They confessed

A.D. 1394. to being alone responsible; and, bravely adding that they had but done their duty according to the Coran and Sunnat, expired under excruciating tortures. The marvel is that the like attempt was so seldom thought of by the Semitic race to restore the country to its native rulers, and stay the barbarous inroad of Turkish slaves who kept still overflowing the land, and subjugating the people to frightful outrage and oppression.

1398. July.
We are told little more of Berkuck's life: but towards its close a dangerous conspiracy illustrates the uncertain temper of the Emirs, and the risks that ever beset the Sultan's throne. A slave of the Treasurer, Ali Bey, was caught intriguing with a slave-girl of the Chamberlain, who punished the offender with four hundred lashes. Aly Bey complained to the Sultan, who failed to call the Chamberlain to account for this assumption of authority. The complainant took the slight so much to heart, that he sought his revenge in an attack on Berkuck's life. For this end he concealed a body of memlukes within his house ready to fall on the Sultan as he returned from the yearly opening of the City canal. But forewarned, before passing the house, Berkuck left his retinue behind and, trotting ahead, passed to the Citadel unrecognised. Aly Bey followed, but only to find the entrance closed. He was seized, and after torture to discover his accomplices, strangled.

His friends, though there was no evidence against A.D. 1393. them, were pursued, and many of them, after the fearful camel-parade, beheaded. Berkuck imprisoned even his own Son-in-law because he had been a friend of Aly Bey. Lost in the discovery that so slight a cause could give rise to so great a danger, Berkuck now regretted his neglect of the Queen's warning not to lean too exclusively on his Circassian memlukes, but rather seek support from a surrounding of Turks and Greek slaves as well. The perilous position at last opened to his eyes affected him so keenly that he did not dare again to quit the Citadel.

In the later years of Berkuck's reign the East again threatened disaster to the Sultanate. After carrying all before him in Central Asia, TIMUR[1] turned his arms westward, and drove Ahmed ibn Oweis out of Bagdad; then marching north he spread devastation over Asia Minor to the shores of the Caspian Sea. Called away by a Mongol insurrection, he returned again triumphant to Persia, inflicting terrible calamities on his road, of which pyramids of heads in Hamadan were a standing witness. A second time he invaded Asia Minor, penetrating as far as Lake Van, and there crushed the Osmanly Bajazet, Chief 1393.

[1] Or Timurlane, born 1336 A.D., descended from a Minister of the Court of Jengiz Khan.

of the Black Weir horde. Now ready to direct the storm against the Egyptian empire, Timur was diverted from the project by another rebellion in the East, and so for the moment Syria escaped.

Although Berkuck suffered little from Timur excepting on the Armenian border, yet communications of a serious nature passed between the two monarchs. Shortly after the capture of Bagdad, the Mongol tyrant sent an envoy to Cairo reminding the Sultan of the bygone hostilities which ended in the peace of Bû Saîd; Persia, having since then fallen to pieces, had now passed under the great Conqueror's sceptre;—" Let there henceforth then be peace between us, and friendly intercourse." Berkuck returned no reply; but afraid of the messenger as a spy had him put to death. At the same time, he received with royal honours Timur's adversary Ahmed ibn Oweis just escaped from Bagdad, loaded him with princely gifts, and took his niece in marriage. But he was still alarmed, and while engaged in measures for the safety of Syria against possible attack, he received a second despatch from Timur, very similar in style to that of Holagu to Nâsir, very long and abounding in quotations from the Coran. The great Conqueror "sent by Heaven to execute vengeance on tyrants of the earth," denounced the wicked murderer of his envoy; while, in his reply, the Sultan scornfully defied him

as an "angel of the Evil one destined for hell-fire," A.D. 1394. May.
and so forth. At last in the middle of the following
year, Berkuck with a strong force started for Syria;
and, assisting Ahmed again to resume possession
of Bagdad, passed on from Damascus to Aleppo.
There he rested for some months; but finding
that Timur had departed north, returned again to Nov.
Cairo. In his later days, Berkuck was so shaken,
as we have seen, by the attack of Aly Bey, that he
took little concern about foreign matters, and before
Timur again came west, he had already passed
away.

In the autumn of 1398 A.D., Berkuck was seized 1399. June.
with dysentery which hung upon him, and in the end
proved fatal. Just before his death in the middle
of the following year, he nominated Faraj, his son by
a Greek mother, with his two chief Emirs, Tagri
Berdy[1] and Itmish as Counsellors, to succeed him.
He died, aged sixty, surrounded by several sons and
daughters, and having reigned, whether as Sultan or
Emir, one-and-twenty years. Extravagant in his
tastes, though yet leaving vast treasures behind,
he had supplied himself with some five thousand
slaves, a magnificent stud, and all the surroundings of a grand Oriental Court. While praised as
an able, wise and benevolent ruler so long as un-

[1] Tagri Berdy was father of Abul Mahâsin the historian.

A.D. 1399. influenced by passion or revenge, and as the founder of many public improvements and institutions, he is equally denounced as ruthless and bloodthirsty whenever occasion roused his jealousy.[1]

He lived in fear not only of Timur, but also of the OSMANLY dynasty a new, and in the end a fateful, enemy to the Egyptian Sultanate. So much depending on this Dynasty in what remains of this story, I propose very briefly to trace its rise, and to mark the position which it occupied at the period under review. To this the following chapter will accordingly be devoted.

[1] The tomb he built for himself still exists outside Cairo. A bridge over the Jordan is mentioned as one of his many public works.

TOMB OF BERKUCK.
(NEAR KOTÂB GATE; PLAIN OF KAITBAI.)

CHAPTER XI

THE OSMANLY DYNASTY

THE birthplace of the Osmanlies lay far away east *12th and 13th Centuries.* in Central Asia beyond the Oxus, from whence Turcomans and Seljukes, first tempted by the Abbaside Caliphs, had been long pouring down upon the West. In their wake, from time to time, there followed hordes of similar race, to aid their arms and share the spoil. One of these, the Ogus tribe, followed the Seljukes in the thirteenth century, and for their services received lands in Asia Minor, where they settled down round about Angora. From *1288.* thence, towards the end of the twelfth century, their Chief, Ertogral, pushed his way onward to the shores of the Bosphorus. He was succeeded by his son Osman[1] who enlarged and consolidated the Osmanly rule; and, on the fall of the Seljukes, became independent Sultan of the western half of Asia Minor. His son Orchan fixed his headquarters at Brousa in dangerous proximity to the Byzantine capital. The

---
[1] Properly Othmân, the *th* being here pronounced as a sibilant.

east of Asia Minor still belonged in part to Persia, and in part to Turcoman chiefs, such as those of the Black and White Weir hordes. There were also throughout the Peninsula a number of small Chiefships, remnants of the Seljuk empire, but now being gradually incorporated in the Osmanly Sultanate. Notwithstanding Orchan's marriage with the Keisar's daughter, hostile relations broke out between the two, and in the middle of the fourteenth century the Sultan crossed the Bosphorus, seized Gallipoli and advanced into European territory. His successor Murâd still moving forward made Philippopolis his western capital. Though he was slain in fighting with the Keisar, the Osmanly sovereignty remained firmly established over an extensive range of country on the opposite shores. Bajazet succeeding, followed with vigour and devotion a like course; and, the Keisar being now subordinate, pushed his arms to the borders of Hungary, where he gained the victory of Nicopolis. Returning east, he engaged his troops in putting down the opposition which had grown up during his absence in Europe, and enlarging his dominions which now extended from the Bosphorus and Cæsarea as far east and north as Siwâs and Tokat.

Had Berkuck joined this conquering Prince and aided him with the Egyptian and Syrian arms, they might have set Timur at defiance, and saved the territories of both from impending disaster.¹ But A.D. 1396. Berkuck feared Bajazet, dreading the Osmanly raids upon his border, and kept aloof; and so Timur was able to take them each separately in hand. Apart from their martial instincts, causes were not wanting to precipitate hostilities between Bajazet and Timur. Each was forward to give the rebellious dependants of the other friendly welcome and help. Ahmed ibn Oweis, for example, driven out of Bagdad found shelter with the Osmanlies; and so with the chief of Erzengan and others. This unfriendly attitude roused Timur to address Bajazet in the vainglorious style of Asiatic conquerors. "The pigeon might as well fight with the vulture, or an ant defy the tread of an elephant, as Bajazet stand before the Conqueror of the world," and so forth;² to which Bajazet answered in the same defiant style. But while Timur fell upon the Peninsula and destroyed Siwâs and its surroundings 1400. with horrid butchery, the Osmanly loitered beyond the Bosphorus at the siege of Constantinople. The trial of arms, however, was not yet. For Timur, instead of moving westward, turned his march unexpectedly south, and (as we shall see below) spent his fury upon Syria and Damascus. Return-

---

¹ Timur used to say that Bajazet was an able leader, but of poor soldiers; while Egypt and Syria had good troops, but badly led.

² Gibbon gives us some of this despatch in his sixty-fifth chapter.

A.D. 1402. ing east by Aleppo, he again laid Bagdad a ruined heap, and then passed the winter at Tebriz. It was
Spring. now that Timur, displeased with Bajazet's treatment of his vassal of Erzengan, concentrated his hordes from Georgia and Persia upon Asia Minor. For some reasons he even now desired peace; and negotiations were the result. His overtures were indignantly rejected by Bajazet, who challenged his
Summer. adversary to battle. They met near Angora, when owing to defection of his troops, Bajazet was defeated, taken prisoner, and (as the story goes) carried about by Timur in an iron cage.[1] For the time his successor, Mohammed ., was able to retain only the northern part of Asia Minor, the remainder being restored by Timur to its various petty Chieftains. Thus weakened, the Osmanly dynasty ceased for the moment to give anxiety to Egypt. But it was not long in recovering the whole territory from the Black to the Mediterranean Sea, and of assuming that hostile attitude which in the end proved fatal to the Mameluke Sultanate.

With this brief introduction the relations of Timur towards Egypt and Syria will now be resumed.

[1] Weil makes some sensible remarks about this iron cage, and comes pretty much to the same conclusion as Gibbon (vol. v. p. 96). Timur is said to have treated Bajazet well till he attempted to escape, and then made him follow the army in what was probably a litter, or sedan chair, surrounded with iron rods like a cage, for security.

CHAPTER XII

FARAJ

1399-1412 A.D.

WE return to Cairo. FARAJ, son of Berkuck, was but thirteen years of age when he began to reign, a wretched time of strife in Egypt and of anarchy in Syria. At the first, there was alarm at the descent of Bajazet on Malatia and other places on the border; but before an army could be sent he had retired. Damascus and other Syrian cities having cast off their allegiance on the ground that the Sultan was a minor, the youth summoned his Law officers and, by their decision, assumed majority. But this made matters no better. Intrigues grew dangerous; the Citadel was closed against the Regent and Tagri Berdy; and they after an open fight fled to Damascus which, with the rest of Syria, was convulsed by rebellion and torn by misrule. At last the young Sultan marched with a powerful army, beat the rebels, and in a way restored peace. The Chief of Damascus, as leader of the rebellion, after long torture for his treasure, was strangled. Four-

[margin: A.D. 1399. June.]
[margin: Oct.]
[margin: 1401. Spring.]

A.D. 1401. and-twenty of the disloyal Governors were beheaded, and others pardoned. Tagri Berdy was among the latter, the Sultan's mother making intercession for him as one of Greek descent.

Autumn. It was now that Timur, after his first invasion of Asia Minor (as related in the previous chapter), turned his arms southward upon Syria, which on the first alarm cried out for help from Egypt. But at the moment all that could be done was to tell the Governors themselves to do the best for their own defence. Timur demanded of them the release of his vassal Itilmish chief of Van, and recognition of himself as Supreme. The demand was answered by the murder of his messengers. On this, Timur came down like a whirlwind upon Syria and defeated the Emirs assembled at Aleppo for its defence. They fled part away to Damascus, and part into the city, which for three days was the scene of murder and outrage. Thence from town to town, the Conqueror passed on carrying destruction in his van. Cairo was now in terror. The tale of Timur's vengeance, and the rapine of his hordes, rapidly filled the ranks

Dec. of the army with which the Sultan reached Damascus just in time to anticipate the approach of Timur. Several encounters followed in which the Egyptians, with Bedouin and Arab help, had the advantage. The two armies remained entrenched for a while beside Damascus, when Timur, anxious it was thought, to avoid the Syrian winter, entered into A.D. 1401. friendly communications with the Sultan, who promised to surrender Itilmish and acknowledge the Khan's supremacy. Satisfied, apparently, the Mongol army began to move away, when the Egyptians fell upon their rear, but were driven back. On this, Timur returned and pitched his camp by the city. Just then a party of the Emirs conspiring against the government, went off in secret to supplant Faraj and seize the unprotected Citadel. The Sultan hastened in pursuit of them, thus leaving Syria to its fate.

The Egyptian army now gradually gave way; the citadel after a month's siege was captured, and the city given over by Timur to flame and plunder. Damascus as the ancient seat of the Omeyyad Caliphate was hateful to the Shiea zealot; but what provoked him to more than Mongol vengeance, was a letter from the Sultan saying that his departure was due to another cause than fear of him, and threatening to return and, like a roused lion, destroy his victim. The wretched city after weeks of conflagration and rapine was left a heap of ruins. Timur then departed and carried with him great numbers of the learned citizens, artists, architects, and workmen, to Samarcand. Retiring by Aleppo and plundering as he went, he vented his fury on July. Bagdad, which had again fallen under Ahmed. Leaving it covered with "towers of the dead," he made his second attack on Asia Minor in which (as we have seen) he took Bajazet prisoner. Towards the close of the following year he despatched an embassy to Cairo demanding, under threat of return, the submission of Egypt and release of Itilmish. The Sultan, then in trouble at home, not only set the prisoner free, but sent an offering of rich gifts, which was acknowledged by the present of an elephant, precious stones and costly robes. Timur also asked that Ahmed and Kara Yusuf of the Black Weir, now prisoners in Syria, might be put to death. This Faraj readily agreed to; but Syria was at that moment so much out of hand that the Emir of Damascus set them free instead; and Timur shortly after dying, the matter went no further.

We carry the reader back to the time when Faraj, leaving Timur before Damascus, hastened his return to Cairo. The conspiracy came to nothing, and every effort was now made to enlist another force against the Mongol army; but meanwhile it had disappeared, and nothing more in that direction was required. During the next few years, the Capital was the scene of dire disorder, one party of Emirs rising against another, and the Citadel being over and again besieged. Syria too, since Timur's departure, had become all but independent. Endeavouring to recover his authority there, Faraj had to retreat before the rebels. These pursuing him, attacked the Capital, but quarrelling as usual amongst themselves, they A.D. 1405. were driven back, and a measure of peace restored.

A new danger now threatened Faraj. The Sept. Circassian memlukes angry at the punishment of certain of their Emirs, and at the favour shown to the Greeks and especially to Tagri Berdy, conspired against him. While Faraj was disporting himself with his slaves in his bath, one of them in their gambols kept him so long under water that, but for the help of a Greek memluke, he had been drowned. Suspecting a Circassian conspiracy, he disappeared by night and hid himself in the house of a friend, who gave out that he had been made away with. The Circassians upon this raised his brother Abdul Aziz to the throne, and made common cause with the Syrian Emirs. But they pressed their hostility too far; and the other party, learning that Faraj was still alive, attacked them. While the fighting raged at the grand entrance of the Citadel, Faraj reappearing entered it with his party by another gate, and taking his enemies in the rear, gained an easy victory. Thus after an interregnum of two or three months Faraj resumed his place; and Abdul Aziz, with another brother imprisoned at Alexandria, was put to death by poison there.

Faraj, now come of age, reigned nearly seven 1405. years more—a wretched tale of conflict with Emirs at home, and revolted Governors abroad. To regain

A.D. 1406. authority in Syria, he led armed expeditions thither every year. But even when his adversaries were defeated, the Sultan was weak enough to be ever restoring them to command again, so that imperial authority fled entirely from his hands. At one time, the Emir Jakam, victorious throughout the greater part of Syria, assumed the title of Sultan with royal honours; but in battle with Kara Yelek of the White Weir, who had encroached upon the Syrian border, this ambitious leader lost his life. Syria now fell under the rule of other Emirs, whose rise and fall and various conflicts it would be profitless to follow. One of these named Sheikh entered Egypt, attacked Cairo and besieged the Citadel, but fled on the approach of troops; and yet after a

1411. year's fighting and rebellion this rebel was not only pardoned, but given the government of Tripoli.

Towards the close of his life, Faraj fell into intemperate and abandoned ways; and in fits of anger would slay, even with his own hand, suspected Emirs and slaves around him. A wife whom he had divorced was sent for by him; and when she came, he rushed at her, cut off her head, and killed her husband.[1] In a tour through lower Egypt, his

---

[1] He is said to have slain "by the dozen." His biographers apologise for him that he did so only after much forbearance, but what a state of society does not this imply!

When the poor divorced wife appeared at his call, he pursued her

tyranny and exactions were so severe as to rouse a conflict in Alexandria; just then a dangerous rising in Syria awakened him from his mad career. For two Emirs, whom he had pardoned, Sheikh and Newroz, now rebelled and assumed an independent attitude. Faraj at once started on his seventh Syrian campaign. His troops began to desert him by the way; but the foolhardy Prince, against the advice of Tagri Berdy, pushed forward his reduced and wearied army by forced march to Balbec. Here a battle took place. Defeated and wounded, Faraj fled to Damascus, where his friend Timurtash (Tagri Berdy having just died) besought him, while yet there was time, to hurry back to Cairo, or even to seek help at Aleppo from the Turcomans around. He refused; and Sheikh approaching in triumph, had him now completely at his mercy. Having taken refuge in the Citadel, Timurtash advised Faraj to escape in the dark with him; but he delayed so long that his friend had to fly without him. Nothing now remained but to surrender. This he did on the sacred promise that his life should be safe; and so he was at the first received with

May. 1411.

as she fled wounded and screaming, and at last beheaded her. Wrapping the body in a sheet, he summoned the husband, and asked whether he recognised it; then rushing at the terrified man, he beheaded him also, and had both bodies buried together. A terrible tale, for by re-marriage they had done nothing wrong either in law or usage, after the Sultan had divorced her as his wife.

A.D. 1411. honour. But having been by common consent, for his evil and tyrannical life, deposed, he was eventually cast into a cell, and by night stabbed to death 23rd May. by one of the Assassin race. The body stript was cast into a dunghill, and after two or three days secretly buried by a citizen at night.

It had been a miserable reign. The devastations of Timur, incessant rebellion in Cairo, Syria convulsed by never-ending conflict of Emirs with their Sultan and with one another,—all this with pestilence and famine to boot, reduced the population (we are told) to one-third of what it had been, and rendered life itself a burden. Repeated attacks of the Franks on Alexandria and the Syrian coast, are hardly to be mentioned amid the confusion of the day.[1] Worst of all in the Believer's eyes, as if to show his contempt of the Moslem law, Faraj had his image struck on the coin of the realm; and to him, amid the long race of Egyptian tyrants, may be awarded the unhappy pre-eminence, of a weak, ungodly and cruel reign.

---

[1] In 1403 A.D. the Franks ravaged Alexandria, and in 1404 A.D. Tripoli. Shortly after, troops from a fleet of forty Cyprian ships landed at Beyrut, set fire to the city, and ravaged the country as far as Sidon and Tripoli.

CHAPTER XIII

THE CALIPH—SHEIKH AL MUEYYAD

1412-1421 A.D.

AT Damascus, Sheikh called a Council which (Faraj being still in the Citadel) nominated ABBAS, the Caliph, who was with the army, to the Sultanate. It was much against the Caliph's will, as he knew that none but a Turk could rule, and that it was but a momentary measure of expediency; he made it therefore a condition that even if ousted from the Sultanate, he should still retain the Caliphate. The announcement that the Caliph had been elevated to the throne was received with shouts of rejoicing throughout Damascus. It was indeed a singular fortune which thus crowned (though it were but in name) the long-neglected Head of Islam; and pious Moslems, anticipating in their simplicity its continuance, exulted at the rejuvenescence of the sovereign Caliphate of bygone days.

They were soon undeceived, for on return to Cairo, the Sultan Caliph was treated as a mere

A.D. 1412. appendage of the State, confined in fact within the Citadel. Sheikh and Newroz together held the reins; but soon the crafty Sheikh induced his fellow to assume the command of Syria, and thus secured for himself unfettered rule at home. A Bedouin outburst was shortly after taken advantage of by his friends to demand that, for the welfare of the State, Sheikh should have the Sovereign name as well as power. Abbas was accordingly deposed, not only from the throne, but from the Caliphate; and sent, with the sons of Faraj, a prisoner to Alexandria, where, eventually released by Sheikh's successor, he lived in privacy.

Nov. SHEIKH was now proclaimed Sultan, with the title Al Mueyyad. Purchased from a Circassian dealer at 3000 pieces by Berkuck, he was rapidly promoted from the courtly page, to be leader of the Meccan pilgrimage and Emir of a thousand. He was then appointed Governor of Tripoli, and after that, as we have seen through bloodshed and rebellion, reached at last the throne. On learning of his investiture, Syria led by Newroz and other Emirs, who professed to recognise the Caliph's sacred right, proclaimed a Holy war against his supercessor. Timurtash with his two nephews took the part of Sheikh against them. But Sheikh feared these three greatly, as having been prominent leaders in the recent turmoils. Ungratefully, therefore, he summoned them on false pretence

to Cairo, where on their being put to death he cried A.D. 1412.
with delight, "Now I am really King, with these
three men away!" Having thus, by imprisonment
or otherwise, got rid of all in Egypt of whom he was
afraid, Sheikh marched against Damascus and there 1414.
defeated Newroz who retired into the Citadel, but March.
surrendered on a solemn oath being recorded in
presence of the Cazie and High officers around, that
he would be spared. Nevertheless, when he appeared,
he was cast into prison on the irrelevant excuse that
the language of the oath had not been understood;
there he was murdered, and his head hung up at the June.
gate of Cairo. His successor, with other Syrian
governors, again rebelled; but the Commandant of
the Damascus citadel remaining firm,[1] the opposition
was put down. In the following year the Sultan 1415.
having again visited Syria, had the disloyal Governors slain before his eyes. The result of this severity,
however, and of his firm administration in Syria
where he passed the winter, was to restore peace
throughout the Province. After the execution of
Newroz, Sheikh visited the cloister of the Syriakus
Soofies, and witnessed their religious dances there,
in penance it is said for his act of perjury.

Asia Minor began again to attract attention. 1417.
Mohammed I. was now regaining the territory of

[1] The citadels throughout Syria were now held by commandants independent of the city governors.

which his Father had been stripped by Timur, but just then he was mainly engaged beyond the Bosphorus. The strongholds on the Armenian frontier had, during the disorder in Syria, cast off their allegiance to Egypt; and so in the spring of 1418 A.D., Sheikh attended by the Caliph[1] and Chief Cazie, marched with a strong force from Aleppo, retook Tarsus and reclaimed the disloyal territory. He then visited with devotion and almsgiving Jerusalem and the Holy places, and returned in triumph to his Capital.

In the autumn of the same year, Syria was thrown into terror by the inroad of Kara Yusuf. It will be remembered that this Chief with Ahmed ibn Oweis, when prisoners in Syria, were set at liberty about the time of Timur's death. Ahmed again got possession of Bagdad, but carrying his arms too far north was attacked and slain by Kara Yusuf. The latter, now Chief of the Black Weir horde, achieved distinguished victories in Kurdistan, and coming into conflict with Kara Yelek of the White Weir at Kalaat Rûm, overthrew and pursued him into Syria. The country was affrighted and Aleppo deserted. The alarm reached even to Cairo, and was so great that the Sultan

---

[1] We find the Caliph in these days following the Sultan with the chief officers of his Court in his military expeditions, but with no authority and simply to grace the train.

gave up the project he was intent upon of a A.D. 1418.
pilgrimage to Mecca. An army was being got
together, when tidings reached that Kara Yusuf
had retired.[1]

The northern border of Syria, however, had 1419.
again fallen away. The Turcomans of Asia Minor,
aided by the remnants of Kara Yelek's scattered
force, not only resumed hold of the frontier, but
retook Tarsus. Ibrahim, the Sultan's eldest son,
was now sent to restore what had been lost. In a
splendid campaign he not only did so, but stretched
his victories as far as Cæsarea and centre of the
Peninsula. He returned in state to Cairo, followed
by a train of captives, and crowned with such
distinguished honour that his Father is said to have
regarded him with envy if not with fear. His
death the following year[2] was the more unfortunate, 1420.
as Egypt was again threatened by Kara Yusuf who May.
demanded back the costly ornaments taken from
him when cast into prison. A force was accord-

[1] The Sultan at this time made some alterations in the military
service, which illustrate the position of the memlukes. The army
was composed of (1) regular troops in the pay of the State; (2) the
memlukes of the various Emirs, who supported them from their fiefs;
(3) the memlukes of the Sultan, paid from the royal domains. The
Emirs had begun to transfer their memlukes to the regular line, and
thus save the expense of their support. To remedy this abuse, the
memlukes were given the choice of either remaining in the service of
the Emir who owned them, or enlisting in the regular army.

[2] Attributed by some to poison at his father's instigation; but by
others this is denied.

A.D. 1420. ingly sent to oppose him; but just then he was recalled to the east by the rebellion of his sons, and he died shortly after. The good tidings, however, little moved the Sultan, for he had been for some time sick; and now on the eve of death,

1421. Jan. he nominated Ahmed, a son seventeen months of age, as Successor, with Altunbogha, his son-in-law still with the Syrian army, as Regent. For fear of disturbances, the last obsequies were carried on in the most abject form. The possessor of millions had for a winding-sheet but the turban of a slave-girl. He died at the age of fifty-five, having reigned eight years and a half. The verdict varies much as to his character. Macrizy is severe; Abul Mahâsin milder.[1] While yet a subject, he had caused much misery through bloodshed, rebellion, and intrigue. But after reaching the throne, by firmness, bravery and wise administration, he restored peace and a measure of prosperity to a much harassed and disabled land. Treachery, as in the Newroz perjury, and assassination, were not wanting; but in

[1] Abul Mahâsin, son of Tagri Berdy, was a favourite at Court, which no doubt influenced his verdict. He tells us that when a child (say about 1414 A.D.) he ran up to the Sultan one day, and asked him for something to eat. Sheikh bade them give him some bread. "That," cried the child, "is food for a beggar; give me some flesh, fowl, fruit or sweetmeats!" The Sultan was so pleased that he gave him 300 dinârs, and a pension ever after. The courtly life which followed may have led to a less unfavourable account both of Sheikh and his successors than we have at the hands of Macrizy and others.

a less measure than in previous days. The nation still cowered under terrible exactions, and there are not even wanting instances in which, by a kind of lynch law, the people rose on their oppressors and executed justice for themselves. A.D. 1421.

The mint value of the precious metals was frequently changed, and the singular device introduced of rating gold, as it came in, at a lower than the market value; and, as it went out in payments, at a higher, so as to receive the more, and spend the less. The Sultan is praised not only as the friend of scholars and himself a poet and musician, but as an exemplary Believer, the princely title by which he is chiefly known being AL MUEYYAD (the Victorious).[1] When Egypt was visited by the plague, the Sultan clad as a dervish, followed by the Caliph and Cazies, and before them the Sheikhs carrying the Coran aloft, and the Jews and Christians their Torat and Gospel, walked to the sepulchre of Berkuck; then, like all around, he bowed his head in prayer upon the bare ground; and afterwards distributed food plentifully to the poor. He did the same after a three days' fast for the rising of the Nile in time of drought and famine; and as one cried out for a

---

[1] That is "Victorious by Almighty help." It is the title by which he is most generally called, and by which the Mosque he founded is to this day known in Cairo. The title also became the name of the faction composed of his memlukes and their followers, of whom we constantly hear in the coming struggles.

A.D. 1421. blessing on him, he answered thus:—" Implore not Heaven's help for me; I am here nought but as one of your own selves."[1]

1416, 1417. During this reign the Franks again attacked Alexandria, carrying off many captives and much booty. It may have been partly on this account that the laws against Jews and Christians were at the present time most rigorously enforced.[2] But such indeed was only to be expected from a zealous Moslem, honoured for the foundation of a College and a Hospital, and above all for the conversion of the Prison in which he was once confined, into a royal Mosque.

[1] Even Macrizy is touched as he tells us this. "Such a man," he says, "were capable of better things, had there been more sincerity and honesty within."

[2] In addition to other severe regulations, the Jews and Christians were now forbidden to have any Moslems in their service.

CHAPTER XIV

AHMED—TATÂR—MOHAMMED—BURSBAI AL ASHRAF

1421–1438 A.D.

ON the death of his father, the child AHMED, not yet a year and a half old, was carried down crying from the Harem, then mounted on a horse, and brought in state into the Audience hall, where with a royal title he was saluted Sultan.[1] In Altunbogha's absence, Tatâr, another Emir named by Sheikh as member of a temporary regency, seized the reins, gained over the army by largesses from the vast treasures accumulated by Sheikh; and then with one sweep sent all in fetters to Alexandria of whom he was afraid. He guided the little Sultan's hand to sign the diploma of regency in his name, and so was

A.D. 1421. Jan.

---

[1] It is amusing to read the titles of these childish Sultans. Thus the present infant was ennobled as *Al Málik el Mozaffar*, "the Conquering Sovereign"; and the next, a boy of ten years, *Al Málik al Záhir Seifuddeen*, "the Victorious King, Sword of the Faith." I have purposely refrained from burdening the page with the magniloquent titles given to the Sultans—slave-boys of yesterday,—according to Eastern wont.

A.D. 1421. recognised as Regent by the Caliph and authorities at Cairo. There was rebellion against him in Syria, and Altunbogha at first holding himself the duly-appointed Regent, joined it; but in the end, he submitted himself to Tatâr and put the rebellious Governor of Damascus to flight. He kept Tatâr duly informed of his success; and when Tatâr journeyed to Syria, welcomed him as Regent as he

May. entered Damascus. With strange ingratitude Tatâr had him fettered, and with many other Emirs of whom he was afraid, put to death. After visiting Aleppo, Tatâr returned to Damascus, where fresh executions took place, and also at Cairo; for by his command all who still adhered to the family of Sheikh were made away with. Then freed from fear of opposition, this blood-stained Emir deposed

Aug. the child Ahmed, and himself assumed the Sultanate. The following month he returned to Cairo, and was received there with outward rejoicings. Shortly after, falling sick, he nominated his son MOHAMMED, a boy ten years of age, as Successor, with Bursbai, a Circassian like himself, Major-Domo, and Jani Beg

Nov. the Regent. He died after a reign of but three months.[1]

[1] Tatâr, as well as Bursbai, was a Circassian slave of Berkuck. He was freed and put into the army by Faraj, and eventually made Emir by Sheikh. The Slave-dealer had him educated in theology and law, for young slaves accomplished in literature, theology, philosophy, or art, fetched all the higher price.

As might have been foreseen, the two Emirs rose A.D. 1421. one against the other. But Bursbai in possession of the Citadel, seized Jani Beg along with his other enemies, and even such friends as he was doubtful of, and had them all imprisoned at Alexandria. Then with the countenance of the Governor of 1422. April. Damascus, he mounted the throne within half a year of Tatâr's death. The opposite faction had been so largely extinguished or sent into exile that there was no opposition, and the deposed boy was given a wife and allowed freely to ride about the city;[1] while even the customary largess to the royal memlukes was dispensed with. BURSBAI made himself popular among other things by fresh edicts against the Jews and Christians; and also by permitting those approaching his person to kiss his hand or the hem of his garment, instead of kissing the ground as heretofore.[2]

For the next year and a half quiet prevailed 1423. Aug. throughout the empire, when in the autumn of 1423 A.D., a sensation was created by the escape of Jani Beg from Alexandria, no one could tell whither, torture and imprisonment notwithstanding. He

---

[1] The families and descendants of past Sultans, hitherto given residence in the Citadel, were about this time removed from it and thereafter lived in the city.

[2] This order was recalled: but instead of as formerly kissing the ground, it was allowed for any one approaching the Sultan first to touch the ground with his hand, and then to kiss it.

A.D. 1423. remained long unknown; but we shall hear more of him hereafter. Syria, compared with the past was loyal. The Governor of Safed, indeed, rebelled on the deposition of Tatâr's son; but at last gave in on a written promise sworn to by the Sultan that he would give him the Chiefship of Tripoli; yet no sooner had the deluded Emir, clothed in a dress

Sept. of honour, given up the citadel, than he was seized and put to death.[1] The following year the same fate befell the rebel Governor of Damascus.

1424. Aug. Syria being now quiet, Bursbai turned his attention to the pirates who had begun to infest the Syrian and Egyptian coast. A number of privateers manned by adventurers bent upon reprisals, sailed to Cyprus, and having plundered and set fire to Limasol, returned laden with captives and booty.

1425. Autumn. Thus encouraged, the Sultan in the following year fitted out a fleet with troops which landed at Famagusta, routed the enemy and, having plundered Larnaca and Limasol, carried off a thousand prisoners and vast booty, with which in triumph they entered Cairo.[2] The Sultan, however, had intended not a raid of this sort, but the conquest of the island.

1426. With this object he now sent a formidable force

---

[1] A hundred of the garrison were executed, and thirty had their hands cut off—a sad example of barbarity.

[2] All were sold; but it is mentioned as a singular proof of Bursbai's humanity that he would not sanction children or near relatives being sold apart from those on whom they were dependent.

which, after seizing Limasol, advanced to Larnaca, A.D. 1426. and having defeated the Cyprian troops, took King Janus prisoner, and with a multitude of captives and spoil of every sort, carried him off to Cairo. They entered in royal triumph, in presence of the Court and foreign Embassies; the booty on camels; the Cyprian crown; the Prince's horse, and captured ensigns; the captive men, women and children; and behind all the King himself who, in clanking chains, kissed the ground at the Sultan's feet,—when falling senseless down, he was borne into the Citadel. In the end, however, the Venetian and other Consuls having arranged his ransom, he was not only set at 1427. liberty, but given a courtly robe and horse, and allowed to retun to Cyprus; henceforth, however, only as the Sultan's vassal.[1]

Some years earlier, the Shereef of Mecca having 1423. rebelled, an army restored the supremacy of Egypt over the Holy city and its seaport Jedda, and this led to a quickened interest in the commerce of the East. Aden had long been the port of traffic, but driven thence by oppressive treatment, an adventurous Captain about this time passed into the Red Sea, and tried various harbours within the Straits

---

[1] The ransom was 300,000 dinârs, with the yearly tribute of 20,000. Abul Mahâsin was present at the entry and, his bigotry notwithstanding, speaks in praise of the King's intelligence and learning, adding that he was acquainted with Arabic.

of Bab el Mandeb.[1] At first the merchants were driven back from these by similar exactions; but better arrangements having been made, and an embargo laid on goods landed at Aden, Jedda at last became the recognised entrance, and Holy Mecca the busy crowded mart for Eastern merchandise.[2] The Sultan, it is true, took pains in every way to prevent the sacred Courts from becoming a house of merchandise; but, as Macrizy says, the traffic all round, and the never-ending hue and cry that at the risk of life all goods must pass through Egypt, sounded in strange discord with the solemn worship of the Kaaba.

For at the present time an ordinance had been put in force that merchandise, from whatever quarter, brought through Arabia, Syria, or Irac, must first be carried either to Alexandria or to Cairo, and there exorbitantly taxed. The Government also assumed the monopoly of eastern spices, and especially that of pepper,—measures which led to complaint and reprisal from the European Powers. Another burden which pressed sorely on the people, especially in time of plague,[3] was the close manufacture and even growth of sugar. In fact the State interfered at

---

[1] Ibrahim he is called, a Captain from Calicut.

[2] 70,000 dinârs are mentioned as the import duty charged on the single entry of a fleet of forty ships.

[3] In time of plague, sugar was prescribed as a medicine or prophylactic.

every point with every branch of trade; and the markets, even of corn and meat, were so lorded over as sometimes to be quite deserted, raising outbreaks as the consequence. Still worse were the outrages of the uncontrolled and wayward memlukes, who mishandled the people to such a pitch that women dare hardly venture out. Exaction was rife all round, the horses of farmers, for example, being carried off for the army. In fact the troubles and burdens throughout the land were then, even in a time of peace, in some respects worse than they had ever been in time of war before.

A.D. 1428.

In the latter part of his reign, Bursbai was in strained relations and frequent warfare with the Powers both in the East and North. Kara Yelek of the White Weir, whom Timur had rewarded for his services by the grant of Siwâs, now came down in force upon the Syrian frontier. An army sent by Egypt to restore order besieged Roha, which was surrendered by Kara Yelek's son on condition of free exit. But the memluke hordes, sweeping through the gates in wild disorder, carried rapine, outrage, and slaughter all before them. The city's fate is sad to read; for the poor dishonoured women were carried off with their children to be sold as slaves at Aleppo. The marvel is that any Christians were left in Armenia or in those parts at all. The attack, however, overreached itself; for in their wild

1429.

A.D. 1430. excess, the army fell clean out of hand, and in confusion breaking up took its way back as it were in flight to Syria. To avenge this attack and the captivity of his son carried off to Egypt, Kara Yelek ravaged again the border cities; and having now the support of Shah Rookh, Timur's son, caused great alarm in Cairo. But pestilence and dearth put a stop to further hostilities for the time.

1431, 1432. In succeeding years, an angry correspondence arose with Shah Rookh, in which he demanded the right of furnishing the Kaaba curtain, to which the Sultan replied in terms of insult and defiance. Countenanced by the Shah, the attitude of Kara Yelek now looked so threatening, that Bursbai 1433. himself headed an army which starting in the spring laid siege to Amid, the capital of Kara Yelek, at the time defended by his sons. After fruitless investment for a month, a hollow truce was made with Kara Yelek, on which the Sultan retired through the ruined Roha, and with triumphal but poorly deserved festivities, re-entered Sept. Cairo in the autumn. Kara Yelek continued his inroad on the border districts; but in the 1434. following year, he made outward submission to Aug. Egypt, and sent in proof thereof not only a gift of horses, but coins struck in the Sultan's name.

The Syrian troops were still in Asia Minor,

having to hold in subjection the Chiefs of Karaman A.D. 1434. and Dulgadir; and it is curious to find that when the son of the latter, on the siege of Marash, was sent a prisoner to Cairo, his wife was deputed thither with rich gifts to obtain from the Sultan the freedom of her son. Just then Jani Beg, after several years' concealment, reappeared. The news was the more startling, as the exile had the countenance of Shah Rookh, with whom the Sultan's relations were now becoming critical. For the Shah had again made demands regarding Mecca, and announced with a solemn oath that his curtain should shroud the Kaaba; to which Bursbai contemptuously replied that he might easily redeem the oath by selling the curtain and giving the proceeds to the poor. Another Envoy now appeared with a courtly robe, and the Shah's command that the Sultan should receive investiture in it as his vassal. The robe was torn in pieces and the Envoy ignominiously cast into a pond. "Tell thy master," said the Sultan, as he bid him go, "that we smile at his demand; and if, to avenge thy disgrace, he appear not in the coming year, we shall hold him the weakest of mankind."[1] To be prepared for any such contingency, a strong force again advanced on Asia Minor; and

1435. April.

1436. Jan.

---

[1] The Envoy, we are told, procured while in Egypt a copy of Macrizy's *History*, which must thus have been already in circulation; and also copy of the *Traditions of Bokhary*.

A.D. 1436. Bursbai hearing that the Shah had made a like imperious demand on Morâd, the Osmanly Sultan, took the occasion for making a defensive alliance against the Shah with him.

1437. In Asia Minor the campaign was eminently successful, and drove back Jani Beg with the Dulgadir Chiefs beyond Siwâs. Jani Beg now fled for refuge to the sons of Kara Yelek, one of whom put him to death and sent his head to Cairo. The Sultan was beside himself with joy, had the head paraded round the City, and then cast into the mud. Kara Yelek himself had also some
1435. Aug. little time before lost his life at Erzengan, while fighting on the Shah's side against the Black Weir Chiefs; and these sent his head likewise to Egypt. But no sooner had Bursbai begun to feel at ease by the removal of these his dreaded enemies, than another son of Kara Yelek, to avenge the death of Jani Beg, attacked and slew the murderer, and opened a fresh campaign against the Egyptians. Bursbai in alarm proposed to take the field himself; but in the end left the command to the Governor of Damascus, who in a prosperous campaign restored peace as far as Erzengan. Egyptian rule thus completely dominated the eastern half of Asia
1438. June. Minor, as Osmanly rule the western. But before the news of this success reached Cairo, Bursbai had already passed away.

Though Egypt under Bursbai prospered on the A.D. 1438. whole, the Sultan yet betrayed in many points the common failings of the Mameluke. He was fond of show; and a single dress of the Sultanah (little else we hear of his domestic life) cost 30,000 golden pieces, —the lot of one but recently a slave! His latter days were embittered by successive calamities,— plague, dearth and locusts. The outrages of the memlukes already noticed, grew worse and worse; not only women but youths were shamelessly seized, till at last the streets were shunned. In the City alone, the plague carried off 300,000 within three months; and the Sultan holding it a punishment for the sins of the people, prohibited females from appearing abroad, and sought to make atonement not only by fresh exactions from the Jews and Christians, but by destroying a Monastery held by them most sacred.[1] With the same object he threw open the prison doors (a strange mode of penance), so that the city was exposed thereby to the depredations of criminals and robbers. The plague at last entered the Citadel, and there seized both high and low,—Princesses, slave-girls, eunuchs, memlukes,—all around. Though the Sultan him-

---

[1] The heavy exactions on the Jews and Christians, which had heretofore been conducted by officials of rank and religious standing, were now placed in the hands of a low vagabond who ground down the poor Christians shamelessly.

A.D. 1438. self escaped the plague, he suffered from other illness; and when his two physicians, honoured and respected men, could give him no relief, he had them both, the reclamations of his Courtiers notwithstanding, beheaded in presence of the city Prefects. Some weeks after, finding the end at hand, he named Yusuf his son Successor, with the Emir Jakmac for his guardian. Then having summoned the Mameluke leaders to his presence, he upbraided them at length, all in the Turkish tongue, for their wildness and excesses, bade them be true to his Son, and so breathed his last.

1438. 1st June.

Macrizy condemns him as a cunning, cruel, avaricious tyrant; and we have seen that, as occasion offered, he did not hesitate treacherously to rid himself of his opponents. All that can be said in his favour is that even in this respect he was not so bad as many who had gone before.[1]

---

[1] Macrizy was not encouraged during this reign at Court, which may possibly have added bitterness to his tone. Abul Mahâsin as a favourite there, is naturally milder. Other writers speak of the Sultan's prayers and fastings as mere hypocrisies.

TOMB OF BURSBAI AL ASHRAF.
(ON PLAIN OF KAITBAI, NEAR CAIRO.)

CHAPTER XV

YUSUF—JAKMAC AL ZÂHIR

1438-1453 A.D.

THOUGH YUSUF was nearly fifteen years of age, the same fate befell him as that of his infant predecessor. Jakmac while simulating devotion to his ward, took possession of the Citadel, and gradually gained over the *Ashrafite* party, or that devoted to the late Sultan's house.[1] The army shortly returning from its Asiatic campaign, the commander Kirkmash was led to believe that Jakmac was labouring to secure the crown for him. And when the deluded General was induced, as a feint for this end, to propose in an

A.D. 1438
1st June.

---

[1] The memluke factions began now to be called by the titles of the Sultans to whom they belonged, or had in times past been attached. Thus while the *Ashrafites* are called after Bursbai al Ashraf (the Exalted); the *Zâhirites* are so called from Berkuck whose title (and that of Jakmac also) was al Zâhir (the Victorious); and the *Mueyyadites* from Sheikh (and also Ahmed) al Mueyyad (the Heaven-helped). These three are the chief factions, which now kept Cairo in continual turmoil. There were also other parties as the *Nâsarites*, or attachés of the Sultan Nâsir. The Ashrafites and Zâhirites were also divided into Old and New.

A.D. 1438. assembly the name of Jakmac for the Sultanate, the Emirs to his dismay with one voice chimed in, and his rival was saluted Sovereign on the spot. Yusuf thus deposed after a reign of but three or four months was imprisoned in the Citadel.

Sept. JAKMAC, a Circassian slave of Berkuck, now aged thirty-five, had risen, like his predecessors, from being a page at Court, to the highest offices of State. To conciliate the unruly memluke hordes, he was obliged to give heavy largess to them all round, not as hitherto only to his own. Kirkmash finding himself overreached by Jakmac, gathered the Ashrafites about him and besieged the Citadel. He was beaten, seized, and sent in chains to Alexandria, where some months after, being condemned to death, he was carried naked into the city and publicly beheaded there. The Ashrafites at large were now visited with pains and penalties, many tortured and slain, and the remainder scattered to distant parts; so that opposition at the Capital was for the moment quelled.

In Syria it was otherwise, and Jakmac would have been wiser if, as advised, he had delayed his assumption of the Sultanate till he had gained favour 1439. there. The Governor of Aleppo, after dissembling Feb. several months, joined the rebellion, proclaimed Yusuf as Sultan again, and took the field. Just then, aided by his eunuch, nurse and slave-girls,

and disguised as a cook, Yusuf escaped from the A.D. 1439.
Citadel, but finding little support, retired into a
hiding-place. Jakmac was greatly disconcerted;
but by torture of the eunuch, nurse and others,
the youth was at last discovered, and taken before
the Sultan, who (better than most of his race)
treated him well; for Yusuf was sent to Alexandria
and, though kept under restraint, settled comfort-
ably there. His reappearance, however, had meanwhile given strength to the conflict in Syria. Much
fighting went on throughout the Province, but both
at Damascus and Aleppo the rebels were defeated;
and the leaders, upstart slaves like their masters,
after being tortured for their treasure, were with
many of their followers cruelly put to death. There May.
was festive rejoicing at Cairo when the head of the
Aleppo Governor was paraded about the city and
at last hung up at the city gate. The Ashrafite
troops engaged in Upper Egypt against the Bedouins
had also been gained over by the conspirators; but
eventually they met the same fate as the disloyalists
in Syria. Rebellion thus put down, the large number
of Emirs still in confinement at Alexandria were, for
safety's sake, distributed in distant parts of the
Empire, and thus by the middle of the year tran-
quillity was again restored.

His hands now free at home, Jakmac, as a
good Moslem, turned his arms against the Franks

A.D. 1440. whose freebooters had begun again to despoil the coast; and, emboldened by the recent successes in Cyprus, sent repeated expeditions against Rhodes.

Aug. The first, after devastating the island of Chateauroux, was attacked by the Knights, and retired

1442. May. with loss to Egypt. A second and more powerful expedition met with no better success. Determined still to crown the Holy war with victory, the Sultan manned a powerful fleet carrying a great body of

1444. June. mariners with 1000 memlukes of his own.[1] They landed and after plundering many villages besieged Rhodes for forty days; but finding no prospect of anything but loss, returned home. And then the Sultan giving up the design as hopeless, entered into peaceful relations with the Order.

The attitude of Jakmac towards the Mohammedan lands around was of the most friendly character. From the various Chiefships of Asia Minor, which had so often thrown off their allegiance, embassies with rich gifts and loyal assurances, were sent, and in royal style received at Cairo. With a daughter of the Dulgadir Chief of Ablestin who accompanied her father's embassy to Cairo, the Sultan contracted marriage; and two other Princesses from Asia Minor, one an Osmanly "Shahzadah," were also taken by him

---

[1] The fleet is spoken of as carrying 18,000 memlukes, so that, making allowance for exaggeration, the force must still have been very large.

to wife. Early in the reign, Jakmac welcomed with A.D. 1440. distinguished honour an Embassy from Shah Rookh followed by a string of camels laden with precious gifts, musk, and Eastern stuffs; to which a fitting response with gifts of Egyptian rarities was made. Later the Shah again sought leave to hang, according to his oath, the Kaaba curtain,—which the Sultan, much against the will of his Emirs, conceded. In the following year, when the widow of Timur came for this pious end, the feeling in the City was so 1443. strong, that her princely following was stoned and plundered as it left the Citadel. The Sultan treated the offenders with condign punishment, and made such amends as satisfied the Queen, and restored confidence with the Shah.

Frequent communications of an amicable kind with costly gifts passed also between the Sultan and the Osmanly Court. Thus with prosperity at home and friendly alliances abroad, the reign of Jakmac may be held the best, and (after the reduction of Syria) the most peaceful, which Egypt had known for many years. There was in it less of torture and assassination. Commerce was still hampered by the previous restrictions, and to these the Shah objected: but they were declared by the Doctors of the law to be just and proper for the due regulation of the trade. The chief blot in the administration was the unbridled outrage of the memlukes which, however, affected individuals more than the community at large. Some very cruel instances of their savage treatment of obnoxious Emirs are given by the historian; and such outbreaks the Sultan, being himself afraid, failed to visit with the punishment he ought. Jakmac was a pattern Mussulman. While Jews and Christians were severely handled,[1] the laws against vice and licentiousness were vigorously enforced. Himself endowed with æsthetic tastes and a lover of beautiful manuscripts, the Sultan cultivated the friendship of the learned. He was kind and liberal, and left but little in his private chest. Fond of the fair sex, besides the Princesses already named, he married daughters of two of the Cazies; and close on fourscore years, he took to himself another bride. When near that age, he was seized with a lingering illness; and after suffering for a year, aware that the end was near, summoned to his presence the Caliph, Cazies, and chief Emirs, announced his resignation, and bade them appoint a Successor. His eldest son described as a noble and learned Prince had died ten years before; and so they nominated as his Successor the only remaining son, by name Othman, and he was done homage to at once. Jakmac died within a fortnight and was followed to the grave by the Court and a multitude of Citizens who mourned

---

[1] As an example of petty interference, they were forbidden to have their turbans made of scarfs longer than seven ells.

the loss of one who for fifteen years had ruled them A.D. 1453. well.¹

---

¹ Early in this reign (1441 A.D.) the historian Macrizy died, and henceforth we miss the profuse details with which his great work, up to the very close of his life, abounds. Besides his office at the head of the Cairo police, he was for some time guardian of an endowment at Damascus, and also employed as a Cazie there. He was never received at Court, and consequently fails to flatter. Henceforth, for another twenty years or so, we are much dependent on Abul Mahâsin.

CHAPTER XVI

OTHMAN—INÂL[1]

1453–1461 A.D.

A.D. 1453. Feb. OTHMAN, son of a Greek slave-girl, though eighteen years of age, fared no better than previous sons of Sultans elevated to the throne. Cruel, vain and avaricious, he fell into the hands of his memlukes; to meet whose greedy demands he had his Chief Minister flogged, tortured and deposed. This shameful treatment roused the indignation of the factions all around. These, with the Caliph's sanction, conspired to depose the young tyrant now gradually deserted by all but his own memlukes, and to raise Inâl, the Admiral of the fleet against Rhodes, in his stead. The Citadel was attacked, and after a week's siege, was entered by Inâl at an unprotected gate,[2] on which Othman fled into his

---

[1] He and Jakmac were both called "Alalâi" from having been bought from a dealer named Aly: they were also named al Zâhir, as signifying the faction they came from.

[2] The "Chain" gate.

Harem. Taken prisoner there, after a reign of but six weeks, he was sent in confinement to Alexandria, but in later years allowed his freedom. *A.D. 1453.*

INÂL, who accepted the Sultanate not without *March.* considerable pressure, was so uneducated that he could not even sign his name. Like his predecessors, he had been the slave of Berkuck; and then, as page of Faraj, freed and gradually promoted to military and naval command. Of a mild and easy nature, he fell into the hands of his memlukes; and to gratify them made such demands upon the treasury, that the Chancellorship not only went a-begging, but high officers of State had to be flogged into accepting it. An expedition having been ordered to the Delta, the Sultan's Circassians insolently demanded more camels, which not being granted, they rose in *1455.* rebellion around the Citadel. There they were *June.* joined by the Zâhirites, who persuaded the Caliph also to join them and propose the restoration of Jakmac's son. This, however, displeased the royal memlukes, and led them to return to their Master, so that eventually the outbreak was defeated, and the Caliph sent a prisoner to Alexandria.[1] The rebels were exiled or incarcerated; and henceforth

---

[1] One begins to notice that the Caliph has not only now much more freedom; but, when loyal, has altogether a better place in society, more honour, and greater influence than in the earlier Mameluke days.

A.D. 1455. all memlukes were ousted from the Citadel, excepting those only of the royal retinue.

The weak hand of Inâl was impotent to hold the licentious memlukes in check who now swarmed in every Emir's employ. Their outrage and tyranny throughout this reign transcend description. They not only ravaged and plundered the country, but thought little of assailing the highest Emirs and ransacking their palaces. The Sultan himself was afraid of his own memlukes. Even the solemn sacrifice of Beiram with distribution of food to the poor, could no longer with safety be held in public, and had to be retired within the Palace walls. Fires were rife,[1] goods exposed in shops seized, and markets deserted; while financial and commercial reforms were dropped at the outcry of uproarious memlukes. The Emirs were powerless to resent attacks upon their own persons. On one occasion the Sultan himself, endeavouring to quell an outbreak in the Citadel, was pursued with stones, and with difficulty escaped barefoot into his Harem; and at the last he was forced to quiet his slaves by conceding their exorbitant demands. The memlukes were now all-powerful, and had officials deposed and changed at pleasure. To redress injustice com-

---

[1] The memlukes accused merchants from Karaman as being incendiaries, and their maltreatment led to reprisals against the Egyptians in the campaign noticed below.

plainants, instead of the Courts, would repair to memluke leaders, who threatened and bullied the accused until their clients got what they wanted. Women were subjected to maltreatment even in the Mosque of Amru; and yet neither Sultan nor magistrates dared interfere. A terrible plague broke out; but the calamity failed to check the wild atrocities. The rioters not only attacked the passing biers, but ravaged the property of the dead, and enriched themselves from their estates. At last the pestilence reached the Citadel, and carried off multitudes of the hated tyrants both within and without its walls;—"the penalty of their vicious lives and a timely safeguard to the Citizens."[1]

But it was not only at home the memlukes ruled; their imperious demands extended even to foreign affairs. We have an instance in Cyprus, still tributary to Egypt. James II., Archbishop of Nicosia, an illegitimate son of the late King, rebelled against Queen Charlotte and fled to Egypt where he was received with honour. The Sultan was at first disposed to support his claim; but after the Queen had submitted her cause, and offered increased tribute, he changed his mind, and prepared a Firman confirming her in possession. The memlukes were displeased,[2] mobbed her Embassy, and created so

---

[1] As Abul Mahâsin in a satire writes.
[2] Perhaps one reason was that James would not be regarded by

A.D. 1460. dangerous a rising that Inâl, unable to resist, equipped a fleet to place James upon the throne. It returned with only partial success, Charlotte having been assisted by Savoy and the Pope. A 1461. second expedition was being fitted out at the time of the Sultan's death; but in the end the Queen retained her throne, and things were left much as before.

Inâl's relations with the Moslem Powers around were of the most friendly kind, and specially so with those in Asia Minor and on the Armenian border. An Embassy arrived from the White Weir announcing a victory over the Black Weir, whose Chief had displeased Egypt by the reception of a rebel governor. The only campaign during this reign beyond that to Cyprus and for the punishment of Bedouin bandits who overran Lower Egypt, was 1457. against the Chief of Karaman who attacked the Syrian frontier, and took possession of Adana and Tarsus. An army was accordingly sent to Asia Minor which, after the siege of Konieh and Cæsarea, devastated the land, sparing neither mosques nor schools. Karaman gave in without fighting, and the following year peace was restored.

Meanwhile, Constantinople had fallen and become the Turkish seat of government, tidings of which as

them as illegitimate; children of concubines and slave-girls being, in Moslem law, equally legitimate with those of married wives.

well as of the succeeding Osmanly victories in Servia, A.D. 1453. 29th May. excited the liveliest joy in Cairo. For several days the success of the Turks, so soon to be their fatal foes, was celebrated by the Egyptians with grand festivity. Repeated embassies with rich presents were exchanged between the two Courts; and the congratulations of Inâl on the Byzantine conquest were conveyed to Mohammed II. in a princely poem, as well as in a versified despatch.

At home the reign of Inâl must be held a lamentable failure from the unchecked outbursts of memluke violence. There was undoubtedly less of tyranny, torture, and murder by the Sultan himself and his officials than before. But no man was safe from the memlukes, and the very thieves and robbers assumed the memluke dress in order that they might the more safely carry on their work. Now for the first time both rich and poor had to protect their properties by trench and wall. The poets of the day decried the reign of Inâl; and all the more decried it, as he was not only niggardly but unlettered. He left a family by a single wife who (strange exception in this history) had not a single rival; but a veil must be drawn over the lives of the Sultan and his Court in other respects too dark to be mentioned here.

Finding his death to be near, Inâl called the 1461. Caliph and Doctors of the law, and motioned in a

A.D. 1461. Turkish whisper, for he could not speak, that Ahmed a son of mature years should succeed; and accordingly homage was at once done to him in the Hall of Audience. Thus at the age of eighty, having reigned eight years, Inâl passed away.

CHAPTER XVII

AHMED—KHUSHCADAM

1461-1467 A.D.

THE accession of AHMED, dignified by the title *Al* _{A.D. 1461. Feb.} *Mueyyad*, was everywhere accepted, and gave good promise for the future. He was thirty years of age and, judged by an Egyptian standard, upright and virtuous. Yet his reign was short and troubled, and one might even say that his very virtues in so depraved an age served but to hasten on the crisis. Bent upon reform, he refused the extravagant demands made by the royal memlukes on his elevation. This so provoked them that forgetting for the moment their party jealousies, they joined the other factions in a conspiracy to dethrone their Master. The Ashrafites were in favour of Janim, Viceroy of Syria and Governor of Damascus, as the new Sultan; the Zâhirites preferred Khushcadam, Major-Domo of the Palace. Ahmed, ill-informed of what was passing, remained inactive, and thus gradually lost the support of his Courtiers. At last, becoming anxious, he

A.D. 1461. summoned them to his presence. But they, fearing his object, assembled instead in the Palace of Khushcadam, and having matured their plans attacked the Citadel. On this Ahmed, after a reign of four months, resigned and was sent to Alexandria, where for a while he remained in fetters, but was eventually released and lived for many years a retired and honoured life.

June.   While the Citadel was yet surrounded, Jani Beg a distinguished Emir persuaded the Ashrafite party of Janim, with the view of securing order for the moment, to proclaim his friend Khushcadam Sultan, telling them that on Janim's arrival the throne would be peacefully given up to him. KHUSHCADAM thus elected to the throne with the title of *Al Zâhir*, was bought by Sultan Sheikh some fifty years before, employed as a page and gradually promoted till he became Governor of Damascus and Commander of the expedition to Karaman. Honoured by Ahmed as the head of his Court, he nevertheless joined the conspiracy against him, and now succeeded to the dignity of his banished Master. He was the first Sultan of undoubted Greek birth, the Circassians having now held the throne over fourscore years.[1]

[1] Lachin is said by some to have been a Greek, but this is questioned by others. Several of the Sultans, as we have seen, had Greek slave-girls for their mothers; but none before the present Sultan had been himself imported as a young slave from Greece. His name is Persian for "Well-paced."

At Damascus the tidings caused great excite- A.D. 1461.
ment. The majority sided with the new Sultan;
but Janim trusting to the summons of his Ashrafite
friends, set out for Cairo to the alarm of Khushcadam who stopped him on the way. Janim, seeing
that he was too late, submitted himself to the new
Sultan, who to please the Ashrafites confirmed him
at Damascus, but without the Viceroyalty of Syria.
Shortly after, still jealous of the Ashrafites, he
placed them all under restraint,—a measure which
raised a rebellion in favour of a powerful Emir, the
Atabeg. With the help of the Zâhirites the danger
was got over; but it so agitated the Sultan that he
deposed Janim, who fearing further trial, fled to
Usun Hasan of the White Weir. That Chief pleaded
in vain for his forgiveness, and taking his part made
an inroad on the Syrian frontier. The Sultan, dreading the return of Janim, prepared a force to pursue
him; but meantime tidings of his death rendered 1463.
its march unnecessary.[1]

We have seen that Khushcadam owed his elevation to the friendship of Jani Beg, who skilfully
outwitted the supporters of Janim. This distinguished Emir having filled high office at Jedda, was

[1] Abul Mahâsin (as we have seen a favourite at Court) sought to
reassure the Sultan when alarmed at this attack, by showing him that
when his throne was much less stable, neither Janim, nor other more
powerful Syrian Emirs could injure him, much less could they do
so now.

A.D. 1463. honoured by the Princes of Arabia, and even of India. Just and generous he was held in high esteem for his splendid liberality; worshipped by the people, his voice was law in all the domestic concerns of Cairo; and whenever he rode abroad, he was attended by an admiring crowd of Zâhirite friends and followers. But all this only served to kindle the hatred of the royal memlukes, and the jealousy of their Master. Khushcadam now turned

Aug. upon the friend to whom he owed the throne. One day as he entered the Citadel, he was set upon by the Sultan's slaves; struck on the head and stabbed in the back, yet still showing signs of life he was dragged by the feet into the Court, and his brains dashed out by great stones. Then they pursued his companion, the Prefect of the City, and slew him with equal barbarity. Khushcadam with his minions, sat in the Hall above, aware of what was going on. By and by he asked the news; "It is all right," was the reply. "Then let us go down," he said; and as they descended he simply desired two winding-sheets to be brought, and the corpses to be washed and buried in them. This act of cruelty and base ingratitude was never forgotten; for apart from Jani Beg's acts of beneficence, the splendour of his festivities, "vying with those of Harun Rashîd," endeared him throughout the city.

The removal of his friend failed to better Khushcadam's position, and he soon began to reap the fruit of his evil doings. The Zâhirites resented the death of their Chief, and were accordingly seized, banished, and imprisoned in Alexandria. Unexpectedly the Sultan found that the other faction, the Ashrafites and Inâlites, to please whom he had been persecuting the Zâhirites, had conspired to murder him, and appoint one of themselves in his stead. Seeing now the error of his ways, he sent for Kaitbai the leader of the Zâhirites, who came surrounded for safety by a body of his clan; but the Sultan received him graciously and throwing himself into his arms, begged him to overlook the past, promising pardon to all whom he had sent to prison. This again angered the Ashrafites, who had rejoiced in the Zâhirite downfall, and had not forgotten the fate of Janim. But it afforded Khushcadam the opportunity of pitting the one faction against the other. Indeed it became now the Sultan's policy to multiply the divisions into which the memlukes had fallen, by alternate favour and flattery to intensify their jealousies, and by playing off the one against the other [1] so to hold his

[1] There were not only the old Ashrafites (those of Bursbai) but the new Ashrafites, called also Inâlites (after Inâl), who were indignant at the favours by which the Sultan now sought to gain over the Zâhirites;—although previously it was very much to please them that he had persecuted the Zâhirites. These latter were very powerful, being the chief source of the cavalry; but the Inâlites were also very powerful. The Mueyyadites, the Sultan's own faction, were a comparatively small body.

A.D. 1463. own. Notwithstanding this, Khushcadam was still helplessly in the hands of his own slaves and the memlukes of former Sultans who formed his bodyguard; for in order to secure their loyalty he was obliged to humour them, and let them have their way even in outrage and excess. For example they would seize the finest horses brought for sale, often without the payment of a dinâr; so that the markets were at times deserted.[1] Such a state of things could not but cause intense dissatisfaction; and, therefore, to ingratiate himself with the Cazies and influential classes, and gain their help in quieting the people, he caused the anti-Christian ordinances to be enforced again with great severity. But as his administration gained in power, he suffered them gradually to fall into abeyance.

1461-1463. To Cyprus the Sultan sent several expeditions, partly to support King James, but mainly to be rid of memlukes whom he feared. Some of these returning without his orders were roughly handled: others came back because they resented the fate of Jani Beg; but these were passed by. One of the Egyptian Commanders, by his contemptuous treatment of the King, so aroused his hostility that he attacked and slew both him and many of the Egyptian

---

[1] Sent on an expedition to relieve Lower Egypt of the Bedouin bands by which it was infested, they carried off all the water-carts of the city, so that for days not a drop of water was to be had.

troops. Charlotte used the occasion to make advances A.D. 1461. to the Sultan; but in the end, the King continuing tributary, things ended pretty much as they began.

The relations of Egypt with the Porte were now 1463. becoming strained. An Envoy bringing a despatch from Mohammed II. couched in language to which Khushcadam took exception, added yet this indignity that, as he approached the royal presence, he refused to kiss the ground, alleging that having just prostrated himself in prayer, it would be an affront to the Almighty. On a subsequent occasion, conforming to the usage, the Sultan was much pleased, and offered him presents for the Porte; but these the Envoy declined, alleging that the dignity of his Court demanded a special Embassy for the occasion. The Sultan showed his displeasure in a contested Karaman succession. The Porte supported 1464. the claim of a son born of an Osmanly Princess, while Khushcadam took the side of a slave-girl's son, who with the help of Usun Hasan defeated his brother; but eventually the latter assisted by Mohammed II., whose conquests now extended far into Armenia, drove the intruder out. Thus, although no actual hostilities transpired, neither Court showed much affection for the other.

In his dealings with the vassal principalities of 1462. Asia Minor, the Sultan was neither wise nor always honest. Thus having desired Usun Hasan to take possession of Kharput, he secretly forbade Aslan Chief of Ablestin to give it up. Shortly after Aslan died by the dagger of an Assassin commissioned by the Sultan. This gave rise to troubles in Ablestin; for the brothers of the murdered Prince fell out. The party favoured by Egypt was opposed by Shah Siwar of Dulgadir, who had the Porte's support. An army was equipped against the Shah, but the result pertains to another reign.

Throughout the Sultanate, but for unceasing Bedouin raids both in Upper and Lower Egypt, peace prevailed at home. By cleverly balancing the humours of the various factions, Khushcadam maintained his supremacy to the end. But the memlukes, especially his own, as we have seen, had life and property at their will, and perpetrated untold barbarities. The revenue was swelled by the sale of offices; and for the Viceroyalty of Damascus 45,000 golden pieces were given. Justice was prostituted, and the accused were sometimes sold into their pursuers' hands. Thus we are told of a Vizier handed over for 70,000 pieces to his enemies, who tortured him till he died. We need not wonder that such a venal and detestable administration gave rise to universal discontent and frequent popular outbursts.

Towards the close of the reign, Bedouin hordes caused terror and disorder not only in Egypt but in

Syria and Arabia where they even plundered the Pilgrim caravans. The standing army had gone to oppose Siwar; and so another was being raised when the Sultan was seized with dysentery and rapidly declined so as at times to be insensible. Hearing that reports of his death had been spread abroad, he was about to punish the Ashrafite memlukes whom he suspected of disloyalty, when on the next day he passed away, and was followed to the grave but by few of his Courtiers. With every class he was unpopular, chiefly for the unrestrained tyranny of his memlukes, but also because of the cruelty, corruption and venality of his reign. He never hesitated to attain his ends by torture or the dagger, or in the last resort by poison. And the fate of Jani Beg was remembered to the last. He left two sons, but of them we hear nothing more.

A.D. 1467.

Oct.

CHAPTER XVIII

JELBAI—TIMURBOGA—KAITBAI

1467–1496 A.D.[1]

A.D. 1467.
Oct.

FOR the next two months, Cairo was the scene of unceasing intrigue amongst the contending factions. The throne was occupied first by JELBAI a Circassian, and then by TIMURBOGA a Greek. Both had risen in the usual way, and were now elevated by Zâhirite influence to the Sultanate. The former was, after

Dec. a couple of months dethroned and sent a captive to Alexandria. The second who followed was of a higher stamp, and had he possessed the means of gratifying rampant factions around him, might have held his place. But the treasury was empty and, bribery apart, conspiracy must spread. The Mueyyads proclaimed one of themselves, Kheirbeg, Sultan; but they were overmastered by the Zâhirites

[1] It was during the reign of Kaitbai that the historian Abul Mahâsin died, 1470 A.D. The sources of our information are now sensibly diminished, and the details few and imperfect. Henceforward, Ibn Ayâs is our only local authority. He lived to see the fall of the Mameluke dynasty, surviving it by eight or nine years.

who raised Kaitbai to the throne. Kheirbeg was A.D. 1467.
sent in fetters to Alexandria, while Timurboga after
his reign of two months was treated honourably, and
given a suitable residence at Damietta.

KAITBAI, who now entered on a protracted reign, 1468. Jan.
was of Circassian birth. He was freed by Sultan
Jakmac, who had bought him as a boy for 50
dinârs. An accomplished spearman, he became a
favourite at Court, and from being Atabek was now at
last raised to the throne. A brave and able ruler,
he owed his safety to an immense retinue of devoted slaves, and could thus deal with the memluke
factions at his will. There were the usual outbursts
from time to time, but party was so balanced against
party that the Government was safe. The chronic
ill was penury. Although Kaitbai refused the
customary succession largesses, money was needed
at the outset for the sinews of war to repel Bedouin
ravages, as well as meet dangers threatening Asia
Minor; and the mode of raising it was fit prelude for
that which was to come. The President of the Council
being held responsible, was robbed of everything he
possessed, and then assessed in a sum which on his
declaring his inability to pay, he was flogged in the
Royal presence. On this producing no effect, the
Sultan himself took the cudgels till the wretched
Emir's blood besprinkled the bystanders. At last,
on agreeing to pay down 200,000 dinârs, the bleed-

ing courtier was not only set at liberty, but clothed in a robe of honour. Such was the rude and versatile barbarity of Kaitbai's Court.

Egypt was now at war with Siwar, Chief of Ablestin, the successor of Aslan, who was assassinated (as we have seen) by the last Sultan. With the Porte's aid, he had recently driven back the Egyptian forces and conquered the border lands as far even as Antioch and Tarsus. Desirous now of peace, Siwar sent all his Egyptian prisoners to Cairo with a pacific Embassy; but the Sultan angry at the defeat of his troops, instead of renewing peace, sent another army against Aintab, which decoyed into a narrow pass and ignominiously defeated, fell back upon Aleppo. In great alarm, Kaitbai resorted to cruel and unworthy means to raise money for a fresh campaign.[1] With difficulty and delay, a third army was at last despatched; but it fared no better than the last, and Siwar began now to assume sovereign airs and call himself the Lord of Syria. Straitened thus, Kaitbai bethought him of the Porte, which at his appeal withdrew its support; and Siwar, thus deserted by his allies, retired into his stronghold of Ablestin. There he offered to surrender as vassal of the Sultan, and on

---

[1] For example, the head Cazie was flogged by Kaitbai's own hands, and the Vizier subjected to torture till the required money was produced.

promise of safe-conduct repaired to the Egyptian A.D. 1472. camp where he was welcomed with apparent honour. But when the Commander was about to clothe him with a robe of honour, they cast instead a chain about his neck ; and of his followers some were cut down, and the remainder carried captive with him to Egypt. At Cairo with grand festivities, followed by singing men and women, and derisive shouts, this Prince of noble mien, clad mockingly in regal robes and seated on a charger, was brought before Kaitbai, who met him with a derisive welcome. The kingly dress was torn off, and the Prince with his kinsmen, bareheaded and with fetters on their necks, were led on camels to the City gate, where they were hung up, and the bodies left for two days a public spectacle. The Sultan justified this horrid treachery by the poor excuse that Siwar had dealt the same to a Syrian Chief. Such were the barbarous morals of the day.

Egypt was still to be kept in alarm from the same quarter by the marvellous success of Usun Hasan throughout the East. In pretended vassalage, he sent repeated embassies to Egypt, and with one 1467-1469. of these the head of the Chief of the Black Weir over whom he had gained a signal victory. Carrying his conquests into Persia and even Central Asia, he despatched to Cairo also the head of the King of Samarcand which, however, Kaitbai, instead of

A.D. 1469. hanging up like others at the city gate, caused reverently to be washed and buried. Returning now to Asia Minor, Usun tried conclusions with the Osmanly forces, took Tokat and overran Karaman, whose
1471–1473. Chief fled to the Porte. On this, Mohammed II. at the head of a powerful army by means of his artillery (little known as yet in the East) inflicted a crushing defeat on Usun. This was not displeasing to the Sultan, for Usun's scattered forces in conflict
1475, 1476. with the Egyptian troops, still ravaged the Syrian border. Usun died soon after, but his son maintained a hostile attitude, beat the Egyptian army attempt-
1482. ing the capture of Roha, and paraded its General's head triumphantly throughout the border Chiefships. In alarm Kaitbai equipped another force for the pro-
1483. tection of Aleppo; but peace before long was restored again.

The Sultan was glad of this, for conflict with the Porte loomed in the North. There was abundant cause for strained relations arising out of disputes in the numerous Chiefships of Asia, and in the appeals of the contending parties now to one and now to
1481. another of the two Powers. But a more serious occasion now transpired. On the accession of Bajezed II., his brother Jem aspired to the throne, and when defeated, found with Kaitbai a princely refuge and the means of pilgrimage to Mecca. Then leaving his family under the Sultan's care, he made with

the aid of Karaman another attempt at the throne. A.D. 1489.
Beaten again, he became the guest of the Grand
Master at Rhodes, who was pressed by Bajazed, by
the Pope, and by Kaitbai, each for his own end,
to give him up. At last he repaired to Rome,
where, in prospect of a fresh Crusade, he met
with a splendid reception from the Pope. To
regain the Pretender, Kaitbai would have conceded much to the Pope, even (it is said) the
cession of Jerusalem. But bribed by the Porte, and
failing in the hope of a religious war, the Pope
kept Jem in durance at Rome, where eventually 1495.
he met his death by poison.

The hostile feelings of Bajazed at the countenance
given by Egypt to Jem, were accentuated by other
causes, such as being hindered from the pious work
of repairing the watercourses along the streets of
Mecca, and the plunder of an Indian Embassy bearing the gift of a precious diamond dagger. Kaitbai
restored the dagger, sending with it also gifts and a
friendly message; but his Envoy was ill received, and
hostilities ensued. Without warning, the Osmanlies 1485,1486.
fell upon the Syrian border, and took Tarsus, Adana
and other cities. Fighting followed with various success; but in the end, Egypt gained the victory in
a bloody engagement near Adana, and carried off a
multitude of captives who, with heads of the slain
were led in triumph into Cairo.

A.D. 1488.   Not long after, war again broke out. Dissension having arisen in the Province of Dulgadir, its Chief obtained the support of Kaitbai, while his brother's cause was taken up by the Porte. On this, a powerful Egyptian army entered Asia Minor, and at 1490. Cæsarea inflicted again a crushing defeat upon the Turks; after which it returned and entered Cairo with great rejoicings carrying the enemy's flags inverted, and followed by a long line of captives in chains. Still Kaitbai was in much alarm lest Bajazed should seek for his revenge; while the treasury was so empty, and the memluke claims so extravagant, that he even threatened at one time to resign. There prevailed also a severe dearth, which was intensified by the Porte's embargo on the passage of products, fabrics, and even slaves, across the 1491. Syrian border. Meanwhile negotiations began again between the two Courts. Bajazed was appeased by an Embassy carrying back the captives taken in the war, and by princely gifts; and all the more readily came to terms, as he was at the moment turning his eyes towards the conquest of Belgrade. Thus the fatal contest was delayed a little longer.

Kaitbai, like Beibars, was fond of travel; and spent much of his time hunting in various parts of Egypt. He journeyed to Aleppo and to the banks of the Euphrates, and stayed for a season at Damascus; but he never led his troops, though once A.D. 1487. about to do so. Penurious at home, he lavished the Imperial resources on the Holy places abroad, and on the seminaries of the chief Provincial cities. He wept on hearing that the Mosque of Medina had been destroyed by lightning, and spent 100,000 pieces on its reconstruction. He had a fellow-feeling with the Moors of Spain; and to save them sent the Monks of the Church of the Resurrection as an Embassy to King Ferdinand with the threat that if he did not spare Grenada, the Churches in the East would be demolished and pilgrimage put a stop to. About the same time, Kaitbai performed with pomp the Pilgrimage to Mecca, and was received on his return with princely rejoicings; and soon after visited the Holy spots at Hebron and Jerusalem where he endowed a school. On his return, and again on the inauguration of a defensive tower at Alexandria, there was given him a royal reception on re-entering his Capital. The streets were laid with carpets, and the Sultanah welcomed her returning husband by lining the road from the Citadel gate to the Palace steps with gold-embroidered silk;—a sad contrast to the misery around.

For the last days of Kaitbai, though of peace abroad, were days of distress at home. The Plague, that curse of Egypt, swept over Cairo with such deadly violence that in one day and night twelve thousand died; the poor Sultan lost his only wife and his daughter also in a single day, a third of the memlukes succumbed, and the city trembled. Two years after, a murrain laid low the camel herds, the staff of the empire. But the crisis of misfortune during Kaitbai's last years was the deadly strife of the memlukes under two hostile leaders, Kansowah Khamsmich and Akberdy.* The Citadel was a constant scene of fighting and riot. Akberdy held the reins; but being outwitted at the last, fled to Gaza for his life, while Kansowah gained his place. Sunk in grief at the desperate outlook, Kaitbai, now eighty-six years of age, took to his bed, and desired his son Mohammed, a lad of fourteen or fifteen years, to be proclaimed Sultan. Soon after he died, having reigned twenty-nine years, the longest term since the days of Nâsir. He owed this protracted Sultanate to his ready address, the skill with which multiplying faithful slaves around him, he bound them by self-interest to himself. In his exactions, he was guilty of monstrous cruelties; as, for example, the High Marshal was lashed by his own hand, and closeted in a turret of the Citadel where he died. Not only Jews and Christians, but merchants and rich citizens were stripped of their property, and even religious endowments had to yield to the necessities of the State, while he sought to make amends by pious services elsewhere. In short he was a grand Sultan, A.D. 1496. too often a cruel tyrant, but withal an exemplary follower of the Moslem faith. He had but one wife, yet many concubines, a Circassian slave-girl being mother of the son who succeeded to the throne.

CHAPTER XIX

AL NÂSIR MOHAMMED II.—KANSOWAH AL ASHRAFY
—JÂN BELAT—TUMANBAI

1496-1501 A.D.

A.D. 1496.
Aug.

WE come now to a restless chapter, for within the next five years there were five accessions to the throne. MOHAMMED II., son of the late Sultan, reigned for two years, a cruel and dissipated youth. Kansowah Khamsmieh[1] having, as we have seen, put his antagonist Akberdy to flight, was now as Atabeg the virtual ruler. To rid himself of his opponents, he proclaimed an amnesty, and when trusting to it they came in, he caused the leaders to be seized and drowned in the Nile. Having by this and suchlike means rid himself of all Akberdy's faction, in a few months he aspired to the throne, and had himself pro-

---

[1] The number of Emirs of this name is somewhat confusing. This one is called also *Khamsmieh*, "the Five hundred one." Then there is Kansowah, the next Sultan, called *Al Ashrafie*; and shortly after Sultan Kansowa *Al Ghury*. There is still another Kansowah Alalfie, who supported Khamsmieh in his attack on the Citadel. And there are several more, the name being a popular one at this time.

claimed Sultan. But when he sought to seize the A.D. 1496. Citadel, he was repulsed and wounded by fireworks from its walls. Failing in a second attack, he fled with his followers to Palestine, but was met at Gaza by Akberdy who had been meanwhile recalled to Cairo. After a desperate fight in which Kansowah was at first the victor, Akberdy aided by Syrian friends put him to flight. Never again seen Kansowah is supposed to have been killed; but as his body was not found, Cairo was for the next few years kept in excitement by reports of the tyrant's expected reappearance. Akberdy thus reinstated, Feb. entered Cairo with grand rejoicings. They were shortlived, for the two factions soon revived their hostile passions; and, assuming each a royal standard, fought mercilessly for weeks, plundering at pleasure all around; and much life was lost. The tumult increasing, Akberdy fled and was pursued to Syria where he attacked Damascus; and eventually, treated as a rebel, took refuge with a son of Siwar in the north. 1497.

The Sultan, as he advanced into youth, began a life of wild libertinism; singing men and women were his companions in night orgies on the Nile; with his slaves and comrades he paraded the streets, attacked men as they passed and entered houses in the dark, so that people had to keep lights burning at their doors, and even women of respectability were not safe. Thus he lost all title to respect.

A.D. 1497. To meet the wild demands of the petulant crowds of memlukes around him, money was extorted by the lash, by torture, and even by the application of burning iron. Wearied at last by such excesses, Mohammed thought of going off to join Akberdy, but he was betrayed, and the dromedary already waiting at his door, seized. He was now watched as a prisoner, while the memlukes carried their outrages to such an excess that no man's life was safe. Careless of the disorder, the young Sultan continued his night debauches till in one of them he was cut down by Tumanbai the Chancellor, and his body with those of his followers left by the roadside. The abandoned youth had alienated every class and died by none regretted.[1]

1498. Oct. To Mohammed succeeded his uncle KANSOWAH AL ASHRAFY, a Circassian slave bought by Sultan Kaitbai, who strangely enough after his purchase was found to be brother of the Sultan's wife Assilbai, Mohammed's mother. He was now twenty-five years old, and being superior to the ordinary run of memlukes, Cairo had a quieter time than usual

---

[1] It is instructive to notice in Weil's preface to vol. v. p. xii., that a contemporary writer praises this youth for his liberality and other virtues, probably because he had himself experienced his generosity. The details, however, given by Ibn Ayâs and others leave no doubt of his abandoned life; and that he should have been praised by any contemporary is rather proof of the depth to which the moral sentiment of the age had fallen.

under his short reign. But he wanted strength to A.D. 1498.
cope with the wild and factious Emirs about him,
and soon succumbed. His friend Tumanbai for a
time stood by him; but at last the Citadel being
stormed, he escaped in female disguise, and being even- 1500.
tually seized was sent in confinement to Alexandria. June.

The next two Sultans, originally like their predecessors Circassian slaves, held office but for a few
months each. JÂN BELAT, aged forty-five and
dignified by his marriage with Assilbai,¹ ruled for
half a year, when Tumanbai who held command in
Syria, advanced on the Capital and, after much fighting captured the Citadel, on which he was saluted
Sultan. Jân Belat was then sent a prisoner to Alexandria and there by order of Tumanbai beheaded.

The love and esteem with which TUMANBAI had 1501.
been before regarded was turned into hatred and April.
terror at the cruelties he perpetrated on coming to
the throne. The chief Cazie, for instance, having
given his official sanction to the last Sultan's
elevation, was on that account deposed, paraded
half-naked about the streets, and then fined heavily.²

---

[1] Assilbai was a slave-girl in Kaitbai's Harem, and having presented him with a son became his Omm Walad, or freed concubine. More is mentioned of her than it is usual to hear of Mameluke ladies. She was so wealthy that hundreds of mules were needed to carry the property to her new residence. After Jân Belat's death she was robbed and ill-treated by Tumanbai.

[2] On hearing of Tumanbai's rebellion, Jân Belat took fresh oaths from the Emirs and memlukes in presence of the Caliph and Judges

A.D. 1501. So also were many banished and some even drowned. Tumanbai married with great festivity another of Kaitbai's widows; but the rejoicing was shortlived. The Emirs gradually fell off; and, attacked in the Citadel, he fled and found concealment in the house of a friend.

Beyond the usual tale of cruelty and extortion, of incessant riot and outrage in the Capital, and repeated rebellion in Syria, there is in these few years little to relate. The chief danger was from the ever-recurring inroads of the marauding Bedouins who kept Egypt and Syria in continual terror. On one occasion having obtained a victory, they even threatened Cairo. But Tumanbai (before his accession) pursued them into Upper Egypt; and having treacherously got possession of their leader, beheaded him. Shortly after, he put the horde to flight, and returned with three hundred captives; these were all hanged, and their women sold as slaves.

on "Othman's Copy of the Coran," the first mention I have met of this exemplar copied out by Othman's hand and lodged by his command in Cairo, like that lately lost in the grand Mosque of Damascus.

CHAPTER XX

KANSOWA AL GHURY

1501-1516 A.D.[1]

ON the disappearance of Tumanbai, the city was disturbed by the mysterious report of Kansowah Khamsmieh's reappearance; and it was not till after some days that the choice of the Emirs and memlukes fell upon KANSOWA AL GHURY. A Circassian slave, he had served Kaitbai as page and valet; was over forty before he was raised to independence as Emir of ten; and then, rapidly promoted to command of Tarsus, Aleppo and Malatia, he became Emir of a thousand, Chamberlain of the Court, and chief Vizier. At first he declined the throne; but being pressed by the Emirs, who swore faithful service, he at last consented. He was now sixty years of age; but, still firm and vigorous,

A.D. 1501.
April.

---

[1] As we approach the close of the history, one misses the rich details of Macrizy and Abul Mahâsin. We are indebted, however, to Ibn Ayâs, who gives an intelligent narrative, but without the fulness of his predecessors. There are also Arabic and Turkish MSS., but of uncertain authority, which supplement his story.

A.D. 1501. soon showed the Emirs that he was not to be overruled by any of them.

The reign began as usual with the removal of all Tumanbai's adherents. As dangerous to the throne, they were laid hold of, imprisoned or exiled and their property escheated; while the opposite party were restored to freedom and raised again to power and office. Tumanbai from his hiding-place was found to be plotting against the new Sultan; after some weeks, betrayed by his friends, he was murdered by the memlukes of an Emir whom he had put to death; and so Kansowa was saved from that danger without arousing the hostilities of his predecessor's party. On the other hand, the remains of Jân Belat were brought from Alexandria where Tumanbai had caused him to be executed, and royally interred at Cairo.

Present danger thus averted, Kansowa turned to the revenue administration. To replenish the empty treasury, exorbitant demands were levied on every kind of property to the extent of from seven to ten months' income; even religious and charitable endowments not escaping. This was exacted with such severity, not only from Jews and Christians, but from every class, as to create outbreaks in the city. In Cairo, the tax-gatherer was pursued with stones, and the Governor of Damascus slain in an *emeute*. Besides depressing duties on commerce and trade, the coinage was largely depreciated; and A.D. 1501. death-rates so heavily imposed that little was left for the survivors. An imprudent Counsellor having suggested a tax on slaves, the Sultan at the first approved; but such a storm was roused against the project that he not only dropped it in alarm, but suffered its author to have his tongue cut out; then, led all naked on a camel through the city, he was flogged and almost stoned to death; a significant mark of the prevailing barbarity, of the Sultan's inhumanity, and of Mameluke notions as to the dignity of their race.

The money thus wrung from the people was lavished first on the memlukes by whose help it had been raised, and then on the purchase of a multitude of slaves on whom, as fresh from abroad, the Sultan could the more safely confide. Next, there was much spent on public improvements; fortifications at Alexandria Rosetta and elsewhere; watercourses in Egypt; a grand Mosque and College at Cairo; and new structures within the Citadel, which was now surrounded by groves of shrubs and flowers from Syria. The revenues were also largely devoted to the beautifying of Mecca, and increasing the supply of water at the Holy shrines and on the Pilgrim routes. But what surpassed all else was the brilliancy of the Court of him who but yesterday had been purchased from the Slave-dealer. It was

A.D. 1501. maintained in the utmost luxury and pomp of equipage, stud, and all surroundings. Fine gold was used, not merely at the royal table, but throughout the Palace down (we are told) to the very kitchen. The Sultan's own dress and toilet were adorned with all that was costly, grand and beautiful; while poets, singers, musicians and story-tellers flocked to the Court, and flourished on the portions of the orphan and the poor.[1]

There is not much of importance to tell of the earlier years of this reign. The outrages of the royal memlukes must have become intolerable, for twice

1502 and 1505. while Kansowa took fresh oaths of loyalty from his Emirs, he also on his own part swore upon Othman's Coran, that he would no more suffer his memlukes to do them harm. We read also of some suspected treason, which led to punishments of more than ordinary barbarism.[2] Till near the close of the Sultanate, much was not done in fighting. The Bedouins made their usual ravages, attacking Kerak and Jerusalem, but were repulsed by the Syrian

1503. Emirs. Rebellion and rival factions at Mecca and Yenbo also rendered measures necessary for chastis-

---

[1] Such is the tale of Ibn Ayás, a witness on the spot, and therefore, though with some possible exaggeration, to be depended on.

[2] One of the victims died under excruciating torture inflicted in hope of further revelations. Greased cloth wound about his fingers was set on fire; his forehead so tightly bound round, that the eyes were forced out; and so on.

ing the Shereefs and restoring order. But the chief A.D. 1501. concern was the fitting-out a fleet which should protect the Eastern seas from Portuguese attack.

For it was at this time that Vasco da Gama, having in 1497 A.D. found his way round the Cape and obtained pilots from the coast of Zanzibar, pushed his way across the Indian Ocean to the shores of Malabar and Calicut, attacked the fleets that carried freight and pilgrims from India to the Red Sea, and struck terror into the potentates all around. The Princes of Guzerat and Yemen turned for help to Egypt. The Sultan accordingly fitted out a fleet of fifty vessels under his Admiral, Hosein the Kurd. Jedda by forced labour was soon fortified as a harbour of refuge from the Portuguese, and Arabia Felix and the Red Sea were protected. But the fleets in the ocean were at the mercy of the enemy. Various engagements took place; in one of these, 1503, 1504. an Egyptian ship belonging to Kansowa, and in the following year a fleet of seventeen vessels from Arabian harbours, were after a hard struggle taken by the Portuguese, the cargo seized, the pilgrims and crew slain, and the vessels burned. The Sultan was affronted and angry at the attacks upon the Red Sea, the loss of tolls and traffic, the indignities to which Mecca and its Port were subjected, and above all at the fate of his own ship, and he vowed vengeance upon Portugal. But first, through the

A.D. 1501. Prior of Zion, he threatened the Pope that if he did not check Ferdinand and Manuel in their depredations on the Indian Seas, he would destroy all his Holy places, and treat Christians as they were
1508. treating the followers of Islam. Foiled in this demand, a naval enterprise was set on foot and carried out with various success. In one engage-
1509. ment Lorenzo of Almeida was discomfited and lost his life; but in the following year the defeat was avenged by a terrible discomfiture of the Egyptian
1513. fleet. Some years after, Alfonso Abulquerque took Aden, while the Egyptian troops suffered disaster in Yemen. Kansowa now fitted out a new fleet to punish the enemy and protect the Indian trade; but before its results were known, Egypt had lost her sovereignty, and the Red Sea with Mecca and all its Arabian interests had passed into Osmanly hands.

The days of the Sultanate were now hastening to a close. There has been little to relate of the Porte for several years, and yet the fatal struggle was at hand. The last war (1490 A.D.) ended, as we have seen, in the defeat of the Osmanly arms. But peace had been restored, and friendly embassies with costly gifts resumed. Yet estrangement, sooner or later, was always imminent owing to the support, by one Court or by the other, of rival claims in Asia Minor and on the Syrian border. Bajazed was

still engaged in Europe when there suddenly A.D. 1501
appeared a new ground of hostility with Egypt.
It arose out of the relations of the two kingdoms
with the Safyide dynasty in the East; and to it we
must now for the moment turn.

The immediate cause of the breach was ISMAIL
SHAH, the Safyide. He was descended, and the
name derived, from Safyuddin, the famous mystic
of Ardebil, whose Soofie tenets spread largely in the
fourteenth century over Adzerbaijan. His house
gained rapid power; expelled by the Black Weir,
they were supported by the White, with whom they
intermarried, so that Ismail Shah was a maternal
grandson of Usȳn Hasan. Enmity, however, having
broken out, Ismail's father was killed in an engage- 1508.
ment with the White Weir, and Ismail still a child
carried with other captives to Istakhr. From thence he
escaped to Lahijan, where he remained hidden among
his kindred and nurtured by them in the ancestral
faith. This he adopted with such enthusiastic zeal as
to become head of the Soofie school. Then rallying
his people around him, and resolved to avenge his
father's death, he fought and defeated the Chief of
the White Weir;[1] continuing his conquests he rose 1499.

---

[1] The fierce intolerance of Ismail's faith may be gathered from the story that he had the body of his enemy roasted and eaten by his followers. He is also said to have had a pig brought up under the name of Bajazed, the utmost indignity a Moslem could devise.

A.D. 1501. to great power in Persia, Khorasan, and even Transoxanian lands. Returning to Adzerbaijan, he became a growing menace to the Porte, not only from his border conquests, but from his people's aggressive creed. Many of the Soofie faith had been arrested or exiled by Bajazed as dangerous to his rule; and Ismail Shah's request, that instead they should be allowed free transit into Europe across the Bosphorus, was rejected. Upon this, Ismail sent an Embassy to the Venetians inviting them to join his arms and recover the territory taken from them by the Porte. Bajazed, angry with the Sultan, complained bitterly that this Embassy had been suffered to pass through Syria. To appease him, Kansowa placed in confinement the Venetian merchants then in Syria and Egypt. And although, fearing reprisals from Venice, he after a year released them, yet the relations between Egypt and the Porte remained peaceful for a time.

On the succession, however, of Selîm to the throne, things took a very different turn. Not only had the attitude of Ismail become more threatening, but Selîm himself was more of the warrior than his Father. The claim of his brother Ahmed, moreover, who had conspired against him, was taken up by Ismail, who sought but unsuccessfully to gain Kansowa also to its support. Selîm, moreover, feared his Shîea subjects, who sympathised with the Soofie zealot, as dangerous to the throne, and A.D. 1501. had them seized and even put to death. Ismail scandalised at the persecution of his followers, stepped forth as their avenger, and thus war became 1513. inevitable. Selîm set out against him, and battle was joined near Tebriz. The fanaticism of the Soofies, which led even to their women joining in the combat, failed against the cavalry and artillery of the Turks, and Ismail after a disastrous defeat fled and escaped. Selîm, his provisions failing, 1514. returned westward and spent the winter at Amasia. In the spring taking the field again, he attacked 1515. the Chief of Dulgadir who as Egypt's vassal had stood aloof, and sent his head with tidings of the victory to Kansowa. Then turning from the Shah, who had found his way back to Tebriz and in vain sought for peace, Selîm overran Diarbekr and Mesopotamia, taking Roha, Nisibin, Mosul and other cities.

Secure now against Ismail Shah, a larger project dawned upon Selîm; it was the conquest of Egypt, and from Syria the invasion must be made. With no anxieties toward the North, he could now safely make the advance, and so in the spring of 1516 A.D. he drew together for this end a great and well-appointed army; and with the view of deceiving Egypt, represented his object to be the further pursuit of Ismail. Kansowa should have been earlier alive to the danger; for the causes of estrangement rapidly multiplied;—another rebel brother of Selîm allowed refuge in Egypt; on Ahmed's death, his young son with a disloyal retinue provided for in Syria; supplies for the Osmanly forces hindered by Chieftains dependent on Egypt; and lastly, though without open coalition, an understanding (to say the least) between the Sultan and Ismail. But Kansowa had lost his opportunity. If at the first he had joined arms with the Soofie Prince, the issue might have been very different; but he was, no doubt, unwilling by such an alliance to countenance, even in appearance, a heresy so hateful to the Moslem world. And, moreover, he was now old, dependent on the factions around him, and never even at the best with any turn for war.

His suspicions at last aroused, Kansowa spent the winter of 1515 A.D. and the spring of 1516 in preparations for an army with which he proposed marching to the disturbed confines of Asia Minor, and thus being ready for all contingencies. When just about to start, an Embassy arrived from Selîm promising, still in friendly terms, to appoint, as he had been asked, an Egyptian vassal to Dulgadir, and reopen the frontier as of old to the traffic of goods and slaves. It was summer by the time that Kansowa started from Cairo with a numerous force, appointed well in all respects but in artillery. Leaving Tumanbeg as local Governor, A.D. 1516. he marched in great pomp with music, singing and festivity. There followed fifteen Emirs of a thousand, besides many of less degree; 5000 of his own memlukes, with the militia; and all this supplemented as he passed along by Syrian and Bedouin contingents; so that they did not want for numbers.[1] The high Officers of State, Caliph, Sheikhs and Courtiers, with Muedzzins, Doctors and Musicians, followed in his train. On the way he received also Ahmed, son of the late Pretender, and carried him along with courtly honours in the hope of drawing over his sympathisers from the Osmanly force. Advancing slowly he entered Damascus in state, with carpets spread in his pathway, while European merchants scattered gold amongst the crowd. After a few days' stay he went forward leisurely, received at Hims and Hamah with festivities, towards Aleppo. Meanwhile another Embassy arrived from the Osmanly camp which, in deceptive guise, brought costly gifts to the Sultan and also to the Caliph and

9th June.

---

[1] The normal strength of the Egyptian army is given at 26 Emirs of a thousand, besides the memlukes of Emirs of a hundred, and of ten. Kansowa, we are told, purchased in all 13,000 slaves. Two thousand of these were now left behind to hold the Citadel.

Of this expedition Paolo Gierro writes:—" Erano col Soldano 14,000 Mamaluchi con altrettanti cavalli di sotto schiavi, si bene instrutti d'armi e di cavalli, e d'altri pomposi ornamenti, che altro piu bel vedere al mondo non era."

A.D. 1516. Prime Minister, with the request of Selîm for a supply of Egyptian sugar and confectionery. It was also intimated that legal pronouncements against the fanatic Ismail had forced him again to prepare for war and take the field. The Chancellor Mughla Beg was sent with presents in return; but by the time he reached the Osmanly camp, Selîm had thrown off the garb of peace; and now to show his contempt of the Egyptians, treated the Embassy ignominiously, and sent back the Chancellor shaven and shorn, and mounted on a lame and wretched animal, with the rest on foot.

At Aleppo, Kheirbeg the Governor, who was secretly with the Porte (though the Sultan, advised of this by the Governor of Damascus, discredited the report), in order to veil his treachery gave him all the more splendid a reception; but the inhabitants were much enraged against the memlukes for the outrages they perpetrated in the city. It was just then that Mughla Beg returning in wretched plight, brought tidings of the hostile attitude of Selîm, and near approach of the Turkish host. All doubt now removed as to what was before them, a fresh oath of allegiance was taken by Kansowa from the Emirs, chief Cazies, and royal memlukes; presents also were distributed to them, which the other memlukes not receiving were much displeased. The Sultan was again warned of Kheirbeg's dis-

KANSOWA AL GHURY

loyalty, and advised to put him out of the way; A.D. 1516. but, dissuaded by the Emir Jân Berdy from what he represented as a proceeding at the moment dangerous, Kansowa failed to do so.¹ The army then set forward, and on 20th August, encamping on the 19th Aug. plain of Merj Dâbik, a day's journey north of Aleppo, awaited there the enemy's approach; for on this plain it was that the Empire's fate was now to be decided. The Egyptians, except the royal memlukes whom the Sultan sought to spare, 24th Aug. fought well; and at one time the Turkish outlook was so bad, that Selîm had thoughts of falling back. But in the end, the Osmanlies, superior both in numbers and artillery, gained the day. Kheirbeg hastened the end by signalling retreat. The Egyptians were soon in full flight towards Damascus for the gates of Aleppo were closed against them but the Caliph and some chief Emirs went over to the enemy. Kansowa himself fell upon the field and his head was carried to the Conqueror.²

---

¹ The Governor of Amlah was here put to death, because he had served Selîm, though under pressure, from which, as soon as it was possible, he loyally returned; while the Sultan, against advice, let Kheirbeg, a much more dangerous man, alone.

² Accounts however vary. Kheirbeg spread report of his death to precipitate the Egyptian flight. According to some the Sultan was found alive on the field, and his head cut off and buried to prevent its falling into the enemy's hands. The Osmanly account is that he was beheaded by a Turk whom Selîm would have put to death, but afterwards pardoned.

A.D. 1516. Selîm, welcomed by the inhabitants as a deliverer from the excesses of the memlukes, entered Aleppo in triumph. The Caliph he received kindly; but the Judges (the Hanefite alone had fled) he upbraided with their inability to check Mameluke misrule. Joined by Kheirbeg and other Egyptian officers, he proceeded to the Citadel, of which the Commandant had with the fugitives disappeared; and to show his contempt of the garrison sent before him a lame soldier with a wooden club, to whom the gates at once were opened. There he found immense treasures which the Sultan and Emirs had placed for safety, but now left behind.[1] Followed with festivity and rejoicing to the great Mosque, he was there prayed for in the Public service. From Aleppo he marched victoriously to Damascus where the utmost terror prevailed. But beyond some attempts to protect the city by flooding the plain around, nothing had been done to oppose the enemy. Action was paralysed as usual by discord amongst the Emirs. Some thought of Jân Berdy as Sultan, others of Kansowa's son. But as the Osmanlies approached, all either went over to them, or fled to Egypt. Selîm

Oct. entered the city about the middle of October; and the inhabitants high and low, only too happy to escape the tyranny of the memlukes,

[1] A hundred million golden pieces is the extravagant sum named.

readily tendered submission to the Osmanly Con- A.D. 1516.
queror.

Kansowa had reigned a little more than fifteen years. Of his private life and domestic administration we know but little, for as we reach the later years of the Sultanate, details become too scanty for a judgment. He could, as we have seen, be cruel and extortionate, but so far as our information goes, there is less to say against him than against most of the previous Sultans.

CHAPTER XXI

TUMANBEG

1516-1517 A.D.

A.D. 1516.
Sept.
Oct.

TIDINGS of the defeat and of Kansowa's death reached Cairo early in September. But the grave issue at hand was long of being realised by either rulers or people; and when it was realised, there could be no more remarkable proof of the utter want of patriotism in the multitude of memlukes, than the difficulty found by Tumanbeg, the governing Emir, in rousing them to a sense of the Empire's danger, or even of bribing them to measures of defence. A month passed, waiting return of the Chiefs from Syria, before steps were taken for the election of a successor to Kansowa. The choice at last fell on TUMANBEG. He long refused the dignity, but was persuaded by a holy Sheikh living near the City, who made all the Emirs swear obedience and loyalty to him. Like his predecessors having been in early youth a domestic slave of the Palace,[1] he

---

[1] Having belonged to the deceased Sultan, he was curiously enough entitled his son,—Ibn Kansowa.

gradually rose to be Emir of a hundred, and then A.D. 1516.
Prime Minister, which office he held until the departure of Kansowa, who left him in charge of
Cairo and Governor of Egypt. The Caliph having
remained behind with Selîm, Tumanbeg was now 17th Oct.
inaugurated by his Son, but without pomp or ceremony, the royal insignia having been lost in battle.
It was a dark and thankless dignity to which, now at
the age of forty, he was called;—Syria gone, the
troops in disorder, the Emirs distracted, the memlukes
a mercenary horde. Yet he ruled well for the time he
held the throne, and was popular throughout the land.

In course of time, the fugitive chiefs, with Jân Nov.
Berdy, arrived from Damascus; but another month Dec.
elapsed before an army could be got together.
Meanwhile, Tripoli, Safed and other Syrian strongholds, besides Damascus, had fallen into the enemy's
hands. It was thus the beginning of December
before the force now raised at Cairo,—delayed and
diminished by the insatiable demands and waywardness of the memlukes,—set out under Jân Berdy in
the forlorn hope of saving Gaza; but before it 17th.
reached its destination, Gaza had already fallen, and
the army was beaten back. During Jân Berdy's
absence an Embassy arrived with a despatch from
Selîm who, boasting of his victories, and the
adhesion of the Caliph, Judges and other leaders
who had joined him, demanded of the Sultan that

A.D. 1516. his supremacy should be acknowledged both in the Coinage and the public Prayers :—" Do this," he said ; " and Egypt shall remain untouched ; else swiftly I come to destroy thee, and thy memlukes with thee, from off the face of the earth." Though the Envoy and his followers were hooted and mishandled in the City, the Sultan was inclined to fall in with the Porte's demand ; but his infatuated Emirs overcame his better judgment, and the Osmanly messengers were put to death.

Tidings of disaster now followed rapidly on one another. Terror and dismay pervaded the City. The treachery of Kheirbeg and many other Emirs made the prospect all the darker. The inhabitants of Gaza having, on a false report of Egyptian victory, attacked the Turkish garrison, were by Selim's order in great numbers massacred. The news of Jân Berdy's discomfiture increased the gloom ; the more so as he himself, shortly after appearing, attributed the defeat not only to the numbers of the enemy, but to the cowardice of his mercenary followers, while even his own loyalty began to be suspected. The Sultan now resolved himself to march out as far as Salahia, and there meet the Turks wearied by the desert march ; but at the last yielded to his Emirs who entrenched themselves at Ridanich a little way out of the city. By this time, the Osmanlies having reached Arish,

were marching unopposed by Salahia and Bilbeis to A.D. 1517.
Khanka; and on the 20th January reached Birkat al
Hajj, a few hours from the Capital. Two days
later the main body confronted the Egyptian en- 22nd Jan.
trenchment; while a party crossing the Mocattam
hill took them in the flank. A battle followed.
Tumanbeg fought bravely. With a band of devoted
followers, he threw himself into the midst of the
Turkish ranks, and reached even to Selîm's tent.
But in the end the Egyptians were routed, and fled
two miles up the Nile. The Osmanlies then entered
the City unopposed. They took the Citadel and
slew the entire Circassian garrison, while all around
the streets became the scene of terrible outrage.
Selîm himself occupied an island close to Bulac.
The following day his Vizier, entering the city, en-
deavoured to stop the wild rapine of the troops;
and the Caliph, who had followed in Selîm's train,
led the Public service invoking blessing on his name.[1]
Still plunder and riot went on. The Turks seized
all they could lay hold of, and threatened death
unless on payment of large ransom. The Circassians
were everywhere pursued and mercilessly slaugh-

---

[1] The Caliph's prayer is thus given by Ibn Ayâs, the epithets being in the dual number:—"O Lord, uphold the Sultan, Monarch both of land and the two Seas; Conqueror of both Hosts; King of both Iracs; Minister of both Holy cities; the great Prince Selîm Shah! grant him Thy heavenly aid and glorious victories! O King of the present and the future, Lord of the Universe!"

A.D. 1517. tered, their heads being hung up around the battle-
26th Jan. field. It was not till some days had passed, that Selîm with the Caliph, whose influence for mercy began now to be felt, having entered the city stopped these wild hostilities, and the inhabitants began again to feel some measure of security.

27th. The following night, Tumanbeg reappeared and with his Bedouin allies took possession of the weakly garrisoned city, and at daylight drove back the Osmanlies with great loss. The approaches were entrenched, and the Friday service once more
29th. solemnised in name of the Egyptian Sultan. But at midnight the enemy again returned in overpowering force, scattered the memlukes into their hiding-places, while the Sultan fled across the Nile to Jizeh, and eventually found refuge in Upper Egypt.

Satisfied with this victory, Selîm returning again to his island, had a red and white flag in token of amnesty hoisted over his tent. The memlukes, however, were excluded from it. They were ruthlessly pursued, proclamation made that any sheltering them would be put to death, and 800 thus discovered were beheaded. Many citizens were spared at the entreaty of the Caliph, who now occupied a more prominent place than ever under the Egyptian Sultanate. The son of Kansowa al Ghury was received with distinction and granted the College founded by the Sultan his father as a A.D. 1517. dwelling-place. Soon after, the amnesty was extended to all the hidden Emirs, who as they appeared were upbraided by Selîm, and then distributed in cells throughout the Citadel. Jân Berdy who fought bravely at Ridanieh, but now cast himself at Selîm's feet, was alone received with honour and even given a command to fight against the Bedouins.[1] Having strongly garrisoned the Citadel, Selîm now took up his residence there, and for security had a detachment quartered at foot of the great entrance gate.

For Tumanbeg had again assumed the offensive. Well supported by memlukes and Bedouins, he had taken up a threatening attitude there, and stopped the supplies from Upper Egypt. At the last, however, wearied with the continued struggle, he made advances, and offered to recognise the Porte's supremacy if the invaders would retire. Selîm thereupon commissioned the Caliph with the four Cazies to accompany a Turkish deputation for the purpose of arranging terms; but the Caliph disliking the duty sent his Deputy instead. When Tumanbeg heard the conditions offered, he would gladly have

[1] There is a great diversity of opinion as to when Jân Berdy either openly or by collusion took the Turkish side. The presumption is that he was faithful up to the battle of Ridanieh, and then seeing the cause hopeless retired and went over to the Porte about the end of January.

A.D. 1517. accepted them; but was overruled by his Emirs, who distrusting Selîm, slew the Turkish members of the Embassy with one of the Cazies,[1] and thus madly stopped negotiations. Selîm upon this, revenged himself by the equally savage act of putting to death the Emirs imprisoned in the Citadel to the number of fifty-seven.

March. The Sultan who had still a considerable following now returned to Jizeh; and Selîm, finding difficulty in the passage of his troops, was obliged to build a bridge of boats across the Nile.[2] Tumanbeg gathered his forces under the Pyramids, and there, towards the end of March, the two armies met. Though well supported by his General Shadibeg he was, after two days' fighting, beaten, and sought refuge with a Bedouin Chief whose life he once had saved, but who now ungratefully betrayed him into Turkish hands.[3] He was carried in fetters into Selîm's presence, who upbraided him for his obstinate hostility and the murder of his messengers. The

---

[1] Because by accusing a memluke to Selim, he had caused him to be put to death.

[2] Wearied with the struggle Selim, we are told, sent an Emir again to see whether terms could not be secured; but it only came to an angry interview with the General Shadibeg, and a struggle in which the Emir was wounded and with his followers fled. Ibn Ayâs, however, does not notice this somewhat unlikely incident.

[3] He was rewarded for the betrayal. But he was afterwards murdered, when the Circassians drank up his blood, and the friends of the late Sultan held rejoicings when his head was hung up in the city.

captive Sultan held a noble front; he denied com- A.D. 1517. plicity in the murder, and spoke out so fearlessly on the justice of his cause and duty to fight for the honour and independence of his people, that Selîm was inclined to spare him, and carry him in his train to Constantinople. But the traitor Kheirbeg, and even Jân Berdy, urged that so long as he survived, the Osmanly rule would be in jeopardy. The argument was specious; and so the unfortunate Sultan was cast into prison, and shortly after hung 15th April. up as a malefactor at the City gate. The body remained suspended thus three days, and then was buried. Shadibeg, similarly betrayed, was at the same time put to death. The sad death of Tumanbai created such a sensation that an attempt was made by an Emir and a body of devoted followers to assassinate Selîm by night. But the Palace guard was on the alert, or the desperate design might have succeeded.

Tumanbeg, forty years of age, had reigned but three months and a half. He left no family; his widow, a daughter of Akberdy, was for her treasure tortured. Both as Governor during Kansowa's absence, and during his own short Sultanate, he proved himself brave, generous and just, and his death was mourned throughout the land. Last of the race he was one of the best. And so with the death of Tumanbeg, the Mameluke dynasty came to its tragic end.

CHAPTER XXII

SELÎM AND THE CALIPH MUTAWAKKIL

A.D. 1517.

Sept.

AFTER the death of Tumanbeg, Selîm stayed still several months in Egypt. He visited the Pyramids and Alexandria; and it was autumn before he marched back to Constantinople. Kheirbeg obtained as reward for his services the government of Egypt, and Jân Berdy that of Syria; while the Citadel, the key of Cairo, was given over to the watchful command of a Turkish Pasha. On his departure, Selîm carried the Caliph with him; a multitude also followed in his suite, amongst whom were the sons of former Sultans and Cazies, many of the learned class, with Sheikhs, officials, builders and handicraftsmen. The City was also denuded of the finest marbles that adorned the Palace and other public buildings. With these, and a great collection of gold and silver plate, ornaments and precious stuffs, a thousand camels were laden, besides what the numberless Pashas, officers and Turkish soldiers were able to spoil Egypt of. The land, too, was A.D. 1517. bereft of its finest horses, mules and camels.

Cairo had now the unhappy experience of falling from an Imperial city to the rank of a provincial town. The people, however, were relieved by Selîm's departure; for during the eight months he resided in Egypt, his hand was little seen except in executions. Leaving the administration to the Viziers and officials about him, he spent his time in wine and the darker indulgences of the East, while the irreligious lives of his followers caused much offence throughout the land.

The son of Ahmed, the Byzantine Pretender who had since Kansowa's defeat remained hid in Cairo, was shortly after Selîm's departure betrayed by his slaves. Afraid of his sympathisers, Kheirbeg had him brought fettered and disguised by night into the Citadel and strangled there. Unpopular at the first with the Emirs and memlukes, Kheirbeg gradually regained their friendship, and was able with their help in some measure to bridle the Turkish Janissaries and Sepahies whose insolence had become intolerable. Once or twice he was called to account, but unjustly so, by the Porte, which had carried off his son by way of hostage to Constantinople. Kheirbeg's administration is praised as upright and successful. He remained true to the Porte until his death (1522 A.D.).

A.D. 1517. Jân Berdy, still Governor of Syria, joined Kheirbeg's successor in an unsuccessful rising against the Porte, but was beaten, and so forfeited his life.

In Syria there continued as before several separate governments or Pashalics; in Egypt only one, the Pasha being changed from Constantinople year by year. The Commander of the forces held the Citadel; but did not interfere excepting on emergency, and after consulting a Dewan composed of the Cazies and other leading men. The change of government gave no relief from the tyranny and exactions which before had ground the people down. Indeed in one respect the land was worse off than for centuries it had been; for the fruit of the soil and of peasant labour, formerly consumed at home, was now in great part carried off to northern shores.

MUTAWAKKIL, the last Caliph of his race, followed, as we have seen, in Selîm's suite to Constantinople, and was held by him there at first in high esteem. This he gradually forfeited by a graceless and unworthy life. Accused of misappropriating the effects of widows and orphans committed to his charge during the attack on Cairo, he was confined in 1520. Sept. the fortress of Sabáa Kuliat outside Constantinople, and so remained till Selîm's death. His successor, Suleiman, permitted him to return to Constantinople, where for some time he lived on a daily stipend of 60 dirhems. Eventually, on formally A.D. 1517. surrendering his title and office into the hands of the Osmanlies he was allowed to retire to Cairo. We hear no more of him but that he joined a rising there and died in 1538.[1]

In virtue of Mutawakkil having resigned to them his office, the Osmanly Sultans assume that the functions appertaining to the Caliphate, those namely exercised by the Omeyyad and Abbaside Caliphs, both spiritual and temporal, have devolved upon them; and therefore that, like these, they are entitled as "Successors of the Prophet" to all the privileges, and bound to perform all the duties appertaining to the office, including Supreme rule over the Moslem world. Were there no other bar, the Tartar blood flowing in their veins would make the assumption altogether out of the question. Even if based on intermarriage with female descendants of Coreishite stock, the claim would be a weak anachronism. The real Caliphate ended with the fall of Bagdad and death of Zâhir, the last Caliph of Abbaside descent; and so did the Fatimide (or schismatic) Caliphate end with its abolition by Saladin. The resuscitation by

---

[1] Ibn Ayâs who continued in Egypt and notices the arrival of persons from Constantinople, nowhere mentions the Caliph's return; so that it must have been after 1522 A.D. when Ibn Ayâs' history ends.

A.D. 1517. Beibars of the sacred office was (as we have seen) a political measure meant to give an air of legitimacy to the throne, and weaken the Fatimide faction which threatened it. The Egyptian Caliphs were possessed of no authority. They were but servants and spiritual advisers of the Crown, fitted at best to grace the Court, and give to each new Sultan an air of religious recognition. The Mameluke Caliphate was a lifeless show; the Osmanly Caliphate is but a dream.

THE CITADEL FROM THE MOKATTAM HILL.

CHAPTER XXIII

THE MAMELUKE RACE

A few closing remarks may be not altogether out of place on the exceptional position and long dominion of the Mamelukes in Egypt.

We search in vain for a parallel in the history of the world. Slaves have risen on their masters and become for the moment dominant. But for a community of purchased bondsmen, maintained and multiplied by a continuous stream of slaves bought, like themselves and by themselves, from Asiatic salesmen; such a community ruling at will over a rich country with outlying lands,—the slave of to-day the Sovereign of to-morrow,—the entire governing body of the same slavish race; that such a state of things should hold good for two centuries and a half, might at first sight seem incredible. But it is the simple truth of the Mameluke dynasty during the fourteenth and fifteenth centuries.

The rise of the race has been traced in Chapter I. as due to the bad example of the Abbaside

Caliphate in summoning barbarous races for its support to Bagdad; an example that was followed by the Anti-Caliphate of Egypt; and which was continued also by Saladin and his followers most unwisely, for their protection against the dangerous community of slaves already so created. The end, as we have seen, was the overthrow of the Eyyubites by the dynasty of the Mamelukes.

But now the parallel with Bagdad fails. There and elsewhere the barbarous races, mingling with the peoples around them, became eventually part and parcel of the population of the land. In Egypt it was far different, and here begins the marvel. For the Mamelukes kept themselves there quite separate and distinct from the races whom they governed. They formed, in fact, an Oligarchy; for while it was the Sultan and Emirs who ruled, still the whole body of memlukes would ever and anon assert supremacy at their will. Their separation from the Copts, an abject oppressed race, and of a different faith, is quite intelligible. But why they held themselves equally aloof from the Semitic races around, is not so easily understood. In Cairo it is true, citizens of those races were comparatively few and uninfluential; while Syria had been depressed and depopulated by two centuries of Crusading warfare. But the Mamelukes were possessed of tracts and cities beyond Syria on the Armenian frontier, and of districts even in Asia Minor; and yet with these, maintaining as elsewhere an entirely separate existence, they had neither domestic nor social relations. It is this singular isolation, from first to last, which distinguishes the Mameluke from all other races, which kept them an integral and independent people, and which may be looked upon as one of the important causes of their long-continued reign.

Of their habits and inner life we have scarcely anything as our guide. To one dark feature we can but distantly allude. And of their Harems and domestic surroundings there is absolutely nothing to go upon but the occasional mention of a Queen or female slave. No doubt female slaves were to some extent imported from Asia as well as Greece, but the mention of such is comparatively rare. Women taken captive in war were, it is true, brought at times in great numbers and, when not kept by their captors, sold as slaves in Egypt. But these (in addition to their own daughters) would hardly suffice as wives and concubines for the multiplying thousands of the Mameluke race. Anyhow, it is certain that as a rule they did not intermarry with the Natives of the land, though marriage with Christian women is permissible in Islam. We read, no doubt, of occasional marriages with daughters of Cazies and other influential residents of Semitic blood in Cairo; but such were comparatively few, and led to no further union with that race. One can only state the difficulty without attempting to explain it.

A remarkable feature of the Mamelukes was that while they held together as a single people, they were divided into many factions each with a leader or patron at its head. A memluke would attach himself with rigid faithfulness to the Sultan or Emir who had bought him; and would devote himself with zeal to his patron's party, and to his family long years even after he had passed away, and even to generations following. Thus we have the *Ashrafites*, the *Zâhirites*, the *Mueyyadites*, etc., so called from the Sultans and leaders whose name they bear. The broils and combats of the various factions so formed, while they often paralysed the administration, at the same time roused an independent and courageous spirit which made the Mameluke feared by those without his circle. It should be noticed also that the Mamelukes were often highly educated. They were brought up in the school both of war and peace; while yet young, they were sometimes proficient in philosophy, divinity and science, as well as in chivalry and arms; and were thus well qualified for high office and command. It was not, however, always so, for we read of Sultans who could not even sign their name; and among themselves they maintained the use of their own Turkish or Circassian tongue.

Yet another feature of the race was their imperfect sense of the hereditary title. The favourite slave might succeed, and was sometimes known even as his master's " son." In the vast majority of cases, however, the succession to the throne was given to the Sultan's son, often a mere child,—shortly, however, to be cast aside by his Atabek or other designing Emir. It is thus that only in the case of Nâsir son of Kilawun the succession continued to the third and fourth generations. The crown, as a rule, was the prize of the strongest, most crafty and overbearing, and often most cruel and unprincipled, of the Emirs. All regarded it as the heritage of the race; and the possible grasp of it, and of the high offices of State, quickened no doubt the interest of all in the perpetuation of the Oligarchy. A still further source of attachment was the vast wealth the Emirs could grind out of the people, as well as the rich fieffs and estates given them by the State, and the grand pavilions which they could thus build for themselves; though these possessions were often held by the most precarious tenure, and lost in the confusion and turmoil of the day.

Cruel and treacherous as a race, there are not wanting instances, though few and far between, of just and upright Rulers, and of true benevolent and honourable men; — many who founded charitable pious and literary endowments, Schools and Colleges for Medicine, Philosophy, Art and Science, and Orphan homes; some who left behind them monuments of their age in beautiful buildings which, however defaced and robbed of ornaments by Ottoman barbarism, still adorn the Capital; as well as a few who checked the scandalous oppression which more or less throughout the Dynasty prevailed against the Jews and Christians. But the vast majority with an almost incredible indifference to human life, were treacherous and bloodthirsty, and betrayed, especially in the later days of the Dynasty, a diabolic resort to poison and the rack, the lash, the halter and assassination such as makes the blood run cold to think of; and that not only for Imperial objects but to extract money from an unoffending people.

To resume;—the wonder is that a foreign yoke so feared and hateful was not long before destroyed. Its continuance, as I have sought to show, arose in chief part from the depressed condition of the Copts; for beside them, there was no sufficient citizenship to match the Mameluke ascendency. The Caliph was their creature, and the Semitic heads of society (though holding all the learned, legal and spiritual offices) were so subordinate and comparatively few as never to venture on any organised antagonism. Why the Fatimide rule had failed to raise up a larger and more powerful Semitic body in Alexandria, Cairo, and Palestine, one cannot say; but so it was. Still more difficult is it to account for the subservience of Syria at large; but, the battlefield of the world, it no longer ventured on any combined and independent policy. Mameluke garrisons held the citadels, and Mameluke governors ruled the land, while Native rule was never thought of. The Bedouins, it is true, were an independent race; but with their roving habits, they never settled anywhere, nor held long together for any common object. With the Mamelukes it was otherwise. Their party-hatred and internal fightings notwithstanding, they were as regards the outer world an integral and united Oligarchy. And though not rooted as in a native soil, yet in course of time everything that was valuable in land had passed into their hands, and they never hesitated to fill their coffers at the expense of those around them. Thus rich and powerful and unscrupulous, they were enabled to hold the people in abject and unquestioned thraldom.

These considerations may, in some degree, help to account for the long-continued Mameluke supremacy in Egypt; but it must still remain one of the strange and undecipherable phenomena in that land of many mysteries.

STOOL OR STAND OF BRONZE, INLAID AND EMBROIDERED WITH SILVER. FOUND IN NÂSIR IBN KILAWUN'S MOSQUE, AND SUPPOSED TO BE OF HIS AGE. PRESERVED IN CAIRO MUSEUM.

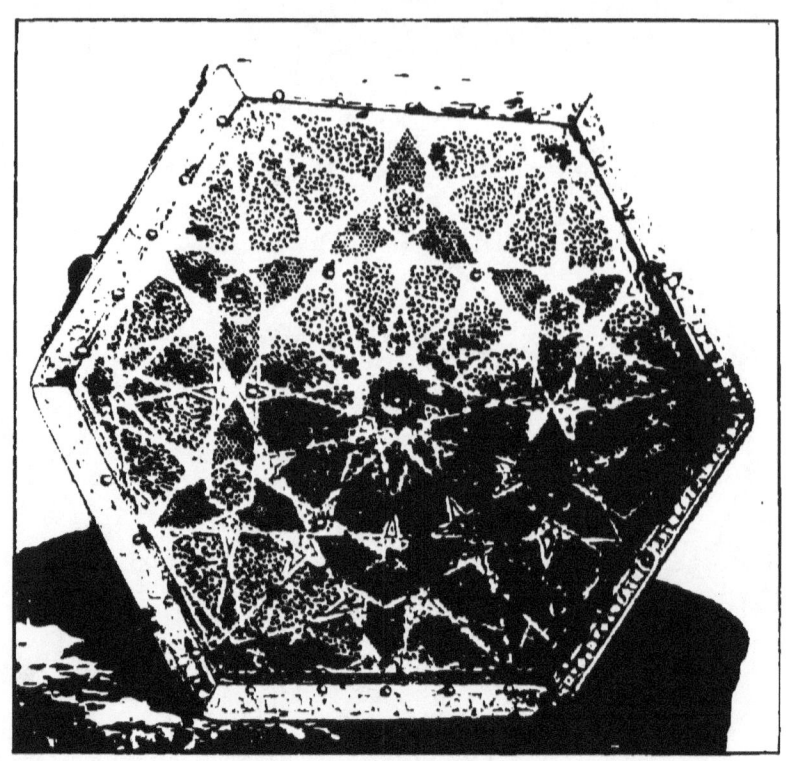

TOP OF THE STOOL IN PREVIOUS PICTURE.

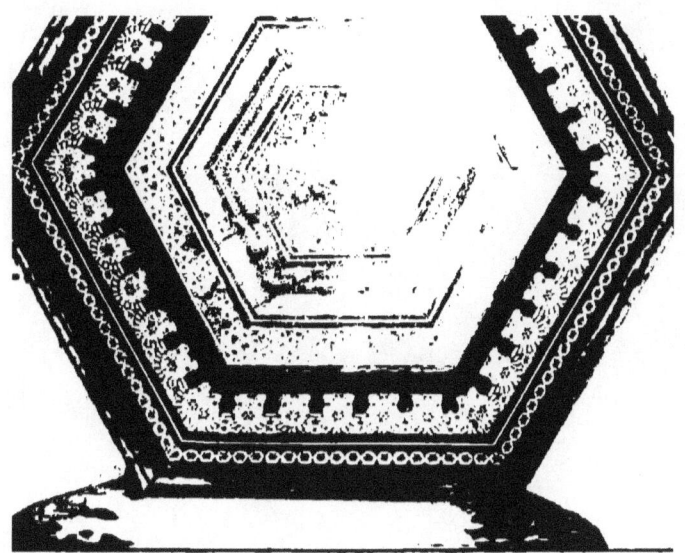

TOP OF A STOOL, INLAID WITH SILVER, FOUND IN THE MOSQUE OF SHABAN, SON OF NÂSIR, AND PRESERVED IN CAIRO MUSEUM.

APPENDIX I

BRIEF NOTICE OF THE MAMELUKES UNDER OSMANLY RULE.

UNDER Ottoman rule, the Mamelukes still maintained their hold upon Egypt; and as the Porte's prestige began from time to time to wane, so likewise did the influence of its Cairo representative; and in the same measure did that of the Beys and their Mamelukes gain ascendency. They remained, as in generations past, a separate race not mingling with those around them; and they still continued to multiply their numbers by the flow of slaves purchased by themselves from Siberia, Circassia and adjoining lands. The head of the Mamelukes came to be called *Sheikh ul Beled*, or "Chief of the Land"; and to gain this office, strife and combat too often embittered the race, and caused fighting and disorder to prevail. The Sheikh when supported by the Emirs was all-powerful; and the Porte, with its local Pashas, must in that case abide by his demands. The virtual ruler was the Sheikh.

[A.D. 1517–1811.]

In the latter half of the eighteenth century, the Porte being then at war with Russia, the famous ALY BEY, as Sheikh ul Beled, gradually reduced the Janissaries, the Osmanly prop; while he increased the number of the Court memlukes till they reached six thousand. Then assuming independent power, he sent back the Ottoman Governor to Constantinople. Victorious also over Syria and the Bedouins, he was recognised as Lord of the Holy places by the Shereef of Mecca, who also conferred upon him the title of Sultan. But, after a brilliant reign, he was eventually betrayed in Syria and slain.

A.D. 1798–1800.

IBRAHIM was Sheikh when Napoleon, to protect the interests of France, took possession of Egypt; but the combined action of England and the Porte forced him to leave it, and then Ibrahim who had fled to Upper Egypt was restored to power.

It is needless here to follow the course of events till at length MAHOMET ALY gained the supreme authority; and fearing the Mamelukes took measures to get rid of them;

1805.
1811.

but the savage act by which he put an end to the leaders of the race did not take place for six years after. The Beys and Emirs were then invited to an entertainment in the Citadel. On their taking leave, the outer gates were closed; and, every way of egress barred, the whole body, said to have been four hundred and seventy in number, were shot down. By further orders, the multitude of Mamelukes in Cairo and throughout the land were pursued, slain or chased abroad. A body escaped to Nubia, but are said to have met the same fate there. The few that survived in Egypt mingled at last with those around them, and are not now, it is said, to be distinguished from the general population.

So ended the Mameluke race, which for generations had lorded it over Egypt, and Cairo enjoyed a rest it had never known before.

APPENDIX II

MEMORANDUM BY HIS EXCELLENCY YACOUB ARTIN PASHA ON THE RELATION OF THE MAMELUKES TO THE GENERAL POPULATION.

(*Being answers to questions put to him by the Author.*)

In your letter you ask me several questions. I will try to answer them to the best of my ability.

1. "The Mamelukes came under the Porte in 1517. Up to that time I imagine they kept altogether a separate and a dominant race?"

Yes, provided that he who deals with their history does not forget that the Mamelukes never pretended to create a race by intermarriage with the inhabitants of the countries in which they held sway. Even with the female consorts of their own race they did not pretend to establish dominant families, or an aristocracy of any kind. A characteristic feature of their moral and social code was that a child should never succeed his father. The slave or mameluke succeeded his slave-master, and became the protector of the lawful family of his master. In many instances he took his master's wives into his own harem; and if he did not slay the children, the perverted habits he allowed them to acquire in the harem brought them to an early grave. The more we approach our own period in history, the more this idea of a democratic slave-soldiery predominates amongst them.

2. "After that, did they keep as distinct as before, or did they at all mingle with the people, Arabs, or other inhabitants of the land, or with populations which came in from Syria, Asia Minor, etc.?"

No, they kept distinct. Continuing to be a body of soldiers holding the country, they held to their paramount principle of not establishing themselves permanently. The maintenance of their political position required them to stand always in the breach. Fighting was their principal interest in life, even with each other, or with the people of the country, in order to keep them down. Leading such an existence, family life was rendered well-nigh impossible. Very few of this soldiery died at home in their own bed; nearly ninety, or perhaps more, per cent. used to die a violent death, and most of them were under thirty or thirty-five years of age. At death, their property, house, goods, female slaves, male mamelukes, children, and, in fact, everything went to their master, to their murderer, or to the State, whichever was the strongest. In the event of the State being the most powerful, everything belonging to the dead man, including his children, was sold for the benefit of the Bait-el-Mâl (Treasury): otherwise, his estate passed into the hands of the foremost and strongest Mameluke chief. Those Mamelukes who lived in retirement and led a civil life, who married, and in the majority of cases had children, were, in the first or second generation, merged into the Egyptian people. Their children were called "Muwellid" (native-born), or nicknamed "Abdullawi," *i.e.* degenerate, or good-for-nothing as soldiers or administrators. You will find in the Chronicles of Gabarti several cases of this absorption. The most prominent is probably that of Abd-el-Rahman Kahia, the master of Ali Bey, in the second half of the eighteenth century. Another example, one you must know by name, is that of Mahmoud Pasha Sami, of the family of Baroudi, who is now in Ceylon with Arabi Pasha. He pretends to be a descendant of the Sultan-el-Ghouri, but is known to be the great-grandson of a Mameluke of Ali Bey (eighteenth century) whom the latter intrusted with the arsenal which he created at Boulak. Even after the death of his master, Ali Bey, this Mameluke kept his post, because of his knowledge of powder-making, bronze gun-casting, etc. Hence his surname of Baroudi, which signifies " powder-maker." His son went on with the concern, and married a Circassian slave: their only child, a daughter, was married to a Circassian male slave, who became the father of Mahmoud Sami. Mahmoud Pasha Sami married a great-niece of Mohammed Ali Pasha, and he has several children by her living. Here is, then, an instance of a family of about one hundred and fifty years' standing in Egypt, sprung from a Mameluke, and of which the main line has been kept distinct from the surrounding population, because the men always married Asiatic slave-girls of their own race, except this Mahmoud Pasha Sami, who (as already explained) married a freeborn girl. But she also had no Egyptian blood in her. Instances of this kind are rare, to my knowledge; but instances of families of less than one hundred years' standing, *i.e.* subsequent to the conquest of Mohammed Ali Pasha, are numerous. Generally speaking, all foreigners, or those of foreign extraction by both parents, prefer to keep distinct from the different dark-hued Egyptians; but there are many instances of their having commingled. There is no fixed rule in the matter, but owing to the difficulty of finding a wife or a husband of the same race or of the same fortune, or owing to the growing keenness in the struggle for existence, the tendency for about twenty years past has been to mix. Furthermore, some thirty years ago, Ismail Pasha changed the official language from Turkish to Arabic. That has had a great effect on the tendencies of the Turks and Circassians—at anyrate of Mussulmans of foreign descent—to approach the Egyptians, and not to treat them as a conquered race, but to try to be accepted as Egyptians by the Egyptians. This sentiment was carried to its extreme in the time of Arabi Pasha's revolution, 1882, when I saw people who had not a single drop of Arab blood in their veins, pretending to be connected with the Arabian prophet's family. This movement is spreading, and in another thirty years I believe it will be difficult to find a pure-bred Turk or Circassian. All of the existing families will have become mixed with Egyptians, and of course the Egyptian blood will prevail, as it has always done. Even in the case of Syrians, Greeks, Armenians, and Christian foreigners in general, who intermarry with Copts, their offspring merges into the Egyptian type, after the intermarriage of two or—at the most—three consecutive generations.

I may here observe, that the idea that foreigners in Egypt cannot have offspring, or rear families beyond the third generation, is absurdly erroneous. To prove this, by an instance which is quite historical, I venture to point to the Ptolemaic family, which came from the mountains of Macedonia to establish itself in Egypt, and had in itself another more serious reason of family decay, namely, consanguinity,—most of those kings having married their sisters,—and still they lived as a strong family for nearly four hundred years, *i.e.* about thirteen or fourteen generations. For an explanation of the difficulty of rearing families in Egypt from the time when the Turkish slaves took the reins of government, practically from the ninth century, we must look first to their military constitution, then to their turbulent life and violent death, and to their intermarriage (when by chance they lived long enough) with Egyptian women, who turned their offspring into Egyptians and merged them into the general public. I am aware that the climate and the country have an enervating effect on foreigners, but I am convinced that by experience and study of the climate, the material life and hygienic conditions will be still further improved, and the scientific comforts of life will allow, as of old, foreigners to live here and multiply better than in many other southern climes. I am told that Kait Bey's family is still living, that some Abbaside offspring exists in Cairo, but those that have been pointed out to me I have found quite Egyptian in form, hue, and mien. One must also listen very sceptically when he hears that such an one is a descendant of such a Sultan, or of any other celebrated Mameluke. Because such an one holds Wakf properties, or part of them, entailed by those Sultans or Mamelukes on behalf of their families—this is no sufficient proof that he is a descendant of the said Sultan or Mameluke; for the Wakfs are entailed, generally speaking, on the children, parents, Mamelukes, white or negro, male or female, and even servants of both sexes, and their offspring right to the end of all the branches. You will thus perceive the difficulty of going back to the origin of anyone existing now, through all the revolutionary epochs in the history of Egypt for the last six centuries, with such scanty means of information.[1]

3. "In 1811 a multitude was massacred in the Citadel by Mohammed Ali; did many escape this fate, and since then are there any traces of their being a distinct race?"

At the massacre of the Mamelukes only the principal chiefs were killed, with their followers. I cannot tell, for a certainty, how many were killed, but at anyrate, from all that I can gather, not more than a couple of hundred, at the utmost, were killed in that celebrated massacre, including chiefs, followers,—who were Circassians by birth,—and their Egyptian servants and grooms. Those Mamelukes who were in the provinces escaped the fate. Many of them, who were in Cairo, were supporters of Mohammed Ali; *they* escaped. Perhaps some thousands

---

[1] The Turkish poet, Fazil Bey (xviii. S.), in his *Zenana Namek*, under the title of "Egyptian" (women), says: "Why do they call Egypt 'mother of the world'? She is only a prostitute who has given herself up each century to all the nations." This fact, which is so conspicuous, alone accounts for not having any solidly stablished families besides the democratic, demagogic institution of the revealed religions, etc.

left the country for Syria and Upper Egypt. In that part of the country they retired first to Dongola, and then to Shendy. Some died there, whilst others took service in the forces of Mohammed Ali that were going to the Soudan in 1824. More than two thousand, under eighteen years of age, belonging to Mamelukes were seized as prizes by Mohammed Ali, according to the law prevailing then that everything belonging to a vanquished foe belonged by right to the conqueror—which principle you will find even in the Bible (*e.g.* David and his son). Those boys were incorporated first in Mohammed Ali's bodyguard as Mamelukes in the school at the Citadel, and afterwards as cadets in the regular army, started by him as early as 1815, in the Cairo citadel, and subsequently transported in 1818 to Assouan, after the revolt of the Albanian troops against the regular army. These boys formed the nucleus of the officers and non-commissioned officers of the four regiments ready by 1824. It is believed that the Mameluke soldiery was about twenty thousand strong in the beginning of Mohammed Ali Pasha's rule. Fighting, death, and exile had reduced them to nothing by the time of the massacre, in comparison with the numbers in Bonaparte's time, which, it is said, amounted to forty thousand. One must bear in mind that owing to the fights and revolutions in Egypt from 1798 up to 1811, the import of slaves from the north had slackened, and also that as owing to the bankruptcy of the chief Mamelukes merchants did not find it in their interest to import slaves, the recruiting of that soldiery had been stopped several years before their entire disbandment by Mohammed Ali in 1811. From 1824 to the present time, the army has been commanded by foreigners, one half of whom, at the very least, were Circassian Mamelukes belonging to the Viceregal family. You find them for the last time in 1881, when Arabi wanted to dismiss them all from the army. Most of those Circassians were bought by the Khedive Ismail, shortly after Shamil, the great and last chief of the Circassians, had been captured and put to death by the Russians. At his death a great number of Circassians emigrated to Turkey and Egypt, and sold their children. Ismail Pasha purchased a considerable number of them, put them in his schools, and eventually improved them into officers. Since a stop has been put to the slave trade, Mamelukes can no longer be found for sale in Egypt. A great many of the Mamelukes, however, are still living, and have posts in the public service. They are generally of Aryan extraction,—Greeks, Circassians, Georgians, Armenians, etc., — and have all the liberty enjoyed by any freeborn man.

Nowhere in Egypt do you find any trace of foreign blood being paramount in the population, either in towns, or in the country. The foreign observer, landing in Lower Egypt, will at first notice the hue of the skin clearer on the seaside, and darker towards Cairo, Cairo being the centre of a great mixture of hues. To my mind, in our own time, as in antiquity, the Egyptian blood has been mixed mainly with Semitic. To the south of Cairo the colour gets darker and darker up to Assouan, where it is almost negro-hued,—the negro element getting the best of it in the course of a few generations. In the north of Cairo the colour is cleared by the mixture of Syrian, Greek, and Turkish blood, without the Semito-negro mixture being ever transformed into a pure Aryan race. An Egyptian race, clearly distinguishable or autochthonous, does not exist, I believe, at least at the present time. It is thus very difficult to assign a colour to the Egyptian. As far as my own knowledge goes, two places are, however, worthy of notice, namely, (*a*) the shores of Lake Menzaleh, where one finds the original type of Hyksos, as shown to us by the monuments, with prominent cheeks, small eyes, large forehead, large nose and scanty beard; (*b*) the north-west of the province of Dakahlieh, bordering the Syrian desert, where you find a pure, or very nearly pure, Semitic type,[1] especially in women. As for the Egyptian type, as shown by the monuments, one meets with it south of

---
[1] Syrian or northern Semites.

Beni Suef up to the cataracts, but all these different kinds are more or less tainted according to their position from south to north.[1]

I think I have given you an answer to each of your queries. I am afraid I have been too long, but you will excuse me, as you well know the difficulty of dealing briefly with these matters.

YACOUB ARTIN PASHA.

CAIRO, *December* 11*th*, 1895.

---

[1] The predominant feature being more or less of the Semitic type.

INDEX

A

Abagha, Mongol leader, 18, 28, 36.
Abbas, Caliph, nominated Sultan, 129.
Abbaside Caliphate, ix., xiv., xix.;
destroyed by Mongols, 10; re-established by Beibars, 14; claimed by Osmanlies, 213.
Abdul Aziz, brother of Faraj, 125.
Ablestin, Mongols defeated at, by Beibars, 28; daughter of Chief marries Jakmac, 152; Aslan Chief of, 170; war with Egypt, 174.
Abu Bekr, son of Nâsir, 85, 87; put to death at Coss, 88.
Abulfeda, ix.; at battle of Merj Soffar, 58; Sultan of Hamah, 84.
Abul Mahâsin, x., 134; position at Court, 134; 148 note; value of his history, 187.
Acre, fall of, xiv. See Akka.
Adana, seized by Moslems, 97; taken by Chief of Karaman, 160; taken by the Osmanlies, 177.
Aden, port of traffic, 141; embargo on goods, 142; taken by Alfonso Albuquerque, 192.
Adil, brother of Saladin, xxiv.; succeeds him, xxvi., 7; extensive rule, xxvi.; his sons quarrel, xxvii., 7.
Adzerbaijan, spread of Soofeeism in, 193.
Aghlabites of Tripolis, 2.
Ahmed, Sultan, son of Nâsir, 84, 88; vices, 88; Sultan, 89; retires to Kerak, 90; deposed and put to death, 91.

Ahmed, Sultan, son of Sheikh, 134; saluted Sultan when a year and a halfold, 137; deposed by Tatâr, 138.
Ahmed, son of Inâl, Sultan, 163; resigns, 164.
Ahmed ibn Oweis, 114; at Bagdad, 115, 119, 132.
Ahmed Mongol, 37.
Ahmed, son of Bajazed II., 194, 197; son betrayed in Cairo, 211.
Ain-Jalût, battle of, 10, 11.
Aintab threatened by Haiton, 23; attacked by Egypt, 174.
Akberdy, Mameluke leader, 180, 182, 183.
Akka, described by Wilken, xxx.; invested by Crusaders, xxv., xxvii. xxviii.; attacked by Beibars, 26; Jehâd against, 39; invested by Khalîl, 44; stormed and burned, xxx., 44.
Aksonker, Regent, 90.
Aktai, 9.
Akush, Governor of Damascus, 64.
Aleppo, attacked by Raimond, xx.; ravaged by Mongols, 34; Timur's victory at, 122; entered by Selim, 200.
Alexandria, ravaged by Venetians and Knights of Rhodes, 98, 99 by Franks, 128, 136; tower inaugurated by Kaitbai, 179; visited by Selim, 210; canal from Fuah to, 79.
Alexius, Kaiser, xvi.
Alfonso Albuquerque takes Aden, 192.
Ali Bey, Treasurer, conspiracy of, 112.

Ali Bey reduces Janissaries, 223; dominant in Syria, 223, 226, 227.
Al Mueyyad faction, origin of the name, 135.
Altunbogha, 89; Regent, 134; submits to Tatâr, 138.
Aly proclaimed Sultan, A.D. 1369, 101; died, 103.
Amalrich, King, invades Egypt, xxii., 6.
Amasia, 195.
Amid, capital of Kara Yelek, 144.
Amru conquers Egypt, 1.
Angora, 117; battle of, 120.
Antioch stormed by Crusaders, xvii.; besieged by Kaiser, xx.; Boemund besieged in, xxv.; stormed by Beibars, xxix., 25; by Ghazan, 56; by Chief of Ablestin, 174.
Arabi Pasha, 226, 228.
Arabia Felix, Nâsir's connection with, 73.
Arabic, adopted in Egypt as official language, 227.
Aradus taken by Egypt, 57.
Archæological Mission, xii.
Ardebil, 193.
Argun, dealings with Pope, 27.
Arish, 204.
Armenia, first connection of Mamelukes with, 23; Haiton seeks aid of Tartars and Crusaders, ib.; devastated from Adana to Tarsus, ib.; raid by Beibars on, 27; oppressed, by Kilawun, 38; attacked by Lachîn, 50; chastised by the Egyptian army, 57, 59; makes peace with Egypt (a Chief embracing Islam), 59; again attacked by Nâsir, 68; by Mongols, 71; by Syrian army, 71; Leo imprisoned, 99; ceases to be a Christian State, 100; persecuted, 143; Inâl's relations with, 160.
Armenians slain at Kalaat Rum, 45; contingent joins Mongols, 58; in Egypt, 228; Armenian Mamelukes in modern Egypt, 231.
Army composed of Mamelukes, 133.

Arragon, Court of, sends embassy to Egypt, 59.
Arsuf destroyed by Beibars, 20.
Artillery of Osmanlies, 176, 195.
Artin Pasha, His Excellency Yacoub, xi., xii., 225.
Ascalon taken by Crusaders, xxi.; given up to Saladin, xxiv.; destroyed, xxvi.
Asendimur, Governor of Hama, 63, 68.
Ashrafite party, 149, 150, 163, 165, 167, 171.
Asia Minor, how divided in fourteenth century, 118; attacked by Timur, 120; again attacked by Timur, 124; by Bursbai, 146; Western half under Osmanlies, Eastern half under Egypt, 146; Inâl's relations with, 160; Egyptians devastate, 160.
Aslan, Chief of Ablestin, 174.
Assassin Race, 70, 128.
Assilbai, Sultanah, 185.
Assouan, governor's cruelty, 100; Mamelukes in, 230, 231.
Atabeg, title, xix., 107, 165.
Ayas, in Armenia, destroyed by Egypt, 71.
Ayla, xxiii., 101.

B

Baalbec, connection of Macrizy with, x.; battle of, 127.
Bab-el-Mandeb, Straits of, 142.
Bagdad, Caliphs of, indifferent to Crusade, xviii.; taken by Seljukes, xix.; Abbaside house destroyed at, 14; Governor proclaims Sultan, 98; attacked by Timur, 113; destroyed by Timur, 120; Timur again vents his fury on, 123; held by Ahmed ibn Oweis, 132.
Bahrite Dynasty, rise of, 13.
Bahrite Mamelukes, 5, 8.
Bajazet, chief of Black Weir, 113, 114.
Bajazet, Osmanly, his conquests, 118; addressed by Timur, 119;

INDEX

defeated at Angora, 120; his "cage," *ib.*
Bajazet II., defeats Jem, 176; hostility to Egypt, 177; insulted by Ismail Shah, 193; arrests and exiles Soofies, 194.
Baldwin, fights Tancred, xviii.; defeated by Moslems, xix.; breaks truce with Moslems, xxi.
Baroudi family, 226.
Bedouins, hostilities with Egypt, 39, 57, 100; overrun Egypt, 160, 170, 171, 173, 186; pursued by Tumanbai, 186; attack Kerak and Jerusalem, 190; help Tumanbeg against Turks, 206; Bedouin chief betrays Tumanbeg to Turks, 208; roving habits, 221.
Beibars I., early history of, 13, 29, 30; defeats Franks at Joppa, xxix., 8; flies from Eibek, 9; bravery of, 11; kills Kotuz, 11; succeeds to Sultanate as first of Mameluke dynasty, xxix., 11, 14; destroys Crusaders' stronghold, xxix.; cruelty to Christians, *ib.*; wise administration, 14; re-establishes Caliphate, 14, 16, 213, 214; treachery and cruelty of, 17, 22, 27, 31; alliances, 18, 19; grants fiefs in Palestine, 20; four campaigns against Crusaders, 19-25; bridges over Jordan, 21; besieges Safed, 22; attacks Armenians, 23; storms Shekif and Jaffa, 25; destroys Antioch and wars against the Crusaders, 25; captures Akkar, 26; fits out a fleet against Cyprus, 26; treaty with Tyre and Akka, 26; last campaign, 28; his faithlessness, 29; death, *ib.*; person and habits, 30; extent of dominions, *ib.*; family, 31; buried, 32.
Beibars II., President of Palace, 53; attacks Bedouins, 57; attitude towards Christians, 60; opposes Sallar, 61; first Sultan of Circassian birth, 63; sues for Nâsir's pardon, 65; is imprisoned at Gaza, 65; cruel end, 66.
Berbers, their connection with the Fatimide Caliphs, 2.
Berekh, Prince of Kiptchak, 18.
Berekh (Mameluke), supreme in Cairo, 102; defeated by Berkuck, and death, *ib.*
Berkuck, Sultan, x.; origin and rise, 98, 105, 106; with Berekh supreme in Cairo, 102; defeats Berekh and puts him to death, *ib.*; deposes Hajy, 103; affair with Caliph, 106; prisoner at Kerak, 107; escapes to Syria, 108; advances on Cairo and again proclaimed Sultan, 109; attacks Mintash, 110; puts Yelbogha to death, 111; plotted against by Ali Bey, 112; fears the memlukes, 113; communications with Timur, puts Timur's messenger to death, 114; marches to Damascus and Aleppo, dies, 115; tastes and character, *ib.*; his tomb, 116; sepulchre visited, 135.
Beshtak, 81 note, 85, 87.
Bernard preaches Second Crusade, xxi.
Bertram of Ghibelet, 39.
Beyrut taken by Crusaders, xxvi.; slaughter at, 41; burned by Cyprians, 128.
Bilbeis, 205.
Birkat al Hajj, 205.
Black Death, The, 94.
Black Weir, 118, 124, 132, 146, 160, 193.
Blue River, 28.
Boemund, besieged in Antioch, xxv.; attacks Hims, 21; attacked by Beibars, 25; admitted to truce, 35; his sister claims the succession, 39 note.
Bokhary, Traditions of, 145 note.
Bonaparte's time, Mamelukes in, 230.
Boulak, 227.
Brousa, Osmanly capital, 117.
Bu Khalil, 102 note.
Bû Saîd, relations with Nâsir, 69.
Bulgaria, route of Crusaders, xv.

Burjites, 5, 40, 48, 53.
Burjite Dynasty, rise of, 103.
Burkhardt, 27 note.
Bursbai, major-domo, 138 ; Sultan, *ib.* ; seizes and imprisons Jani Beg, 139 ; edicts against Jews and Christians, 139, 147 ; treachery of, 140 ; attacks pirates, *ib.* ; destroys Roha, 143 ; alliance with Morâd, 146 ; beats back Jani Beg and Dulgadir Chiefs, 146 ; dies, *ib.* ; his failings, 147.

C

Cæsarea besieged, xxii., 20, 29, 160 ; Egyptians defeat Turks at, 178.
Cairo, 2, 3 ; Saladin's capital, 7 ; attacked by Pelagius and Louis, xxvii., 8 ; plague in, 49, 147 ; Black Death, 94 ; attacked, 126 ; sacked by Turks, 205, 210 ; sinks to provincial town, 211.
Caliphate of Bagdad, xviii.; indifferent to Crusades, *ib.*; rule over Egypt, 1 ; connection with rise of Mamelukes, 3 ; fall of, 3, 14 ; influence on Egypt, 8 ; re-established by Beibars, 14, 16.
Caliphate, Egyptian, a shadow, 16, 64 ; Caliph banished to Upper Egypt, 84 ; prestige abroad, 91 ; Caliph appointed Sultan, 129 ; deposed, 130 ; follows Sultan in military expeditions, 132 note ; sent a prisoner to Alexandria, 157 ; improved position under later Mamelukes, 157 note ; goes over to Selim, 199 ; public prayer of for do., 205 ; greater prominence under Turks, 206 ; accompanies Selim to Constantinople, 210 ; end of, 212 ; office given up to Osmanlies, 213 ; baseless assumption of, by Ottoman Sultans, 214.
Caliphate, Fatimide. See Fatimide.
Camel, parading on, description of the torture, 102 note.

Castile, Kilawun treats with, 38.
Catapults used at siege of Akka, 44.
Charizmian hordes, xxix., 7.
Charlotte, Queen of Cyprus, 159, 160.
Chateauroux devastated by Egyptians, 152.
Children's pilgrimage, xxvii.
Christian wife of Abagha, 37.
Christians, favoured by Zenky, xx.; well-treated by Saladin and Adil, xxiv., xxv.; at Jerusalem slain by Charizmians, xxix.; at Damascus, 11 ; at Cairo, 15 ; oppressed by Beibars, 19 ; led in triumph, 20 ; restrictions on, 21, 59, 136 and note, 139, 154, 159 ; favoured by Argun, 37 ; missionaries received in Persia, 37 note ; Kilawun intolerant to, 38, 40, 41 ; indignities offered to, 44 ; protection of, proclaimed by Mongols, 54 ; slain at Aradus, 57 ; populace attack, 60 ; edict against, *ib.*; persecuted, 68, 74, 75, 76 ; treatment by Nâsir, 76 ; by Tengiz, 77 ; in Damascus, 83 ; ill-treated by Salih, 96 ; abused by Yelbogha, 99 ; persecuted, 180, 192, 220 ; in Armenia, 143 ; Copts, exactions on, 147 ; in modern Egypt, 228.
Cilicia attacked, 99.
Circassian, origin of Burjite Mamelukes, 5 ; Regent, 92 ; dynasty, 103 ; long tenure of the throne, 104, 184, 185 ; memlukes, 93, 107, 125 ; slaughtered by Turks, 205 ; by Mahomet Ali, 224, 229 ; officers in Egyptian army, 230.
Circassians emigrate to Turkey and Egypt in modern times, 231 ; recent nationalisation of, in Egypt, 227, 228.
Clement v., Pope, 69 note.
Cœur-de-Lion, xxv.
Colleges, Al Azhar, 2 ; erected by Kilawun, 41 ; founded by Sheikh, 136 ; by Kansowa al Ghury, 206.
Commerce of the East, revival of, 141.
Conrad heads the Second Crusade,

xxi.; attacked by Cœur-de-Lion, xxv.
Constantinople, besieged by the Crusaders, xxvi.; besieged by Bajazet, 119; becomes Turkish capital, 160.
Copts, 216; depressed condition of, 220; intermarriage with, 228.
Coran, Othman's, at siege of Damascus, xxi. note; 186 note; 190.
Council of Placenza, xv.; of Clermont, *ib.*
Crusades, the, connection of Mameluke dynasty with, xii.; First Crusade, xvi.; causes of failure, xvii.; Second Crusade, xxi.; Third, xxii.; defeated by Saladin, xxiv.; Fourth Crusade, xxv.; Fifth, xxvi.; Sixth, *ib.*; Seventh, xxvii.; last Crusade and loss of Antioch, xxix.; end of Crusade, xxx., 44; cause of failure, xxx.; effect of, on Europe, xxxi.; Crusaders friendly with Mongols, 19; vindictive treatment by Kilawun, 40; by Khalil, 44, 46; remnant destroyed at Aradus, 27.
Currency arrangements by Nâsir, 55 note; by Sheikh, 135.
Cyprus, Cyprians attack Egypt, 98; burn Beyrut, 128; defeated at Larnaca, 141; Bursbai attacks island, 140; it becomes tributary, 141; rebellion in, 159; expeditions against, 159, 168, 169.

D

Dakalieh, province of, Semitic type of race in, 231.
Damascus, never taken by Crusaders, xviii.; attacked by Zenky, xx.; besieged by Crusaders, xxi.; taken by Nureddin, xxi.; by Mongols, 10; spared by Ghazan, 54; panic on approach of Mongols, 58 note; rebels against Faraj, 121; attacked and sacked by Timur, 119, 122, 123; viceroyalty of, sold, 170; Kansowa enters in state, 197; taken by Selîm, 200.
Damietta, defence by Saladin, xxii.; besieged in Sixth Crusade, xxvii.; attacked by Louis, xxix.
Danit, battle of, xix.
Death-rates imposed by Kansowa al Ghury, 189.
Diarbekr overrun by Selîm, 195.
Dietrich of Flanders joins Crusade, xxii.
Dilghadir, Chief of, 100, 145, 146, 152, 170, 195.
Dongola, battle of, 28; Mamelukes retire to, in modern times, 230.
Druses attacked by Egypt, 59; rising of, 72; tenets of, *ib.*
Duties on trade imposed by Kansowa al Ghury, 189.

E

Edessa, xvii.; stormed by Zenky, xx.; independence of, xxxi.
Edward II., 69 note.
Egypt, conquered by Amru, 1; by the Fatimides, 2; invaded by Baldwin, xviii.; invaded by Nureddin and by Amalrich, xxii., 6; Saladin and Adil succeed to power in, xxii. *et. seq.*; Selîm's designs against, 195; spoiled by the Turks, 211; Pasha sent yearly from Constantinople, 212; recent commingling of races in, 227-9; adaptibility of foreigners to residence in, 228; ethnology of, 227-231; predominance of Semitic blood, 231.
Eibek, Sultanate of, 8; defeats Nâsir, 9; death, *ib.*
Emessa, 11.
Endowments (Carât), 51 note.
Ertogral, Chief of the Ogus, 117.
Erzengan, Chief of, 119, 120; battle of, 146.
Extravagance, in Nâsir's Court, 81, 82; of Shaban's Court, 92, 93; of Bursbai, 147.

INDEX

Eyyub, Sultan, xxviii., 7.
Eyyubite Sultanate, xii.; fall of, 3, 8.

F

Famine, 49, 50; Nâsir's measures in, 79, 101; Sheikh's measures in, 135; in Bursbai's reign, 144; in Kaitbai's reign, 178.
Faraj, Sultan, x., 115, 121; fights Timur, 122, 123; sends gifts to Timur, 124; unhappy rule, 125; cruelties, 126, 128; yearly campaigns in Syria, 127; defeated at Baalbec, *ib.*; surrenders, *ib.*; strikes his image on coin, 128.
Fatimide Caliphate, origin, 2; hold Jerusalem, xvii.; fall of, xiv., xxii.; defeat Aghlabites, 2; conquer Egypt and Southern Syria, 2; remove seat at Cairo, 2; fall into hands of Turkish Viziers, 2; connection with Mamelukes, 3; end of, 7.
Fazil Bey, poet, quoted, 229 note.
Female society, state of, under Nâsir's reign, 83 note, 88 note.
Ferghana lineage of Ibn Toghej, 2.
Fostat, Mosque of, 1, 2 note.
Frederick II. crowned King of Jerusalem, xxviii.
Fuah Canal, 79.
Fulco, King, xx.

G

Gabarti quoted, 226.
Gallipoli, 118.
Gaza, visited by Black Death, 94 note; battle of, 109; taken by Turks, 203; massacre at, 204.
Genoa, Kilawun makes commercial arrangements with, 38.
Georgia, Adil extends rule to, xxvi., 7.
Georgian contingent joins Mongols, 58; in modern Egypt, 231.

Ghazan, ruler of Persia, 50; advance of against Nâsir, 54; retires, 55; embassies to England and France, 56, 57; dies, 59; character, *ib.*
Ghorians, xix.
Godfrey elected King, xvii.
Gold, fall of value, 55; rating of, 135.
Grandmaster of Templars taken captive at Hittin, xxiv.; tries to save Akka, xxx.; shelters Jem, 177.
Greeks oppose Crusaders, xxv., xxvi.; G. Mamelukes, 165, 231.
Grenada, 179.
Guzerat, sovereigns of, seek help from Egypt against Portuguese fleet, 191.

H

Haiton, King of Armenia, defeated by Beibars, 23; submits, 24.
Hâjy succeeds to throne, is slain, 91, 93.
Hâjy II., Sultan, 103; deposed, *ib.*; restored, 107; resigns, 109.
Hakem, Fatimide Sultan, xv.
Hamah, Abulfeda made Sultan of, 84.
Harim besieged by Armenians, 23; Beibars retires on, 28.
Hasan the Greater, 70; the Less, *ib.*
Hasan, Sultan, 93; defeats Yemen troops and Turcomans, 95; deposed and confined, *ib.*; re-appointed, 96; imprisoned, 97.
Hawks, Nâsir's love of, 82.
Hebron visited by Beibars, 21; by Kaitbai, 179.
Hejaz invaded by Rainald, xxiii.
Henry VI., xxvi.
Hims attacked by Boemund, 21; battle of, 36.
Hittin, battle of, xxiv.
Holagu, 10; cruel capture of Damascus, 10; destroyed the Abbaside Caliphate at Bagdad, 14.
Honfroi, xxiii.
Horses, prices given by Nâsir, 82 note.

INDEX

Hosein the Kurd, Admiral, 191.
Hospital erected by Kilawun, 41; founded by Sheikh, 136.
Hospitallers quarrel with Templars, xxix.; defend Arsuf, 20; attacked by Kilawun, 35.
Hungary, on Crusaders' route, xv.; Bajazet pushes his army to border of, 118.
Hyksos, Egyptian type of feature, 231.

I

Ibn Ayâs, ix., x., 49 note, 83 note, 184 note, 187 note, 190 note.
Ibn Batuta, ix.
Ibn Khallican, the historian, 34.
Ibn Toghej, 2.
Ibn Toghluk, his embassy to Egypt, 73, 91.
Ibn Tulûn, 1.
Ibrahim, son of Sultan Sheikh, campaign in Asia Minor, 133.
Ibrahim Sheikh, supported by England, 224.
Ikshidite line, 2.
Ilghazy takes Antioch, xix.
Ilkhan Dynasty, 59; Ilkhan Oweis, 98.
Import duties under Bursbai, 142.
Inâl, besieges Rhodes, 152; Sultan, 157, 158, 160; foreign relations, 160; rejoices at Byzantine conquest, 161; death, 162.
Inâlites, 167.
Income-tax, 188.
Indian Embassies, 73, 91, 177.
Ismail, Khedive, 230.
Ismail Pasha, 227.
Ismail Shah, the Safyide, 193; zealot of Soofie sect, 193; embassy to Venetians, 194; opposes Porte and champions Sooficites, 195; defeated, 195; coalesces (secretly) with Sultan, 196; legal pronouncement against, 198.

Ismail, Sultan, 90, 91.
Ismail, uncle of Eyyub, xxviii.
Ismailians, 2 note.
Ismailites, in Syria, 26; subject to Egypt, 27.
Itilmish, Chief of Van, 122; released by Faraj, 124.
Itmish, 115.

J

Jakam, Emir, and Sultan of Syria, 126.
Jakmac, 148, 149; Sultan, 150; fights Franks, 151; welcomes embassy from Shah Rookh, 153; a pattern Mussulman, 154; zeal and learning, ib.
James II., Archbishop of Nikosia, 159.
Jân Belat, Sultan, 185; swears on Coran, 185, 186 note; beheaded at Alexandria, 185; interred at Cairo, 188.
Jân Berdy, 199, 203; beaten at Gaza, 204; opposes Selim at Ridanieh, 207; goes over to him, ib.; governor of Syria, 210; rebels against Porte and forfeits his life, 212.
Jani Beg, Regent, 138; imprisoned at Alexandria, 139; escapes, ib.; reappears, 145; put to death, 146.
Jani Beg (second), distinguished supporter of Khushcadam, 165; Khushcadam puts him to death,166; memlukes resent his death, 168, 171.
Janim, nominated Sultan, 163, 164; deposed, 165; flies, ib.; dies, ib.
Janissaries, insolence of, 211; reduced by Ali Bey, 223.
Janus, King of Cyprus, taken prisoner, 141; ransomed, ib.; vassal of Sultan, 141.
Jebela, 72.
Jedda, 141, 142, 165, 191.
Jelbai, Sultan, 172.

240 INDEX

Jem, rebels against Bajazed, 176, 177; received by Pope, 177; poisoned, *ib.*
Jerusalem, King of, xiv.; taken by Seljukes, xv.; by Crusaders, xvii.; attacked, xxi.; taken by Saladin and desecrated, xxiv.; given over to Frederick II., xxviii.; attacked by Mongols, xxviii. note; destroyed by Charizmians, 7; visited by Beibars, 21; by Sheikh Sultan, 132; by Kaitbai, 179, 190.
Jews, attacked by Crusaders in Germany, xvi., xxi.; attacked also by Egyptians, 11; join in procession of Abbaside Caliph, 15; persecuted by Beibars, 31 note; favoured by Argun, 37 note; protected by Ghazan, 54; restrictions and edicts against, 59, 136, 139, 147 note, 154, 180, 220.
Jizeh, 206.
John I. of Castile, 99 note.
John, King, adverse to advance on Cairo, xxvii.
Joppa, battle of, xxix., 8.
Jordan, bridge of Beibars, 21; stoppage of stream, 21 note; bridged by Berknek, 116 note.
Joscelin, xx.
Joscelin II. dies in prison, xxi.

K

Kaaba curtain, 144, 145; hung by Shah Rookh, 153.
Kairowan, Aghlabites of, 2.
Kaitbai, 167; Sultan, 173; cruelty, 174, 175, 180; receives Jem, 176; supports Dulgadir, 178; travels and character, 179, 180, 181; visits Mecca and Jerusalem, 179; dies, 180; descendants, 228, 229.
Kalaat Rûm, stormed, 45; Weir hordes fight at, 132.
Kamil, xxviii.
Kansowa al Ghury, Sultan, 187; brilliant Court, 189; maritime proceedings against Portuguese, 191; relations with Ismail Safyide, 194; dies fighting against Selim, 199; character, 201.
Kansowah Khamsmieh, 180; Atabeg, 182, 183.
Kansowah, surname, 182.
Kara Sonkor, governor of Aleppo, 63, 68, 70.
Kara Yelek, 126, 143, 144, 146.
Kara Yusuf, 132, 133, 134.
Karaman, Chief of, 145, 160, 169.
Kausun, Emir, 81 note, 85, 87, 88, 89.
Keisar, relations with Crusaders, xvi., xx.; joins in attack on Aleppo, xx.; Beibars makes friends with, 18; Murâd slain while fighting, 118.
Kemisbogha, governor of Cairo, 110 note.
Kerak, Prince of, attacks Egypt, 9; stormed by Beibars, 18, 33, 35, 90, 91, 190.
Kesrawan, 59.
Ketbogha, Emir, 46; deposes Nâsir, 47; deposed by Lachin, 47; Sultan, 48; resigns, 49.
Ketbogha, Mongol, 10; slain, 11.
Khalil, Sultan, 42; kills Vizier, 43; cruel character, 43, 46; destroys Akka and ends Crusade, 44; assassinated, 45, 46.
Kharput, 170.
Khedive Ismail, 230.
Kheirbeg, Emir, 172, 173.
Kheirbeg, governor of Aleppo, 198; joins Selim, 200; governor of Egypt, 210, 211.
Khusheadam, 163; Sultan, 164; cruel treatment of Jani Beg, 166, 171.
Kilawun, 9, 33; Sultan, 34; attacks Mongols, 35; opposes Crusaders, 38; Jehâd on Akka, 39; character, 40, 41; benevolent institutions, 41; family, 42; dynasty ends, 103.
Kiptchak, Prince of, 18, 37, 50, 51, 55.
Kirkmash, 149, 150.

Knights Templars and Hospitallers, xxiv., xxix.; cruelly treated by Khalîl, 44; of Rhodes attack Egypt, 98, 152.
Konieh besieged by Egypt, 160.
Kotlubogha, 88, 89, 90.
Kotlushah commands Mongols, 57.
Kotuz, Vicegerent, 9; Sultan, 10; campaign in Syria, 11; killed by Beibars, *ib.*
Kujuk, Sultan, 87; deposed, 88; strangled, 92.

L

Lachîn, Regent, 47; Sultan, 49; attacks Armenia, 50; assassinated, 51, 52, 164 note.
Lahijan, 193.
Larnaca plundered, 140, 141.
Latakia seized by Kilawun, 38.
Library, public, at Cairo, 41.
Limasol plundered and burned, 140, 141.
Lorenzo of Almeida defeated at sea, 192.
Louis IX., or Saint Louis, xxi., xxix.; attacks Damietta and taken prisoner, xxix., 8.
Lydda, bridge of, 21.

M

Macrizy, historian, x., 100, 134, 136, 142, 145, 148, 187.
Mahomet Aly, 224, 227 *et seq.*
Malatia, 68.
Mamelukes, 1; rise of, 4, 215 *et seq.*; segregation, 216, 219, 225 *et seq.*; relation to Egyptians and subsequent history, 23, 225 *et seq.*
Mangu, 10.
Manuel, sea exploits, 192.
Marash, 145.
Massîssah, 27; seized by Moslems, 97.
Mecca, attacked by Rainald, xxiii.; Yemen contests for its supremacy,
40; Nâsir's interest in, 71, 72; embellished by Nâsir, 80, 81; victory over Yemen troops at, 95; Hasan defeated at, 96; rebellion at, 141; commercial centre, 142; repair of water-courses, 177; Kaitbai visits, 179; beautified by Kansowa, 189; disorder at, 190, 191; passes into Osmanly hands, 192.
Medina, xxiii., 71, 72; mosque destroyed by lightning, reconstructed by Kaitbai, 179.
Memluke, the name, 1; Bahrites and Burjites, 5, 8, 9, 10; divisions of memlukes, 167; their barbarities, 170, 171, 178; succumb to plague, 180; deadly strife among, *ib.*; extortion and cruelty of, 184, 198; slaughtered in Cairo by Turks, 206.
Mengu-Timur, Abagha's brother, 36.
Menkutimur, Mameluke, 50, 51.
Merj Dâbik, battle of, 199.
Merj Soffar, battle of, 58.
Mintash, 107, 108, 109, 110; cruel death, 111.
Mission Archæologique, 81 note.
Moghîth, Prince of Kerak, 17.
Mohammed I., Osmanly, 120, 131.
Mohammed I., Sultan, 97.
Mohammed II., Sultan, 180; his licentious character, 183; killed, 184.
Mohammed II., Osmanly, 169.
Mohammed, Sultan, son of Tatâr, 138.
Mongols, xiv.; invade Palestine, xxviii.; attack Jerusalem, *ib.*; overthrow Bagdad, 10; defeated at Ain-Jalût, 10, 11; friendly relations with Crusaders, 19; pursued by Beibars, 27; fall on Syria and Damascus, 34, 57, 58; dealings with Papacy, 37; converted to Islam, *ib.*; attacked by Khalîl, 45; ravages by, 53; defeat Egyptians and seize Damascus, 54; second inroad beaten back, 57, 58.
Moors of Spain, Kaitbai's sympathy with, 179.

242 INDEX

Mosul taken by Selim, 195; Zenky, chief of, xix.; subdued by Saladin, xxiii.
Mucoucus, 1.
Mucyyadites, the, 167, 172.
Mughla Beg, Chancellor, 198.
Murâd, Osmanly, 118; Bursbai's alliance with, 146.
Murrain of camel herds, 180.
Mutawakkil, Caliph, 106; M. the last Caliph, 212; resigns title to Osmanlies, 213; dies at Cairo, *ib.*

N

Naphtha at siege of Safed, 22.
Naples, 19.
Nashju, 75, 76.
Nâsir, the Eyyubite, of Syria, 8, 9; flies from the Mongols, 10.
Nâsir, son of Kilawun, 42, 47; second reign, 51-53; defeated by Mongols, 54; but inflicts severe reprisal on them in turn, 58; resigns, 61, 62; third reign, 66; kills Beibars, 66; visits Mecca, 68; peaceful relations with Persia, 69; supports Hasan the Greater, 70; suppresses Druses, 72; territory in North Africa, *ib.*; relations with India, Constantinople, Pope, and France, 73; supports Christians in Cairo, 74, 76; impartiality, 74, 75; marries Tengiz' daughter, 77; treacherous end of Tengiz, 78; wise measures, 79, 83; public works, 79, 80, 81; extravagance, 81-82; appreciates learning, 84; his sons' vices, 84; death, 85, 219.
Nazareth Church destroyed by Beibars, 19.
Negro element in Egyptian population, 231.
Nejimeh, Cilician fortress, 50.
Newroz, Emir, rebels in Syria, 127; proclaims Holy war against Sheikh, 130; murdered, 131.
Nicæa taken by Crusaders, xvi.

Nicopolis, victory of, 118.
Nile, 63; Nâsir's works on, 80.
Nile, Fast at failure of, 135; Selim's bridge of boats over, 208.
Nisibin taken by Selim, 195.
Noweiry ix., 17, 21 and 22 note; present at battle of Merj Soffar, 58.
Nubia, attacked by Beibars, 27; subjected to Egypt, 28; Kilawun's campaigns against, 39; Nâsir's expedition against, 72.
Nureddin defeats Crusaders, xx.; devastates Palestine, xxi.; sends Shirkoh to Egypt, xxii.; dies, xxiii.; compared with Saladin, xxvi.

O

Ocljeitu, Mongol, 37, 68, 69.
Ogus tribe, 117.
Omeyyad Caliphate, 213.
Orchan, Osmanly, 117.
Orfah, *see* Roha.
Orphan Asylum of Kilawun, 41.
Ortok, house of, xiv.; take Antioch, xix.
Osman, son of Ertogral, 117.
Osmanly Turks, become unfriendly to Egypt, 100; dynasty, 116-118; besiege Constantinople, 119; weakened by Timur, 120; Egypt's alliance with, 146, 153; take Constantinople, 160, 161; attack Syria, 177; defeated at Cæsarea, 178; victory at Merj Dâbik, 199; march on Cairo, 204; enter Cairo, 205; rule in Egypt, 212.
Othman, Sultan, his Greek origin, 156; deposed, 157.
Othman's copy of Coran, 186 note, 190; exhibited at siege of Damascus, xxi. note.
Ottoman. See Osmanly.

P

Paneas, defeat of Franks at, xxiii.

Paolo Gierro quoted, 197.
Papacy and Crusades, xxv.; Pope supports Sixth Crusade, xxvi.; ban against Frederick II., xxviii.; effect of Crusades on, xxxii.
Patriarch of Bagdad beheaded, 18.
Pelagius, Cardinal, xxvii.
Pepper monopolised by Sultan, 142.
Persia, 51-55, 59.
Pestilence, 144, 147.
Peter the Hermit, xv.
Philip of France, xxv.
Philip the Fair, 37 note, 69 note.
Philippopolis, 118.
Pirates, 140.
Plague in Cairo, 147, 159, 179.
Poll-tax imposed on Nubia, 28.
Pope, Nâsir's dealings with, 73; keeps Jem Osmanly in durance,177; threatened by Kansowa al Ghury, 192.
Porte, Egypt's relations with, 169, 174; embargo on goods passing Syrian border, 178; menaced by Ismail Shah, 194.
Portuguese destroy Egyptian fleet, 191, 192.
Pullanes, xxiii., xxv., xxviii. note.
Pyramids, 7; battle at, 208; visited by Selîm, 210.

Q

Quatremere, his translation of Macrizy, 21.

R

Raimond routed in Armenia, xviii.
Raimond of Antioch, xx., xxi., xxiv.
Rainald, xxii., xxiii., xxiv.
Red Sea, traffic in, 141; attacked by Portuguese, 191, 192.
Remusat quoted, 69 note.
Rhodes, Knights of, 98, 152, 177.
Richard Cœur-de-lion puts Akka garrison to death, xxv.

Ridanieh, battle of, 204, 205.
Ridhwan, xviii.
Rogers of Antioch, xix.
Roha (Orfah or Odessa), besieged, 143; Egyptian army beaten at, 176; taken by Selim, 195.

S

Safed, besieged, 22; rebuilt, 23; Governor rebels, is seized and put to death, 140.
Safyide dynasty, 193.
Safyuddin mystic, 193.
Saîd, Sultan, 32.
Saladin, xxi. note; Lord of Egypt, xxii.; victorious against Franks, xxiii., 7; slays Rainald and Knights, xxiv.; takes Jerusalem, ib.; fighting at Akka, xxv.
"Saladin's Tenth," xxv.
Salahia, 204.
Salamia, battle of, 54, 110.
Salih, Sultan, 95, 96.
Sallars, Regent, 53; attacks Bedouins, 57; opposes Beibars II., 61; cruelty and avarice, ib.; welcomes back Nâsir and is starved to death, 67; popularity and wealth, ib. note.
Saluting Sultan, fashion of, 139.
Samarcand, Timur carries educated Damascenes to, 123; Chief of, defeated by Usan Hasan, 174.
Sawakin. See Suakin.
Selîm, Osmanly Sultan, ix., 194; embassy to Egypt, 196; victory at Merj Dabik, 199; enters Aleppo, 200; Cairo, 204; occupies Citadel, 207; offers terms to Tumanbeg, 207; puts Emirs to death, 208; visits Pyramids, 210; licentious life in Egypt, 211.
Seljukes, xiv., xv., xvii., xviii.; dynasty ends, xx., 19, 117, 118.
Sepahies, insolence of, 211.
Shabân, Sultan, 91; slain, 92.
Shabân II., 97; strangled, 101.

244 INDEX

Shadibeg, General, 208, 209.
Shah Rookh, Timur's son, 144; claims right of Kaaba curtain, 145; embassy to Cairo, 153; Queen Mother hangs Kaaba curtain, *ib.*
Shamil, Circassian chief, 230.
Sheikh, besieges Cairo, 126; governor of Tripoli, *ib.*; rebels, 127; Sultan, 130; treacherous death of Newroz, 131; visits Soofie cloister, 131; attacks Armenia, 132; obsequies, 134.
"Sheikh-ul-Beled" title, 223.
Shicku, 96 note.
Shiea faith, 2 note, 15, 72; opposed by Beibars, 25; Timur's zeal for, 123; Shieas persecuted by Selim, 194, 195.
Shirkoh, xxii., 6.
Shnjai, 47, 48.
Sicily, 38.
Sinjar, battle of, 95.
Sis, Armenian capital, ravaged, 24, 27; peace restored, 59; Leo prisoner, and Sis annexed, 99.
Siwar of Dulgadir, 170, 171.
Siwar of Ablestin, opposes Egypt, 174; cruelly slain at Cairo, 175.
Siwâs, 118, 119.
Sonkor, governor of Damascus, 34.
Soofies, 131, 194, 195.
Soudan, 230.
Spain, 19.
Suakin, 30, 72, 100.
Sugar, monopoly, 142; prophylactic in plague, 142 note.
Syria, xiv., 54, 55, 124–128, 221.

T

Tagri Berdy, x., 115, 121, 122, 125, 127.
Tancred and Baldwin, xviii.; supreme in Syria, *ib.*
Tarsus, 97, 132, 133, 160, 174, 177.
Tatâr, 138; Regent, 137; kills Altunbogha, Sultan, 138.

Taxes imposed by Kansowa, 188, 189.
Tebriz, 59; Timur winters at, 120; battle, 195.
Tell Hamdun fortress, 59.
Templars, slain by Saladin, xxiv.; internal dissensions among, xxix.; make a stand at Akka, xxx.; two thousand beheaded by Beibars, 22; their Armenian stronghold stormed, 24; attacked by Nâsir, 57.
Tengiz, Governor of Damascus, 76; Nâsir marries daughter, 77; put to death, 78; his daughter and grandson, 95.
Tertosa (Tartus), 57 note.
Timur or Tamerlane, 113; his messenger put to death, 114; attacks Syria, 119, 122; and Bajazet in Asia Minor, 120; victory at Aleppo, 122, 123; sacks Damascus, 123; embassy, 124; his widow in Egypt, 153.
Timurboga, Sultan, 172, 173.
Timurtash, Emir, 127, 130.
Timurtash, Mongol, 69; his son Hasan the Less, 70.
Tokat, 118.
Trade, interfered with by Bursbai, 143; by Jakmac, 153.
Tripolis, xxix., xxxi., 25, 39 note, 72, 126, 128, 203.
Tulunides, 2.
Tumanbai, 184; Sultan, 185; murdered, 188.
Tumanbeg, Governor, 197; Sultan, 202, 203; beaten by Turks, 205, 206; battle at the Pyramids, 208; hanged, 209; high character, *ib.*
Tunis, xxix., 73.
Turan Shah, Sultan, xxix., 8.
Turcomans, xix., xx., 3, 5, 73, 95, 117, 118, 133.
Turkish abolished as official language, 227.
Turks. See Osmanlies.
Tushtumur, 89; beheaded, 90.
Tushtumur, Prime Minister, 101, 102.
Tyre, xix.; Beibars' treaty with, 26.

INDEX

U

Usan Hasan of the White Weir, 165, 169, 176 ; defeated by Mohammed II., 176, 193.
Uzbecs, 69, 70.

V

Van, Chief of, 122.
Van, Lake, 113.
Vasco da Gama, 191.
Veit, King, xxiv., xxv.
Venetians, 98, 194.

W

Wakf entails, 229.
Walter, First Crusade, xv.
Watson, Colonel, on stoppage of Jordan, 21.
Weil, History of Caliphs, ix., xi., xiv., 22 note, 120 note, 184 note.
Weir hordes, Black Weir, 118, 124, 132, 146, 160, 175, 193 ; White Weir, 118, 126, 132, 143, 160, 165, 193.

Wilken's History of Crusades, xiii., xxx., 39 note.

Y

Yelbogha al Jahjawy, Emir, 97, 98, 99.
Yelbogha al Nâsiry, Atabeg, 107, 108, 110, 111.
Yemen, embassies from, 38 ; defeated at Mecca, 95 ; seeks help against Portuguese, 191.
Yenbo, risings at, 190.
Yurat leaders, 54.
Yusuf, Sultan, 148, 149.

Z

Zâhir, last Abbaside Caliph, 213.
Zâhirites, 35, 157, 163, 165, 166 ; pitted against Ashrafites, 167 ; influence in appointing Sultan, 172.
Zenky defeats Crusaders, xix., xx.; storms Edessa, xx.
Zion, Prior of, 192.

ERRATA

P. 73, l. 15, margin, *for* 1881, *read* 1330.

P. 102, l. 16, *for* Berkuck, *read* Berekh.

P. 209, l. 15, *for* Tumanbai, *read* Tumanbeg.

SMITH, ELDER, & CO.'S PUBLICATIONS.

THE LIFE OF LORD LAWRENCE. By R. BOSWORTH SMITH, M.A., late Fellow of Trinity College, Oxford; Assistant Master at Harrow School; Author of "Mohammed and Mohammedanism," "Carthage and the Carthaginians," etc. Revised and Cheaper Edition, being the Sixth Edition. Two Vols. large crown 8vo. With Two Portraits and Two Maps. 21s.

LIFE OF SIR HENRY LAWRENCE. By Major-General Sir HERBERT BENJAMIN EDWARDES, K.C.B., K.C.S.I., and HERMAN MERIVALE, C.B. With Two Portraits. 8vo, 12s.

LIFE OF LIEUT.-GENERAL SIR JAMES OUTRAM. By Major-General Sir FREDERIC J. GOLDSMID, C.B., K.C.S.I. Second Edition. Two Vols. demy 8vo, 32s.

THE LIFE OF MAHOMET. From Original Sources. By Sir WM. MUIR, K.C.S.I. Third Edition. With a new Map and several Illustrations. 8vo, 16s.

THE MERV OASIS: Travels and Adventures east of the Caspian during the Years 1879-80-81, including Five Months' Residence among the Tekkes of Merv. By EDMOND O'DONOVAN, Special Correspondent of the *Daily News.* In Two Vols. demy 8vo. With Portrait, Maps, and Facsimiles of State Documents. 36s.

MERV: A Story of Adventures and Captivity. Epitomised from "The Merv Oasis." By EDMOND O'DONOVAN, Special Correspondent of the *Daily News.* With a Portrait. Crown 8vo, 6s.

ESSAYS ON THE EXTERNAL POLICY OF INDIA. By the late J. W. S. WYLLIE, C.S.I., India Civil Service, sometime Acting Foreign Secretary to the Government of India. Edited, with a brief Life, by Sir W. W. HUNTER, B.A., LL.D. With a Portrait of the Author. 8vo, 14s.

THE ANNALS OF RURAL BENGAL. From Official Records and the Archives of Ancient Families. By Sir W. W. HUNTER, LL.D. Vol. I. The Ethnical Frontier. Fifth Edition. Demy 8vo, 18s.

BY THE SAME AUTHOR.

ORISSA; or, The Vicissitudes of an Indian Province under Native and British Rule. Being the Second and Third Volumes of "Annals of Rural Bengal." With Illustrations. Two Vols. demy 8vo, 32s.

A LIFE OF THE EARL OF MAYO, Fourth Viceroy of India. Two Vols. Second Edition. Demy 8vo, 24s.

THE LIFE OF HIS ROYAL HIGHNESS THE PRINCE CONSORT. By Sir THEODORE MARTIN, K.C.B. With Portrait and Views. Five Vols. demy 8vo, 18s. each.
*** Also a "People's Edition," in One Vol., bound in cloth, 4s. 6d.; or in Six Parts, 6d. each. Cloth cases for binding, 1s. each.

MORE LEAVES FROM THE JOURNAL OF A LIFE IN THE HIGHLANDS, from 1862 to 1882. Fifth Edition. With Portraits and Woodcut Illustrations. 8vo, 10s. 6d.
*** Also the Popular Edition, with Portrait and Woodcut Illustrations, fcap. 8vo, 2s. 6d.

ENGLISH PROSE: Its Elements, History, and Usage. By JOHN EARLE, M.A., Rector of Swanswick, formerly Fellow and Tutor of Oriel College, Professor of Anglo-Saxon in the University of Oxford. 8vo, 16s.

THE HISTORIC NOTE-BOOK. With an Appendix of Battles. By the Rev. E. COBHAM BREWER, LL.D., Author of "The Dictionary of Phrase and Fable," "The Reader's Handbook," etc. Crown 8vo, over 1000 pp., 7s. 6d.

HAYTI; or, The Black Republic. By Sir SPENSER ST. JOHN, G.C.M.G., formerly Her Majesty's Minister Resident and Consul-General in Hayti, now Her Majesty's Special Envoy to Mexico. Second Edition, revised. With a Map. Large crown 8vo, 8s. 6d.

THE REIGN OF QUEEN VICTORIA: A Survey of Fifty Years of Progress. Edited by T. HUMPHRY WARD. Two Vols. 8vo, 32s.

UNDERGROUND RUSSIA. Revolutionary Profiles and Sketches from Life. By STEPNIAK, formerly Editor of "Zemlia i Volia" (Land and Liberty). With a Preface by PETER LAVROFF. Translated from the Italian. Third Edition. Crown 8vo, 6s.

ENGLISH LIFE IN CHINA. By Major HENRY KNOLLYS, Royal Artillery, Author of "From Sedan to Saarbrück"; Editor of "Incidents in the Sepoy War," "Incidents in the China War," etc. Crown 8vo, 7s. 6d.

WALKS IN FLORENCE AND ITS ENVIRONS. By SUSAN and JOANNA HORNER. With numerous Illustrations. Two Vols. crown 8vo, 15s.

LONDON: SMITH, ELDER, & CO., 15 WATERLOO PLACE, S.W.

A SELECTION FROM SMITH, ELDER, & CO.'S PUBLICATIONS.

THE LIFE OF SIR JAMES FITZJAMES STEPHEN, BART., K.C.S.I., a Judge of the High Court of Justice. By his Brother, LESLIE STEPHEN. Second Edition. With 2 Portraits. Demy 8vo, 16s.

AN ARTIST'S REMINISCENCES. By RUDOLPH LEHMANN. With Portrait. Demy 8vo, 12s. 6d.

RECOLLECTIONS OF A MILITARY LIFE. By General Sir JOHN ADYE, G.C.B., R.A., late Governor of Gibraltar. With Illustrations by the Author. Demy 8vo, 14s. net.

OUR SQUARE AND CIRCLE; or, The Annals of a Little London House. By "JACK EASEL," sometime *Punch's* Roving Correspondent. With a Frontispiece. Crown 8vo, 5s.

OFF THE MILL. By the Right Rev. G. F. BROWNE, D.C.L., Bishop of Stepney. With 2 Illustrations. Crown 8vo, 6s.

FIFTY YEARS; or, Dead Leaves and Living Seeds. By the Rev. HARRY JONES, Prebendary of St. Paul's; Author of "Holiday Papers," etc. Second Edition. Crown 8vo, 4s.

HISTORY OF THE UNITED STATES. By E. BENJAMIN ANDREWS, D.D., LL.D., President of the Brown University. 2 Vols. With Maps. Crown 8vo, 16s.

A SHORT HISTORY OF THE RENAISSANCE IN ITALY. Taken from the Work of JOHN ADDINGTON SYMONDS. By Lieut.-Colonel ALFRED PEARSON. With a Steel Engraving of a recent Portrait of Mr. Symonds. Demy 8vo, 12s. 6d.

THE LIFE AND LETTERS OF ROBERT BROWNING. By Mrs. SUTHERLAND ORR. With Portrait and Steel Engraving of Mr. Browning's Study in De Vere Gardens. Second Edition. Crown 8vo, 12s. 6d.

THE JOCKEY CLUB AND ITS FOUNDERS. By ROBERT BLACK, M.A., Author of "Horse Racing in France." Crown 8vo, 10s. 6d.

A COLLECTION OF LETTERS OF W. M. THACKERAY, 1847-1855. With Portraits and Reproductions of Letters and Drawings. Second Edition. Imperial 8vo, 12s. 6d.

LIFE OF FRANK BUCKLAND. By his Brother-in-Law, GEORGE C. BOMPAS, Editor of "Notes and Jottings from Animal Life." With a Portrait. Crown 8vo, 5s.; gilt edges, 6s.

NOTES AND JOTTINGS FROM ANIMAL LIFE. By the late FRANK BUCKLAND. With Illustrations. Crown 8vo, 5s.; gilt edges, 6s.

AN AGNOSTIC'S APOLOGY, and other Essays. By LESLIE STEPHEN. Large crown 8vo, 10s. 6d.

HOURS IN A LIBRARY. By LESLIE STEPHEN. Revised, Rearranged, and Cheaper Edition, with additional Chapters. 3 Vols. Crown 8vo, 6s. each.

LIFE OF HENRY FAWCETT. By LESLIE STEPHEN. With 2 Steel Portraits. Fifth Edition. Large crown 8vo, 12s. 6d.

A HISTORY OF ENGLISH THOUGHT IN THE EIGHTEENTH CENTURY. By LESLIE STEPHEN. Second Edition. 2 Vols. demy 8vo, 28s.

THE SCIENCE OF ETHICS: An Essay upon Ethical Theory as Modified by the Doctrine of Evolution. By LESLIE STEPHEN. Demy 8vo, 16s.

LIBERTY, EQUALITY, FRATERNITY. By the late Sir JAMES FITZJAMES STEPHEN, K.C.S.I. Second Edition, with a new Preface. Demy 8vo, 14s.

GERALD EVERSLEY'S FRIENDSHIP: A Study in Real Life. By the Rev. J. E. C. WELLDON, Headmaster of Harrow School. Fourth Edition. Crown 8vo, 6s.

SHAKSPEARE COMMENTARIES. By Dr. G. G. GERVINUS, Professor at Heidelberg. Translated under the Author's superintendence, by F. E. BUNNETT. With a Preface (by F. J. FURNIVALL. Fifth Edition. 8vo, 14s.

SHAKSPEARE: certain Selected Plays abridged for the use of the Young. By SAMUEL BRANDRAM, M.A. Oxon. Fourth and Cheaper Edition. Large crown 8vo, 5s.

SHAKSPEARE'S PREDECESSORS IN THE ENGLISH DRAMA. By JOHN ADDINGTON SYMONDS. Demy 8vo, 16s.

THE GAMEKEEPER AT HOME. By RICHARD JEFFERIES. New Edition, with all the Illustrations of the former Edition. Crown 8vo, 6s.

WILD LIFE IN A SOUTHERN COUNTY. By RICHARD JEFFERIES. Crown 8vo, 6s.

THE AMATEUR POACHER. By RICHARD JEFFERIES. Crown 8vo, 5s.

WOODLAND, MOOR, AND STREAM: being the Notes of a Naturalist. Edited by J. A. OWEN. Third Edition. Crown 8vo, 5s.

ROBERT ELSMERE. By Mrs. HUMPHRY WARD. Popular Edition, crown 8vo, 6s.; Cheap Edition, crown 8vo, limp cloth, 2s. 6d.; Cabinet Edition, 2 Vols. small 8vo, 12s.

By the same Author.

THE HISTORY OF DAVID GRIEVE. Popular Edition, crown 8vo, 6s.; Cheap Edition, crown 8vo, limp cloth, 2s. 6d.

MARCELLA. Fourteenth Edition. Crown 8vo, 6s.

IN STEVENSON'S SAMOA. By MARIE FRASER. Second Edition. With Frontispiece. Crown 8vo, 2s. 6d.

THE HAWARDEN HORACE. By CHARLES L. GRAVES, Author of "The Blarney Ballads," "The Green above the Red," etc. Third Edition. Small post 8vo, 3s. 6d.

THE STORY OF GOETHE'S LIFE. By GEORGE HENRY LEWES. Second Edition. Crown 8vo, cloth, 7s. 6d.

THE LIFE OF GOETHE. By GEORGE HENRY LEWES. Fourth Edition. With Portrait. 8vo, 16s.

LONDON: SMITH, ELDER, & CO., 15 WATERLOO PLACE, S.W.

www.ingramcontent.com/pod-product-compliance
Lightning Source LLC
Chambersburg PA
CBHW030819230426
43667CB00008B/1292